Date:
This can be requ
Renew onli

DIVINE RIGHT?

Divine Right?

The Parnell Split in Meath

David Lawlor

CORK UNIVERSITY PRESS

First published in 2007 by
Cork University Press
Youngline Industrial Estate
Pouladuff Road, Togher
Cork, Ireland

British Library Cataloguing in Publication Data
A CIP catalogue record for this book is available from the British Library.

ISBN 978-1-85918-426-4

Typesetting by Red Barn Publishing, Skeagh, Skibbereen, Co. Cork
Printed by ColourBooks Ltd., Baldoyle, Dublin

www.corkuniversitypress.com

For my wife
Mary Cryan

and in memory
of my friends
Mary McNally
and her brother
John Cantwell

Contents

Acknowledgements

My father, Joe Lawlor (may God be good to him) bequeathed among many gifts a love of the past — despite one of his great sayings that 'there won't be a word about any of us in a hundred years'. But it was the late Garrett Fox who, as my senior colleague on the *Meath Chronicle* in the 1960s, sowed the seed for this book. Garrett gave me his copy of the *North Meath election petition of 1892,* knowing from it of my family's involvement in the Parnell split in Meath and correctly guessing that they would be the last to tell me about how we had gone 'against the priests'. A few decades later, when I had the opportunity to begin research, I received invaluable advice and guidance from Dr Bill Vaughan of the history department of Trinity College Dublin and from Seamus MacGabhann, who in his spare time from the English department of NUI Maynooth is editor of *Ríocht na Midhe* (the journal of Meath Archaeological & Historical Society). I must thank Dr Carla King and all the staff of the history department of St Patrick's College, DCU, where I did a master's degree. I owe an enormous debt of gratitude to Professor Tom Dunne of Cork University Press for his patience and kindness in helping me to convert a thesis into a book.

Ethna Cantwell helped me greatly by reading my manuscript. Ken Davis, editor of the *Meath Chronicle,* has been very supportive, as has Seamus Shortall, co-biographer of Pierce Mahony, along with Iva Pocock, Mahony's great-great-grand-daughter. Phil Smyth, Eva Ryan (née Rowan), Helen Fulham, Hugh Gibney, Richie Brady and Tommy Conway all assisted me with photographs. My brother Bill, Phil O'Neill and Jim O'Donnell were always available to advise, as was Noel Tierney of the Parnell Society and Niamh Carty, who has researched the life of Bishop Matthew Gaffney. I also wish to thank Bishop Michael Smith for access to Meath diocesan archive and Meath priests: Fr Gabriel Flynn, who loaned me his research notes on Bishop Thomas Nulty and the land question; Fr Paul Connell of St Finian's and Fr Pat McManus (St Columban's) who went to a lot of trouble to provide me with photographs; Fr Gerry Rice, Monsignor John Hanly and Fr Ambrose Macaulay of Belfast, who kindly gave me the benefit of their research experience.

All of the staff of the National Library, where I did much of my research, could not have been more helpful, especially Joanna Finegan in prints & drawings. I would also like to thank my former classmate, Andy Bennett, and the staff of Navan library, together with that of Dublin diocesan archive, the manuscript library in Trinity College and those in the National Archives. My wife, Mary, gave me great encouragement, despite the amount of my time that was absorbed in this project. My apologies to anyone I have omitted to thank. Any mistakes are my own.

David Lawlor
June 2007

Foreword

This is an especially stimulating book for anyone interested in the huge changes that have taken place in Ireland in the last 120 years. The Parnell split has been somewhat erased from public memory by the subsequent split over the Treaty, but in some ways it tells us more about who we were than does the Treaty split, because it involved the electorate more directly.

The County Meath described in David Lawlor's book is in many ways familiar. The descendants of many of the protagonists are still very present in the county. But it is also very different. The willingness of the Catholic clergy to involve themselves so directly in politics will surprise most readers. But it was explicable then by recent history. Daniel O'Connell would never have been able to organise his successful mass political movements in favour of Catholic Emancipation or the abolition of Tithes without the organisational support of the Catholic clergy. So it is not surprising that the clergy became involved in the arguments at the heart of the Parnell split.

As the material in this book demonstrates, these arguments were not solely or even mainly about Charles Stewart Parnell's private life. They were about whether the Irish Parliamentary Party should ally themselves with the Liberals, as the only party likely to deliver Home Rule, and therefore take Liberal objections to Parnell's continued leadership seriously, or whether, on the other hand, they should support his continued leadership and oppose both Liberals and Conservatives in the Commons. This is a type of dilemma that faces Irish Nationalist MPs in Westminster even to this day.

It is interesting to note how support in Meath broke down between the Parnellites and the anti-Parnellites. The towns of Trim, Navan and Kells supported Parnell, but the rural areas supported the anti-Parnellites because their priority was the land question and they believed (wrongly) that only the Liberals could meet their demands on that.

It is sad to read of the personal hardships encountered by some of the protagonists. The two Meath anti-Parnellite MPs, Michael Davitt and Patrick Fulham, were both unseated as a result of a Parnellite petition alleging undue clerical influence on their election. The costs

of fighting those cases bankrupted both Michael Davitt and Patrick
Fulham. This seems very harsh as neither was personally responsible
for all or most of the actions of their clerical supporters.

The Parnell split influences some matters in County Meath up to
this day. The Diocesan Seminary, St Finian's, is in Mullingar, not Navan,
due to the Bishop's negative views of Navan, arising from the attitude
of Navan voters during the controversy. The involvement of the Sisters
of Mercy in the management of Our Lady's Hospital in Navan also arises
from a direct political initiative taken by the Bishop at this time.

Many Meath families reading this book will be prompted to look up
personal associations. In my own case, I found at home an 1893 cutting
from the *Drogheda Independent* of a letter to the editor, co-signed by my
twenty-three year old grandfather, defending the Parish Priest of
Dunboyne, Fr Brady, against charges by Dunboyne Parnellites that he
had given an unduly political sermon during the South Meath by-
election that year.

John Bruton,
EU Ambassador to the United States of America
August 2007

Preface

Historians agree that in the power vacuum after the fall of Parnell, the Catholic bishops and clergy consolidated their influence on Irish politics. This was certainly true in Meath but, remarkably, the dramatic events of the split there — which made national headlines at the time — have never been recounted. People of the county which had sent an unknown Parnell to Westminster in 1875 continued to hold him in great affection after the O'Shea divorce revelations in 1890. But Bishop Thomas Nulty and his clergy, who had been instrumental in Parnell's entry to politics, turned bitterly against him. In the angry clash between priests and people, Dr Nulty imposed anti-Parnellite candidates in local elections and turned the church into a political machine to ensure their success. He nominated Michael Davitt, founder of the Land League, to oppose North Meath's Parnellite MP, Pierce Mahony, in the general election of 1892, warning in his famous pastoral that no Parnellite could remain a Catholic. When Davitt won the election — as did his anti-Parnellite colleague, Patrick Fulham, in South Meath — the Parnellites had little difficulty in persuading the courts to unseat them because of 'undue clerical influence', but the anti-Parnellites narrowly won the ensuing by-elections.

Extensive research in local and national newspapers, confidential police reports and private papers compensate for the absence of a major source, owing to the burning of Meath's diocesan archive by Bishop Gaughran in 1909 over fears of an unrelated scandal. Such study reveals how Bishop Nulty claimed a 'divine right' to instruct his flock how to vote. He and his clergy preached that the issues in the split were religious or moral questions, on which their teachings must be obeyed, but then claimed election results as *political* victories. As well as dividing their flock, they provoked violent hostility from local Catholic farmers, shopkeepers and workers who had grown confident of their ability to take over the running of political affairs from the Protestant landlords then in the midst of being expropriated under the Land Acts. This led to a temporary alliance between the Parnellites and these Tories against the bishop and his priests, which, however, only served to aid the churchmen's victory, which was followed by political apathy.

Afterwards, the diocesan seminary was transferred from Navan to Mullingar, in the more congenial Westmeath half of the diocese, where a new cathedral was later built.

This account describes how the contesting of local and parliamentary elections in Meath cemented the bitter divisions of the split, particularly so in the case of the conflict between Davitt and Mahony. Much of this animosity could have been avoided if a Parnellite proposal to divide the two Meath seats between each side had not been rejected by Bishop Nulty and his clergy. This mirrored the failure to agree nationally not to contest seats which either side was sure to win in the highly divisive 1892 general election, thereby postponing any chance of party re-unification to the end of the decade. The Meath experience challenges the view accepted by most historians that priests could lead their people only in the political direction that they wished to go and were unable to impose a political view of their own. While Tim Healy, Parnell's chief adversary in the split, hailed the clergy as natural leaders in a Catholic–Nationalist supremacy, evidence of clerical interference, particularly in Meath, damaged the prospect of Irish self-government being realised through Gladstone's second Home Rule bill. That was lost in the Lords in 1893, along with hopes for a free and united Ireland in which diverse traditions could be reconciled.

It is idle to speculate about the utterly different kind of Ireland which might have emerged if the split had not occurred and if Parnell had succeeded in securing a measure of Home Rule. Many nevertheless regard him as the founder of the modern Irish state and so his followers' conflict with the Catholic church during the split may be considered as a painful part of Irish people's growing up as independent citizens. Unfortunately, it was a stage of development which was not successfully completed, allowing that church to maintain a dominant role in many areas of national life that would otherwise be politically directed. This account, which uses participants' own words to chronicle what actually happened during the split in Meath and which also attempts to place events there in a national context, demonstrates how such clerical influence was established and maintained at a time of social revolution when the role of priests in politics was publicly debated as it would not be again until the waning of Catholic church influence. This, in our own time of unprecedented prosperity, has exposed an ethical vacuum which our political immaturity renders us peculiarly ill-equipped to fill by, for example, creating a civic morality which would sustain real communities and replace the anarchy of self-interested individuals and groups fighting to uphold their privileges.

Chronology

1875

Parnell elected MP for Meath in by-election on death of John Martin, MP

1880

Parnell re-elected for Meath but opts to sit for Cork; he is elected Irish Parliamentary Party leader

1882

Michael Davitt elected MP for Meath as a protest while in prison, but deemed ineligible by the Commons

1886

Pierce Mahony and Edward Sheil elected unopposed for North and South Meath; Gladstone's first Home Rule bill defeated in Commons

1890

17 November — William O'Shea granted divorce from Katharine because of her adultery with Parnell; Bishop Nulty returns from Rome to Navan

19 November — Navan town commissioners support Parnell's leadership by 9 votes to 4

20 November — Meath National League convention in Navan, attended by 35 priests, unanimously affirms Parnell's leadership; Pierce Mahony, MP, conveys Meath's allegiance to national rally in Dublin

25 November — Parnell re-elected party leader

26 November — Liberal leader, W.E. Gladstone, publishes letter saying Parnell must go

28 November — Parnell issues manifesto renouncing alliance with the Liberals in favour of 'independent opposition'

1 December — Mahony supports Parnell in Irish Party debate in Committee Room 15 at Westminster

3 December — Standing committee of Irish hierarchy condemns Parnell's leadership

6 December — The split: majority of party desert Parnell (thereafter called 'seceders', who dub Parnellites 'factionists')

13 December — *Drogheda Independent* becomes anti-Parnellite at instigation of director/priest and commences attack on Mahony

1891

February — Navan board of Poor Law guardians passes anti-Parnell resolution

1 March — Parnell's visit to Navan

March — After failing to agree terms with Bishop Nulty, Navan Parnellites hold their own in Poor Law elections, despite clerical pressure, which Dublin Castle merely notes

April — Bishop Nulty reins in his clergy; he attacks Navan Parnellites and returns the offerings of some, as they join landlords to try to change the chairmanship of Navan guardians; priests begin to establish anti-Parnellite federation branches in Meath; Navan guardians black the Parnellite *Meath Reporter*

May — Navan guardians condemn Pierce Mahony by 10 votes to 7 for allegedly insulting Irish priests. Tim Harrington, MP, says in Mullingar and Parnell himself repeats in Belfast that Bishop Nulty told Tim Healy, MP, after the divorce verdict that he supported Parnell: denials by both Fr Michael Woods and Dr Nulty

16 June — Navan Parnellite rally calls for clerical moderation in Meath

1 July — Hierarchy formally condemns Parnell's leadership and his followers' hostility to church authority

July–October — Navan clergy try to separate Parnellites from their labourer supporters

26 July — Pierce Mahony in Nobber defends role of priests in politics

30 July — Parnellites attack Navan parochial house, illuminated for the release of MPs Dillon and O'Brien, who declare against Parnell, as does the *Freeman's Journal*

16 August — Parnell's visit to Kells

6 October — Death of Parnell

October — Pierce Mahony is active in launching the *Irish Independent* and is spoken of as the new party leader, but he realises he must fight for his North Meath seat

November — Priests propose that a nun replace the deceased matron of Navan workhouse, but Parnellites join Protestant landlords in voting against her, while Bishop Nulty denounces landlord extermination of his Meath flock

23 December — Michael Davitt defeated by John Redmond in Waterford by-election

1892

January — Bishop Nulty denounces Parnellites and urges his clergy to oppose them in forthcoming general election

February–June — Moderate anti-Parnellites fail to agree a deal on Parnellite seats in a bid to reduce animosity in the general election

March — Navan Parnellites routed in Poor Law elections, having been castigated by clergy for opposing nun as matron of workhouse

24 April — Michael Davitt re-enters Meath politics at Slane, where Fr Woods correctly predicts that Navan Parnellite defeat marks the end of Mahony's career

1 June — Michael Davitt and Patrick Fulham selected for North and South Meath at anti-Parnellite convention in Navan, after which Davitt is struck by a stone on the head during protests

16 June — Pierce Mahony and James Dalton selected for North and South Meath at Parnellite convention in Trim

26 June — Michael Davitt's scurrilous attack on Pierce Mahony

3 July — Bishop Nulty's famous pastoral: No Parnellite can 'remain a Catholic'

6 July — Bishop Nulty awoken by Navan rowdies

7 July — Bishop Nulty formally nominates Michael Davitt, who dubs Pierce Mahony 'grandson of the Kerry souper'

10 July — James Lawlor calls Bishop Nulty 'a liar' and walks out of Navan cathedral; 150 police separate rival rallies in Navan

13 July — Patrick Fulham wins South Meath by 81 votes, but James Dalton threatens election petition

14 July — Serious rioting in Navan on polling day in North Meath

15 July — Michael Davitt wins North Meath by 403 votes; Pierce Mahony blames Bishop Nulty for his defeat and calls on Parnellites to stop subscribing offerings to his clergy

3 August — League in Dublin decides to lodge petitions against the election of both Davitt and Fulham

August — New parliament meets and 80 Irish Home Rulers join with Liberals to end Tory government; parliament prorogued to January to enable Gladstone prepare his Home Rule bill; Bishop Nulty in Mullingar repeats Mahony 'souper' slur

8–9 August — South and North Meath election petitions lodged

11 November — Fr John Fay, PP, Summerhill, sentenced to month in jail for disparaging petitions

16 November — South Meath petition opens in Trim

30 November — Petition judges find for James Dalton and unseat Patrick Fulham, mainly because of Bishop Nulty's pastoral

15 December — North Meath petition opens in Trim

23 December — Petition judges find for Pierce Mahony and unseat Michael Davitt

30 December — A.J. Kettle proposes disenfranchisement of Meath until clerical power is curtailed

31 December — John Redmond and Michael Davitt each publish English magazine articles on priests in politics to try to assuage British public opinion

1893

6 January — Parnellite convention in Trim re-selects Pierce Mahony and James Dalton to contest fresh Meath elections, amid fears of renewed clerical opposition

17 January — Anti-Parnellite convention in Navan selects James Gibney and Jeremiah Jordan to contest North and South Meath

24 January — Pierce Mahony assaults barrister Matt Kenny, MP, in the Four Courts for insulting his mother

27 January — Sir Henry James, MP, issues a pamphlet using the petitions' evidence to show that Irish priests control 80 constituencies; Michael Davitt ridicules his claim that priests could influence illiterate voters

29 January — Parnellites attack opponents returning to Navan from a Healy meeting in Gormanlough

31 January — Irish members squabble over issuing of Meath writs as parliament re-assembles

2 February — Unionist MPs raise Meath clergy's actions as reason to deny Home Rule

6 February — Meath elections fixed for 17 and 21 February; Pierce Mahony seeks votes of fellow Protestants

13 February — Gladstone introduces his second Home Rule bill, which Unionists and Conservatives oppose vehemently, many citing Meath example of clerical influence; Edward Burke, Navan Parnellite, dies of wounds received in police baton-charge

18 February — Jeremiah Jordan defeats James Dalton in South Meath by 69 votes

22 February — James Gibney defeats Pierce Mahony in North Meath by 258 votes

28 February — At Meath assizes, William Mongey is acquitted of assaulting Michael Davitt in Navan on 1 June 1892; Fr P. Clarke, curate, Kingscourt, is found guilty of assaulting Owen Reilly, Rahood, in Nobber during polling on 14 July, but is released on bail; twelve Navan people are bound to the peace for rioting on 14 July, but two of them are imprisoned for a fortnight for assaulting policemen

1 March — Fr Christopher Casey, curate, Dunderry, is acquitted of assaulting Patrick Byrne, Knockumber, in Navan on 14 July while protecting an anti-Parnellite voter from the mob

2 March — Bishop Nulty begins his *apologia* in Kells, grieving at divisions in Meath

9 March — Bishop Nulty laments lack of subscriptions for new church in Trim, but says they will beat Parnellites again

March — All Parnellite candidates defeated again by the bishop's nominees in Navan Poor Law elections after clergy raise the nuns issue again

25 March — Bishop Nulty issues pamphlets defending his pastoral and his priests

April–February 1894 — Michael Davitt's and Patrick Fulham's bankruptcy proceedings over their refusal to pay costs of the petitions

April — Philip H. Bagenal's *Priest in Politics* argues that the second Meath elections proved that Parnellite independence could not withstand clerical influence

June — James Dalton returns to Australia

5 July — John Redmond concedes that the Catholic church is 'omnipotent in Irish politics'

September — Home Rule bill is passed by the Commons but lost in the Lords and allowed to drop by Gladstone

1894

Gladstone resigns and Liberals abandon Home Rule

1895

Pierce Mahony fails to be elected MP for St Stephen's Green, Dublin

1898

Death of Bishop Nulty (24 December)

1899

Monsignor Matthew Gaffney, parish priest of Clara, named Bishop of Meath (May); death of Luke Smyth (December)

1900

Irish Party re-unites under John Redmond; Bishop Gaffney announces moving St Finian's seminary from Navan to Mullingar, where a new cathedral is also to be built

1904

Deaths of Francis Sheridan and William Lawlor

1905

Bishop Gaffney resigns (August)

1906

Monsignor Laurence Gaughran, parish priest of Kells, named Bishop of Meath

1908

St Finian's college opens in Mullingar (January)

1930

Bishop Thomas Mulvany opens St Patrick's classical school in Navan; deaths of Pierce Mahony and Laurence Rowan

Chapter 1

The Parnell split and priests in politics

On 17 November 1890, Ireland was shocked when Captain William O'Shea was granted a divorce from his wife Katharine on the grounds of her adultery with Charles Stewart Parnell, the Protestant landlord from Avondale in Co. Wicklow who had become 'the uncrowned king of Ireland'. In the 'new departure', Parnell by 1879 had obtained the support of the Fenians and of Davitt's Land League for his goal of Irish self-government. For ten years he led the Irish parliamentary party at Westminster to what seemed the verge of obtaining Home Rule, now endorsed also by the Catholic church and by the British Liberal Party, which he converted to his cause in 1886. Within three weeks of the divorce, however, the Liberals rejected the alliance under his leadership, the Catholic hierarchy in Ireland condemned him as leader and the majority of the Irish Party (44 to 27) deserted him after a bitter debate in Committee Room 15 at Westminster. Parnell took his case to the Irish people, but lost three tough by-elections in Kilkenny, Sligo and Carlow before dying, aged 45, in the arms of Katharine, now his wife, in Brighton on 6 October 1891. His death did not end the split, which persisted between the Parnellites and a much weakened Irish Party — itself divided into factions led by Tim Healy and John Dillon — until they re-united under John Redmond in 1900.

A significant feature of the split was the clumsy way in which the difficulties that the divorce caused the Liberal leader, W.E. Gladstone, with nonconformist (Presbyterian, Methodist, etc.) opinion in his party were conveyed to the Irish Party. When a letter from Gladstone was not read to the party meeting which re-elected Parnell as leader, he published a second letter saying that Parnell would have to go. The latter predictably rejected such dictation and his followers from then on contrasted their independence to their opponents' abandonment of their leader at Gladstone's insistence. The Irish Catholic bishops, who had remained silent to avoid being accused of interfering in politics, condemned Parnell's leadership only when it became clear that most

1

of his party would reject him. This enabled the Parnellites to accuse the bishops of ignoring the moral issue and reacting only to Gladstone's letter, so their objection could be construed as being purely political. When Parnell issued a manifesto renouncing the liberal alliance, his followers reverted to their pre-1886 stance of 'independent opposition' in Westminster. This independence was just as important at home in rejecting 'clerical dictation' from bishops and priests who were trying to regain political influence in the developing power vacuum. Otherwise, Protestants in Ireland and British people considering Irish demands for self-government would be convinced that Home Rule would become 'Rome rule'. In any case, why should Ireland, having got rid of a Protestant ascendancy, now submit to a clerical one?

As F.S.L. Lyons remarked in his biography of Parnell in 1977, James Joyce used the fall of Parnell repeatedly to express his revulsion for what he called the Irish paralysis — and its sources: priestly power, moral cowardice and social hypocrisy.[1] (A much earlier biography by R. Barry O'Brien is an affectionate account also well worth reading.)[2] Lyons, later provost of Trinity College, and the political analyst, Conor Cruise O'Brien, were the first professional historians to write about the split in the 1950s, both making forensic use of original sources in their books on the Irish Party.[3] They showed how the bishops and clergy, naturally active in Daniel O'Connell's campaigns for Catholic emancipation (granted in 1829) and against the tithes tax which funded the established Protestant church (abolished in 1837), continued to agitate for repeal of the 1801 union with Britain and to act as an 'election machine' for the Irish Party, becoming particularly important in selecting home rule candidates.[4] But they maintained that bishops' and priests' direct political influence was much less than their spiritual and moral authority. Otherwise, the Land League, the new departure and the Parnellite movement, which they initially opposed, would never have been successful.

However, after 1888, when the Irish Party faced down Rome's condemnation of the plan of campaign (which forced landlords to improve conditions for tenant farmers), its MPs developed a new attitude of independence towards many of the churchmen. With the fall of Parnell, however, the influence of the clergy became decisive. While Cruise O'Brien was at pains to contradict the traditional view that his followers deserted him at the command of the bishops, he said 'the sight of Parnell hounded down by the Catholic priests confirmed the fears and intensified the revulsions of northern Protestants and disgusted also those English liberals who had always feared a clerical ascendancy'. But, he added, 'English men and Protestants easily forgot that the spectacle which repelled them was one which they themselves had been the first — after Parnell himself — to bring about'.[5]

In *The Fall of Parnell* in 1960, Lyons observed that all this was hardly surprising, because 'when the crisis had been touched off by moral offence, the bishops would have been open to severe criticism if they had not spoken'.[6] He quoted Archbishop Croke of Cashel: 'You cannot support Mr Parnell's leadership without giving public scandal, condoning his offence and thus disturbing the landmarks of social morality.' Catholics knew it was the church which decided which issues fell within the realm of faith and morals and that the church spoke through its bishops. Lyons described this as the weakest link in the Parnellite argument. 'This whole dispute was an Irish variation on a theme which was common enough in late nineteenth century Europe — the reaction of modern man against the claims of the church, which usually expressed itself in anti-clericalism.' Also, the Parnellite appeal to Fenian sentiment was a challenge which the church dared not ignore.

In 1960 also, J.H. Whyte, later the author of *Church and State in Modern Ireland* (Dublin, 1971), made the point, much repeated afterwards, that in the nineteenth century 'the Irish clergy could lead their people only in the direction they wanted to go', although he acknowledged that 'leadership was provided by the clergy'.[7] But Whyte added that education and prosperity were changing this, so that 'ordinary people were beginning to be capable of running their politics for themselves: The growing up of the Catholic laity provides the main cause of the decline of clerical influence'. Support for Whyte's view came from Virginia Crossman's and William Feingold's description in, among other works, *The Revolt of the Tenantry,* of Catholic farmers taking the place of landlords on the Poor Law boards of guardians in the 1880s.[8] They constituted an emergent rural elite which would make a strong contribution to the shaping of an indigenous Irish political system in the split and its aftermath. (Boards of guardians were responsible for levying rates on property-owners to run the workhouses and fund relief for the poor. Landlords were 'ex-officio' members, but half the membership had to be elected). But Whyte acknowledged that the split checked this process. 'The violence with which so many clergy threw themselves into the struggle against the Parnellites can at least partly be ascribed to a feeling that this was their last chance to restore their now rapidly waning authority in political matters.' The present study challenges Whyte's thesis and will demonstrate that in Meath at least the clergy were able to lead their people in a direction that they would not otherwise have gone. A pointer to the reason for the persistence of Whyte's thesis may be seen in Professor Tom Garvin's account in 1998 of 'the strange death of clerical politics in UCD'.[9] Garvin said Whyte's book, *Church and State*, 'seriously understates the context of clerical power at that time and earlier. John . . . was concerned to defend his church [which] . . . chose however to view him as a danger.' His resignation from UCD resulted from 'clerical politics and bullying' in 'a crippling structure of external, non-academic clerical control' under Archbishop John Charles McQuaid.

From universities in the United States, Emmet Larkin, son of Irish emigrants and biographer (though no relation) of the Irish labour leader, James Larkin, developed the thesis throughout the 1970s and 1980s that Parnell created the modern Irish state.[10] He recounted the formation in the autumn of 1884 of an informal clerical–nationalist alliance, by which the Irish Party would pursue the hierarchy's claims for Catholic education. This partnership worked so well that by 1886 Parnell, the church and the party comprised the de facto Irish government and 'the British state had finally lost the great game it played for so many centuries in Ireland'. In the first Home Rule bill in that year, Gladstone proceeded to seek to invest with legal form what Larkin characterised as the new state, while the plan of campaign consolidated the nationalist–clerical alliance, making the bishops part of the consensus of the leader and the party — but bound by that consensus, as demonstrated by their refusal to endorse Rome's condemnation of the plan.

When Lyons published his biography of Parnell in 1977, he highlighted the strains in this new relationship:[11] The party represented an alternative source of authority from which, should Home Rule materialise, would presumably come the government of Ireland. The church was bound to regard a secular agency of this kind with jealousy and suspicion, so the divorce crisis offered it an unprecedented opportunity for reasserting its leadership 'on impeccably moral grounds'. The bitterness of Parnell's supporters ensured that anti-clericalism would not be avoided, but this was limited to a minority. Larkin concluded in 1979 that in the Parnellite crisis and its aftermath, a basic readjustment took place in the distribution of power within the governing consensus, which proved to be permanent and which also contributed to the fundamental stability of the political system. 'The bishops would never again be taken for granted by their lay allies and would continue to be an integral part of the Irish political system almost down to the present day.'[12]

D. George Boyce, in his *Nineteenth Century Ireland, The Search for Stability* in 1990, noted that clerical pressure was resisted in the cities and towns, 'where Parnellites showed a vehement loyalty to their chief'. But in the countryside the clergy could still sway the public against Parnellites, who were denounced as adulterers. The church, having been pushed into the background, could use the opportunity to re-assert its primacy. 'It is hardly surprising then that Parnell's last struggle should leave scars of the deepest kind.'[13]

As far as Meath is concerned, Larkin has shown that north Leinster was an area 'where the clergy were prone to assume a very active role in national and local politics between 1850 and 1880' and the influence of Rome-oriented Cardinal Cullen of Dublin was minimal.[14] E.R. Norman, in the *Catholic Church and Ireland in the Age of Rebellion*, has also shown how the bishops and clergy of Meath had been conspicuous in the tenant farmer agitation of the 1850s and 1860s.[15] Patrick Corish's synopsis in *Archivium Hibernicum* of the Kirby papers in the Irish College in Rome cites many examples of Cullen's exasperation with the political involvement of Bishop Nulty's immediate predecessor, Bishop John Cantwell (died 1866) and his priests.[16] Paul Connell, in his *The Diocese of Meath under Bishop John Cantwell* in 2004, remarked how 'their zeal led to what Cullen in particular feared most — public acrimony between priests and people in the chapels — Cantwell had let the genie out of the bottle'.[17] Whyte noted that the most convincing evidence that priests played a decisive part in the selection of candidates was that at one point in certain constituencies they did away with the participation of the laity altogether. 'This curious practice was first seen at the Meath by-election of 1855 and it continued intermittently in that and other constituencies for over twenty-five years.'[18] Cruise O'Brien instanced a number of such occasions in Meath, where he appeared to accept the clergy's assertion that they were voicing the wishes of their people, rather than imposing their own views.[19]

The only published study of the split in Meath, by C.J. Woods in *Ireland under the Union* in 1980, is a numerical analysis of voting in parliamentary elections.[20] He maintained that both the level of clerical activity and the fine balance of votes for each side in Meath were untypical of elsewhere in the country. In the towns, the priests' influence was rivalled by that of greater numbers of 'Catholic professional and prosperous business men who, like the priests, had education, leisure and financial independence, enabling them to engage in public affairs' and by the petite bourgeoisie who had earlier swelled the ranks of the Fenians and the Land League. In rural areas the Parnellite case 'was not much heard'. Woods's conclusion was that the Catholic clergy contributed to the defeat of the Parnellites in 1892, not by 'hectic electioneering', but by steady influence. The present study, which is different in that it examines the actual extent of clerical electioneering, will suggest otherwise.

In *The Modernisation of Irish Society,* Professor Joe Lee in 1973 noted that 'in 1892, there is little evidence that even the unprecedentedly vigorous clerical intervention influenced many voters to change their minds. Bishop Nulty of Meath gave drunkards and prostitutes a rare episcopal leg-up by exalting them above Parnellites, but this did not deter 48% of Meath voters from asserting their preference for traditional theology.'[21] Lee later warned that Larkin's central thesis that Parnell established the modern Irish state, although audacious and challenging, reduced in importance the Easter rising, the war of independence, the treaty and the civil war. Lee also maintained that the bishops' political influence was limited to the areas of sexual behaviour and education.[22]

Sean Connolly, reviewing the work of some of these historians in 1985 in *Religion and Society in Nineteenth Century Ireland,* noted that between 1853 and 1892 no less than nine Irish MPs were unseated on the grounds of undue influence by Catholic priests in their election, leading many to allege that the clergy were the real controlling force behind Irish popular politics. But he agreed with the more cautious assessment of most historians that priests' political role 'depended less on their ability to dictate the opinions or actions of their congregations than on their unique suitability for the role of local agents and organisers. This became clear on those occasions when priests chose to support unpopular individuals or movements or to oppose popular ones.'[23] However, James Loughlin, in *Gladstone, Home Rule and the Ulster Question* in 1986, was one of many to comment since the split on the ammunition which events in Meath gave to unionists.[24]

K.T. Hoppen, in his *Elections, Politics and Society in Ireland, 1832–85* in 1984, found that 'the more the detailed workings of individual political communities in Ireland were examined, the more striking and important seemed the gap between local realities and the rhetoric of national politics'.[25] Irish politics were often profoundly localist in both content and style, so that the 'bright political fireworks' of O'Connell, Parnell or the men of 1916–21 were merely punctuation marks, against which 'limited goals and local priorities' could count for more. Considering the issue of clerical influence, Hoppen felt that it must include 'the gradual moulding of opinion' as well as the simple alteration of votes. Its impact depended, not only on popular identification and sympathy, but also on outright intimidation and spiritual coercion. 'It functioned most effectively when constricted and directed by powerful external political forces, such as those led by O'Connell and Parnell'. Clericalism was not the issue here, but rather the confessional nature of Irish life, which deepened as the century progressed.[26]

A.C. Murray found Hoppen's ideas a useful framework for his 1986 study of Bishop Nulty's bitter but successful battle for control of Westmeath politics with John P. Hayden, editor of the *Westmeath Examiner,* which centred on the reform of sanitation in Mullingar.[27] (Archbishop Croke of Cashel acidly remarked of Bishop Nulty in November 1891, as he bade farewell to politics: 'Tis a pity the Meath man does not take this view of life. He is close to 80 and might well give up his "Mullingar waterworks" and cease muzzling his parish priests').[28] Farmers and shop-keepers followed Bishop Nulty, while Hayden's followers became Parnellites, but Murray argued that even before the defeat of the Parnellites in 1892 the people of Westmeath 'were prepared to accept clerical dictation and reject a secular concept of nationality'. This 'challenges the truism that the people drove the priests before them in politics'. The present study, while reaching a similar conclusion, does not draw upon Hoppen's analysis because in Meath, as we shall see, local issues were subordinated, indeed used, in the all-out battle for supremacy in the split.

The latest historian to concentrate on the split is barrister, Frank Callanan, biographer of T.M. Healy. The publication of his work on Parnell in the early 1990s coincided with the centenaries of the split and of Parnell's death, at the same time as a solution based on consent was again being sought for the northern problem. So it is not surprising that Callanan highlighted Parnell's inclusive vision of a Home Rule Ireland against Healy's Catholic nationalist view, the one which prevailed. Healy celebrated the adherence of the church to the anti-Parnellite cause: 'The clergy, sprung from and endowed by the peasantry, were thus assumed into what Healy conceived to be the nationalist governing class, native and Catholic, which would supplant the usurping Anglo-Irish caste to which Parnell belonged', Callanan wrote.[29] 'The prospects for a clear demarcation of church and state . . . perished in the split. There succeeded a confusion of roles and an imbalance between the secular political leadership of nationalism and ecclesiastical power . . . The enhanced political influence of the church was at the price of an increased overtness in its exercise and of a deepened conflict between power and spirituality, both of which portended a coarsening of the role of the Irish church.'

In his book, *The Parnell Split*, Callanan said it 'was the first and in some respects the definitive confrontation between church and nation in modern Irish politics . . . [Parnell] protested vigorously against the menace of a confessional nationalism . . . His uncompromising delineation of the proper limits of ecclesiastical influence and secular nationalist politics . . . was a question of state . . . The supremacist Catholic Home Rule Ireland which he charged his Healyite opponents with seeking to bring about, he dismissed as a travesty.'[30] The split tore the country apart, with Parnell insisting that the independence of the Irish Party could not be compromised either by Gladstone or the Catholic church and Healy articulating an aggressive Catholic nationalism which defined one of the dominant idioms of modern Irish politics. Parnell also 'vividly warned of the dangers of sectarian excess within nationalism'. Asking whether Home Rule was ever really feasible, faced with British political obstacles, the overwhelming power of Catholic nationalism and the unyielding opposition of Ulster unionism, Callanan concluded 'Parnell's was a far more fragile political project than he made it appear'.[31]

The northern troubles continued to make clear just how catastrophic was the failure of that project. Lyons, in *Culture and Anarchy in Ireland* in 1979, lamented the fact that the Catholic–nationalist supremacy in the Republic precluded the Anglo–Irish caste, which it had emaciated, from mediating in the bitter conflict between it and Presbyterian unionists in the north.[32] Cruise O'Brien, in *States of Ireland* in 1972 and in *Ancestral Voices* in 1994, has meditated gloomily on this same fusion of Irish nationalism and Catholicism and particularly on its further refinement by Patrick Pearse into a 'sacral nationalism' which is completely different from Tone's secular enlightenment republicanism and which, in battling towards its goal of a united Ireland, was utterly intolerant of the identity or aspirations of any other Irish grouping.[33]

Chapter 2

Bishop Nulty's 'divine right'

On 17 November 1890, the day of the O'Shea divorce verdict, 72-year-old Bishop Thomas Nulty returned from Rome to Navan, of which he was parish priest and where he resided, as well as living in Mullingar.[1] He was escorted by the band of the Catholic Young Men's Society (CYMS) and a large segment of his 4,000 parishioners to the front of St Mary's church, in which he had been consecrated 26 years earlier. An address of welcome was presented by future protagonists, Luke Smyth, the 59-year-old farmer, bakery owner and chairman of Navan town commissioners, and Francis Sheridan, a farmer, hardware merchant and chairman of the wider-based Navan board of Poor Law guardians. Replying, Bishop Nulty condemned the replacement of tillage by cattle-grazing, because it reduced the number of people on the land. More radically, he attacked the process of tenant farmers becoming owners of their land. 'These peasant proprietors will be all landlords and they will be just as anxious to maintain landlordism as the old landlords,' he declared with considerable foresight.

Son of a tenant farmer near Oldcastle, the bishop detested landlordism, having witnessed the misery of 700 evictions in one day near Mountnugent, Co. Cavan, as well as burying 11 people a day as a curate in Trim during the famine.[2] The insights gained had led him to advocate nationalisation of the land, along with Michael Davitt and inspired by the political essays of James Fintan Lalor (1807–1849), whose idea of making land reform the engine of political change the conservative Parnell had adopted. In his *Back to the Land* pamphlet in 1881, Bishop Nulty had proclaimed that 'no individual or class of individuals can hold a right of private property in the land of a country: The people of that country, in their public, corporate capacity, are and must always be the real owners of the land.'[3] At different times he also contradictorily advocated peasant proprietorship, as had Lalor, who had characterised Irish landlords as England's garrison. Lalor wrote 'the entire soil of a country belongs of right to the people of that country and it is the rightful property not of any one class but of the nation at large'.[4] Michael Davitt ceased active advocacy of land nationalisation in Ireland from 1882, when Parnell ruled it out because, as the Land League founder recalled in 1904 in his *Fall of Feudalism in Ireland*, 'the farmers and priests were more favourable to the less radical plan' of peasant proprietorship.[5]

As the two principal Irishmen to advocate the radical option of land nationalisation (whereby farm rents would fund social services for all) to a deeply conservative society in which tenant farmers were gaining ownership of the soil in the social transformation that was the Land War, both Nulty and Davitt were branded communists.[6] The bishop that day in Navan was candid about previous reprimands by Rome for being the first member of the hierarchy to support both Parnell and the Land League.[7] But 'this time, I had nothing to fear . . . there was no contention of any kind'. *Ecce sacerdos magnus* (behold the great priest) was 'intoned by the priests in their soutanes' as he proceeded to a 'banquet' in his 'palace', as the clerically dominated *Drogheda Independent* referred to the adjoining parochial house. It and many people referred to Navan's church as a cathedral, because of its close association with Dr Nulty. One of his predecessors, Dr Patrick Plunkett, who was consecrated in Paris in 1779, had lived in Navan also for the following 48 years, as he re-established Catholic structures throughout the diocese in the wake of the Penal Laws. He opened St Finian's diocesan seminary in the town in 1802 and was buried in the parish chapel in 1827.[8] Bishop John Cantwell (1830–66), to whom Dr Nulty would become co-adjutor, opted to live in Mullingar.

In his defence of the Land League in 1881, Bishop Nulty had shown that his political involvement stemmed at least partly from pastoral concerns.[9] He advocated tenant farmers being allowed to organise openly and legally because 'Ribbonism or Fenianism are by no means the worst of the secret confederacies' which they would otherwise join. During a long career, 'especially while acting chaplain at two jails for seventeen years', he had warned that such secret organisations were condemned by both reason and religion and that their objectives were worthless or wicked; that, by joining, one ceased to be a member of the Catholic church, that those who swore them in were perjured traitors and that they would probably end up on the convict ship or the gallows. 'These warnings were at all times acknowledged to be salutary, charitable and well-intentioned, but invariably they made no practical impression whatever.' The men he addressed felt that they would be able to avenge their country's wrongs and rid it of oppression; their inevitable fate failed to deter 'the unbroken stream of similarly misguided youths who followed'. (For an account of local land issues of the period, see Peter Connell, *The Land and People of Co. Meath, 1750–1850.*)

Two days after Bishop Nulty's homecoming, at a special meeting of Navan town commissioners, his neighbour, 76-year-old William Lawlor, farmer, bakery owner and brewer, proposed a resolution, which was seconded by John Spicer, miller, and passed by 9 votes to 4, that 'as this county was first to elect him and since we have had no reason since then to complain of his political life, we record our unabated confidence in the matchless leadership' of Parnell.[10] The town council's support for Parnell had been unanimous at the beginning of the year, after O'Shea had lodged divorce proceedings. But that had been in the then widespread belief that 'the machinations of his enemies will meet in the future with the defeat and opprobrium which they have met in the past'[11] — a reference to Parnell's recent vindication by a government commission after letters alleged by the London *Times* to link him with the Phoenix Park murders in 1882 were proven to have been forged by the Dublin journalist, Richard Pigott, who had then shot himself.

Navan convention with 35 priests supports Parnell

The next day, 20 November 1890, as public debate raged on the divorce verdict and its political implications, an important meeting took place in Navan, the outcome of which would sustain Pierce Mahony's and even Parnell's stance, while causing much embarrassment to Bishop Nulty and his clergy. The Irish National League, created in 1882 after the government suppressed the Land League, was the Irish parliamentary party's local organisation and a convention of its Meath branches and public bodies, attended by 35 priests, unanimously reaffirmed Parnell's leadership, on the motion of Luke Smyth, seconded by Francis Sheridan.[12] North Meath MP, Pierce Charles de Lacy Mahony, aged 40, was a member of a Kerry land-owning family and had been educated at Oxford and Cirencester agricultural college.[13] One of 13 Protestant members of the 80-strong party, and one of only four of those Protestants to remain loyal, he said 'he would never turn his back' on Parnell. Patrick Fulham, a member of Drogheda guardians from Donore, who would successfully contest the 1892 general election in South

Meath as an anti-Parnellite, said 'they would stand by him to the last'. Fr Hugh Behan, parish priest of Trim, said he 'was not ashamed to mention his name', having as a curate proposed Parnell for Meath in 1875. Fr Michael Woods, Bishop Nulty's administrator in Navan and secretary to the meeting, said over £2,358 was collected in Meath for the Tenants' Defence Association. Mahony had lunch with Bishop Nulty before returning to Dublin, where he told a crowded Leinster Hall meeting in support of Parnell that 'the priests and people of royal Meath had that day met in conference and had asserted their undying allegiance to Mr Parnell as their leader'.[14] Mahony again instanced the Navan meeting when he supported Parnell on 1 December in the fateful debate on his leadership in Committee Room 15 at Westminster.[15]

Back home, the declaration of the hierarchy's standing committee, signed by the four archbishops and nineteen of the bishops on 3 December, that Parnell was unfit to lead on moral grounds, was not signed by Bishop Nulty.[16] But two days later the *Freeman* stated that since its publication Dr Nulty had authorised Archbishop Walsh to attach his name.[17] Such hesitancy points to some soul-searching by one who had previously opposed his fellow bishops on both Parnell and the Land League. Further evidence of Bishop Nulty's attitude at this time is provided by Patrick O'Brien, a Parnellite MP who, following his defeat in the 1892 general election, became party organiser in Meath after the 1893 by-elections — and an avowed enemy of Dr Nulty. He remarked that the bishop had fought hard to defend Parnell at a meeting of the hierarchy in Dublin, as he told a priest when he returned to Mullingar regretting that 'a majority of the bishops decided against him'.[18] (Margaret Leamy, in *Parnell's Faithful Few* in 1936 stated the Parnellite belief that a previous meeting of the bishops to that of their standing committee 'agreed to take no action' on the divorce crisis.)[19]

Bishop Nulty's stance in the divorce crisis would become, as we shall soon see, a national issue. He would later reveal how he was 'stunned' by Parnell's disgrace and this must account for his initial hesitation. But he must also have been affronted by the deceit of the man he regarded as a protégé and this would at least partly account for his subsequent bitterness. Only two years previously, the bishop had written of his meeting in Navan in 1875 with Parnell, who 'came to elicit my approval and support' for the Meath seat:[20]

'At a single interview . . . he revealed such extraordinary powers of intellect . . . that I . . . committed myself to him with the fullest trust and confidence . . . As I was thus the first Irish bishop who had absolutely committed himself to Mr Parnell, so I should naturally be the very last to abandon him.' (Parnell was duly nominated on the proposals of Fr T. Lynch and Fr Michael Tormey at private and public meetings in the CYMS Hall and on the Fair Green, respectively, where he pledged himself to tenant rights and Home Rule. After canvassing every parish, he won the Meath seat with 1,771 votes.[21] For an account of his entry into politics, see R.F. Foster, *Charles Stewart Parnell, the Man and his Family* (Sussex, 1976, pp. 140–46).

The name of Fr Christopher Mullen, parish priest of Moynalty and the only Co. Meath priest publicly to remain a Parnellite throughout, appeared in the *Freeman* on 8 December as a member of the Parnell leadership committee in Dublin.[22] But as support for Parnell started to wane, the *Drogheda Argus* of 6 December published a letter from Fr Peter Kelly, parish priest of Slane, complaining of pro-Parnell coverage in that paper and in the *Freeman*.[23] When the *Drogheda Independent* of 13 December carried a letter from Fr W.P. Kearney, curate in Oldcastle and a director of the paper, stating 'the bishops and priests of Ireland can never again touch him with a forty foot pole' and calling on both Parnell and Mahony to resign,[24] the paper abruptly changed its editorial line decisively to oppose Parnell. Even the neutral *Argus* praised Davitt, a former Fenian, as the first to call for the leader's resignation because he 'saw that if Home Rule was ever to be won by parliamentary methods and not by those evolutions on an Irish green hillside which Parnellism effectually discredited and of which no-one now dreams out of a lunatic asylum, Mr Parnell should go or at least efface himself for some period'.[25]

Fr Mullen, addressing his 'fellow parishioners' in Moynalty, took the opposite view:[26] They could complain if Parnell was a Catholic, but they would be ungrateful cowards not to follow the man who had left the aristocracy 'and joined the people of Ireland in a struggle for independence'. The church had opposed John Martin, Parnell's immediate predecessor as MP for Meath (the Protestant nationalist was elected in 1871 although opposed by a clerical nominee, having been twice defeated in Longford by the priests' candidate, after a successful election petition). But the clergy, even the bishop, had wisely changed their political opinions and supported Martin. Then, with the aid of Parnell they drove the landlords from parliament — 'the wolves from minding the sheep. The same will happen again. We will all unite under Parnell and become a burst of agitation.' He had 'raised a despondent people', forming a constitutional movement 'which brought the government to its knees' and he would 'lead us to the promised land'.

But an anti-Parnellite resolution was soon submitted to Navan guardians by Laurence Rowan, a 40-year-old farmer and shopkeeper in Stackallen, between Navan and Slane, who would soon emerge, along with the chairman, Francis Sheridan, as a major agent of the clergy in local politics.[27] His motion supported the majority of the parliamentary party in deposing Parnell and censured the *Freeman* for supporting the minority, thereby undermining the basic principle of party unity. Sheridan at this stage merely regretted the board becoming a party in creating a division. On 17 December Mahony wrote to the *Freeman* rejecting Fr Kearney's call on him to resign and reminding him of the 35 priests' support at the Navan meeting, since which nothing had happened except Gladstone's letter and 'I should deem it no honour to represent even royal Meath as a follower of any English party.'[28] Fr Kearney's response in the *Drogheda Independent* reminded Mahony that in fact two significant events had occurred: Parnell had published 'his foolish manifesto', denouncing the liberal alliance and attacking his former colleagues, who had been working in the cause while he was 'pursuing his peculiar pleasures', and the Irish hierarchy had issued their condemnation of his leadership.[29] A reader, M. English of Kilmessan, raised the temperature further, writing to the *Argus* of 20 December that the MP had no mandate to support Parnell from his Meath constituents, who 'with their noble priests, will sit in calm counsel and send Mr Pierce Mahony home to mind his Kerry kine, which would be far more fitting business for him than eulogising a convicted adulterer with all the stench of the divorce court fresh upon him'.[30]

Another indication of Bishop Nulty's changed stance was an *Irish Times* report of 23 December that Fr E. O'Reilly, curate, presiding at the Mullingar League, said that Parnell's opponents now included the bishop, 'who had got Parnell elected for Meath'.[31] In his confidential report to Dublin Castle for December 1890 (preserved in the National Archives in Dublin), Captain Robert Stokes of the Midland Division (Kildare to Sligo) of the Royal Irish Constabulary (RIC) noted 'the majority of priests are taking an active part against Mr Parnell throughout the division. In Meath the people are about equally divided.'[32] However, the *Argus* reported that a public meeting called by Navan branch of the Gas Workers Union in Market Square passed resolutions supporting

Parnell and endorsing the actions of Pierce Mahony and Edward Sheil, his 39-year-old fellow-Parnellite MP in South Meath.[33] Similar resolutions were passed at a Labour meeting in Trim.

The *Drogheda Independent* hammered Mahony in its first issue of 1891.[34] Quoting from the *Insuppressible* (the short-lived weekly published by the anti-Parnellites after Parnell forcibly regained control of *United Ireland*), it referred to him as an ex-land commissioner 'who fixed impossible rackrents'. He was never heard of 'until in 1886 he was mysteriously introduced as a man willing to take £200 a year for a seat in parliament while on the look out for better things'. At the end of January the paper published a letter from Fr Kelly of Slane, stating that as one of the 35 priests at the Navan convention he did not express support for Parnell, that he was for Home Rule and therefore against Parnell and calling on Mahony to resign.[35] Another straw in what would swiftly become a gale was *The Nation's* report of 24 January quoting Tim Healy, MP, announcing in Mullingar, where he had stayed with Dr Nulty, that he and the party had the support of the bishop.[36] This is significant because Healy would later contend that Bishop Nulty had disavowed Parnell two months earlier. But Mahony, campaigning with Parnell in Limerick, said that if they were to win Home Rule tomorrow by sacrificing their leader they would rather do without it and if they took it upon such terms their children would curse their memory.[37] Referring at another meeting to the 35 priests at the Navan convention, he said those resolutions of support would hardly have encouraged Parnell to resign. Also, Parnell 'would have treated the manifesto of the Irish bishops with regard and respect if it was only promulgated a little more than a fortnight sooner'.[38]

In early February 1891, Luke Smyth presided at a public meeting in Navan at which William Lawlor, the only town commissioner who was also a guardian, proposed support for Parnell.[39] A Parnell leadership committee was formed, 'consisting of the town commissioners, shop-keepers, farmers, artisans and labourers',[40] which began to prepare for a visit by Parnell on Sunday, 1 March.[41] But Navan guardians peremptorily carried Laurence Rowan's anti-Parnellite resolution, with only Michael Denning dissenting. Francis Sheridan denied the latter's charge of inconsistency, as 'he would not go into the company of an adulterer or into that of any party that would try to sustain the influence of such a man'.[42] At the next meeting, Lawlor complained about the lack of notice for the resolution and Denning proposed rescinding it, warning of the 'bad feeling' it engendered.[43] To taunts about his support for

Parnell, the landlord, magistrate and former nationalist MP for Meath, Robert H. Metge, retorted 'he is now turned upon by men who would lick his boots but a short time ago and for what anyone here would perhaps be guilty of if subject to the same temptation. I say the greatest curse of this country, next to drunkenness, is the curse of cant and hypocrisy.' Denning's motion was carried by 9 votes to 7, but Rowan indicated he would seek to reverse this at the next meeting.[44]

Parnell's visit to Navan

The *Freeman* described Parnell's meeting in Navan on 1 March 1891 as the largest in Meath since O'Connell's time, special trains conveying more than 3,000 people.[45] When he was recognised by the throng outside the station, he was carried to a wagonette. The horses were unharnessed and the vehicle was pulled along the streets of the town, which were spanned by arches of evergreens, the houses being decorated with laurel boughs. From every window handkerchiefs were waved and in response Parnell waved his hat, until he reached the Russell Arms hotel, where he was presented with addresses. The first was read by town clerk, James Lawlor (whose father, William, had ensured his appointment to the £58-a-year post when chairman of the town commissioners in 1887, thus giving the now 44-year-old official a freedom which he would fully use to act independently).[46] Approved by 10 votes to 3 by the town commissioners, the address concluded 'in your hour of trial, when enemies sought to destroy you, when friends deserted and betrayed you, when you looked around for a friendly hand to help you, we formed for you a bodyguard to defend, protect and sustain you and, regardless of the consequences to ourselves, we will be to you, faithful leader of the Irish race throughout the struggle for the restoration of Ireland's long-lost rights, as fearless and true as the plains of our country are green'.[47]

Luke Smyth told the meeting on the Square that the issue now was whether they would have an independent party in the Commons or one 'pinned to the tail of Gladstone'. He appealed for tolerance of those townspeople who opposed them. After William Lawlor proposed a vote of confidence in his leadership, Parnell controversially declared: 'Men of royal Meath, perhaps some day or other in the long distant future, someone may arise who may have the privilege of addressing you as men of republican Meath. Of that future I know nothing and should predict nothing here.' Highlighting his reversion to holding the balance of power in the Commons, having abandoned the liberal alliance,

Parnell continued: 'I have to go back to the days of Frederick Lucas, who as your representative first planted the banner of independent opposition which I see before me and which I have faithfully upheld.' Meath had also returned an upholder of independence in 'Honest John' Martin, who had defended John Mitchel in the Commons as Mahony and Sheil defended him in Committee Room 15. But 'if I had not had a colleague in number 15 committee room, I would have gone back to the Irish people to get their verdict. I refuse to submit to any other judgement.' He remarked on the town commissioners' support from Navan, Kells and Trim, Athboy 'very nearly united' and Moynalty with 'the gallant Fr Kit Mullen, the old disciple of independent opposition for whom I was not good enough in '75, but who thinks me nothing worse of the wear today' and the Gaelic clubs of Meath, 'who to a man have rallied to our side'.

Mahony yet again referred to the priests' allegiance at the Navan convention, 'when they knew everything about Mr Parnell in that English court'. He regretted that no priests were present, but John Redmond, MP, reminded the meeting that 'when Parnell started the land movement the bishops of Ireland were against him and the great body of the priests were either hostile or apathetic'. In matters of politics, every man amongst them had just as much liberty of thought and action as any bishop or priest. But Redmond, acutely conscious of the organisational vacuum created by clerical non-involvement in Parnellism, urged the formation of a branch of the National League in Navan and that Parnellites should run for election to public boards. (In a contemporary report to the Castle, among the chief secretary's papers preserved in the National Archives, the resident magistrate in Navan, Albert Meldon, noted that the league was 'moribund' and the district 'most peaceable').[48]

At a banquet in the courthouse later, Parnell more reflectively addressed his closest local followers on their rift with the Catholic clergy and on the need to involve Protestants in nationalist politics:

> Whenever the priesthood may have been uncertain or whenever the people may have been weak, the people of Meath have never been wrong . . . But we are standing here at the parting of the ways. This fight is one which I should gladly have avoided . . . and let us not disguise it from ourselves that the result will be a severe and bitter struggle. I believe . . . that all creeds within our country will be united as a result of these

issues which have now been knit and which must be fought
out. I have always had full confidence in my Catholic fellow
countrymen . . . But there are many of my Protestant fellow
countrymen who do not share my feelings . . . They will not
lose by casting in their lot with their common country and . . .
one of the most important results of the fight in which we are
now engaged will be that many of these alarms which they now
feel will be dissipated.[49]

The *Freeman* reported that the MPs who accompanied Parnell were
impressed by the order and discipline of the meeting.[50] The *Irish Times*,
while dismissing Parnell's reference to republican Meath as a bid to be
associated with 'advanced nationalism', agreed 'there was no
appearance of any hostility or opposition'.[51]But Laurence Rowan told
Navan guardians 'I can scarcely walk the streets [of Navan] now
without being insulted. I find that those who were loudest in their
demand that Mr Parnell should visit Navan, instead of being out to
welcome him when he came, were behind their counters taking in their
2 pences and 4 pences from the poor fools that came in from the
country on their invitation.' William Lawlor: 'It is a great infliction
upon a man listening to this.'[52] Although James Everard and Henry
Loughran were later prosecuted at Navan court for breaches of the
licensing laws on this occasion,[53] there is no evidence to sustain the
anti-Parnellites' — particularly the clergy's — frequent attribution of
drunkenness to their opponents. The *Drogheda Independent* minimised
the Navan demonstration as 'a few thousand youths with a sprinkling
of staider men'.[54] It went to the trouble of calculating that the 'few'
politicians from Navan, Trim, Kells and Athboy represented a total of
only 9,029 people, against a population of 87,000 in Meath. There
were no addresses from the guardians of Navan, Dunshaughlin,
Oldcastle or Kells, apart from six nationalist guardians in Kells, and no
league branches except Moynalty. 'For the first time in perhaps a
hundred years, the familiar figure of the loved saggart aroon [beloved
priest] was conspicuous only [by] its absence from a political . . .
gathering in Navan.' Parnell's speech it condemned as 'full of mischief
in alluding to republican Meath'.

Clerical surveillance had failed to prevent people attending Parnell's
meeting in Navan. Fr Kelly's letter to the *Drogheda Independent* stating
that only seven people from Slane were there and a further two from
the adjoining parish of Monknewtown was a clear signal to

parishioners that they were being watched.[55] RIC District Inspector Alan Bell secretly reported from Mullingar for March: 'Bishop Nulty and his priests warned his people not to attend in the strongest terms. . .[56] One of the Meath priests, Fr Mullen . . . was fully prepared to attend . . . But Bishop Nulty summoned him to Mullingar on the day before and held him here all Sunday and thus frustrated his intentions.' Bell's RIC superior, Captain Stokes, noted that while the clergy were succeeding in bringing the people on their side against Parnell, his meeting in Navan was very large.[57] In Meath and Kildare, people were about equally divided, but 'if an election occurred soon in either county, he would find it extremely difficult to return his nominee in consequence of the opposition . . . from the priests.'

To counteract such influence, the *Freeman* ran a campaign to show 'the bishops have not always been the best of guides in political matters. They have often chosen the anti-national side.'[58] It quoted a clever letter from one of Bishop Nulty's predecessors, Bishop Patrick Plunkett. From Navan, dated 29 October 1799 and addressed to Castlereagh, the Irish secretary who secured the union, it indicates how different the roles of priests and people in Meath were almost a century earlier:

> The Roman Catholics of Meath are too near Dublin and too much accustomed to listen to the opinions of the Protestants of Meath to be as yet willing to declare in favour of the union. They are not strangers to the principal arguments used to oppose it and many of them believe these arguments to be unanswerable. The clergy depend upon the people and they say here they would act imprudently did they wound the feelings of their respective flocks by stepping beyond their own sphere and abetting a system to which the people are not yet reconciled. 'We cannot separate from our parishioners', add they. 'On political questions, it becomes us rather to follow than to lead.' To this kind of reasoning, my lord, I must confess it is not easy to reply. For my part, I will heartily join the Roman Catholics of Meath the instant they will show a disposition to declare in favour of the union. Until then, your lordship perceives, I must content myself with defending and supporting the measure when opportunities offer of doing so with advantage.

Navan Parnellites fail to negotiate terms with bishop

The annual Poor Law elections in Navan followed Parnell's visit, with the retiring Parnellite, Michael Denning, apologising at his last meeting for stating that he was 'no priest's man'.[59] There were eight candidates for the five seats, Bishop Nulty simply nominating the four remaining outgoing guardians, who comprised two Parnellites (William Lawlor and Patrick Keogan) and two anti-Parnellites (Francis Sheridan and John Rice), but also Michael Lightholder, an anti-Parnellite. The Parnellites, in the hope of ousting their opponents, also nominated Lawlor and Keogan, along with Luke Smyth, George Jones and Thomas Nugent, thus creating a contest. The *Irish Times* reported on 12 March that with a view to avoiding a serious conflict with the bishop and clergy, 'ten of the principal supporters of Mr Parnell in the town yesterday visited him at the palace, Mullingar, but the bishop, it is understood, would make no terms and is determined to support his nominees against all comers. The feeling on both sides is daily becoming more embittered.'[60] Indeed, when Laurence Rowan's anti-Parnellite motion again came up at Navan guardians, Lawlor pleaded with the chairman not to accept it, because 'the matter has been already well thrashed out and public feeling outside the board is very strained'.[61] But Rowan replied that before Parnell's meeting the town commissioners had adopted a resolution supporting him, so the guardians should let the public know *their* feelings: the commissioners represented nobody but themselves, while the guardians represented the opinion of Co. Meath, he contended. After bad-tempered exchanges, in which Lawlor denied trying to bully the chairman, Francis Sheridan, Rowan's resolution was carried by 8 votes to 6. Lawlor, amid laughter, handed in notice of a rescinding motion.

By 17 March, the RIC in Navan were reporting on the very strong Parnellite feeling in the town and its vicinity, 'the principal opponents being the clergy, who however did not publicly declare their opposition, and a few of the well-to-do traders in the town and some of the farmers'.[62] The opposing resolutions at Navan guardians had engendered 'very bad blood' on both sides and the Parnellites were determined to unseat their opponents in the election. Providing background, the police recalled that Bishop Nulty had long 'assumed to himself' the right to nominate guardians and was therefore 'very much annoyed' at the Parnellite nominations. He wrote a letter which was read at all masses in Navan on 8 March, denouncing the Parnellites' attempt to remove his 'divine right'. The priests, especially Fr Woods, spoke 'very strongly' in support of the bishop. This unnerved most of the Parnellites, who decided to form a deputation to the bishop comprising: Luke Smyth, Thomas Nugent TC, John McKeever TC, P. McNamara TC, P. Finegan TC, James Lawlor, Patrick Smith (publican), Joseph Cregan (publican), George Jones (miller) and Christopher Quinn (whitesmith).

> But the bishop would not listen to their arguments. They then asked [him] would he direct the clergy not to interfere or speak on the subject of the election. He replied he would do no such thing but that he would direct them to advise the people to vote for his nominations. On their return from Mullingar, Luke Smyth notified that he would not go on with his candidature but the others taunted him with being a coward and that resolved [him] to go on. The bishop wrote another letter to the clergy here complaining of the offensiveness of the deputation, especially of five of them, and one of them actually lectured him on his duty as bishop. The letter was read at all the masses on the 15th and the priests spoke against the new nominations, as also at all the masses today . . . It is generally believed that with the exception of Luke Smyth none of the new candidates will be elected.

On receipt of this police report, the Castle under-secretary sought details of the election result from the RIC inspector general and enquired whether the bishop's letter had been published in the newspapers. A memo from Navan RIC on 31 March replied that the result was 'to leave the representation just as it stood before the election, viz. three Parnellites and two anti-Parnellites, all being old guardians except Smyth, who replaces Denning. Lawlor and Keogan, being nominated by both parties, headed the poll. Luke Smyth is . . . a large employer of labour and very popular and were it not that his principles are so strongly opposed by the Catholic clergy he would . . . have headed the poll.' In fact there had been a re-count following priests' objections to some of Jones's votes, threats of an appeal to the local government board (LGB) and of a sworn enquiry before Smyth took the last seat instead of Lightholder, as the Parnellites got two-thirds of the votes.[63] Turning to the Castle's second request, Navan RIC reported that the bishop's first letter had not been published 'and no copy can be obtained. It was very strong and is resented by large numbers of the better-class Catholics as arbitrary and claiming powers to which the

bishop has no right. This view was put forward by the deputation and
. . . Mr Jones boldly taxed the bishop with advocating taxation without
representation.' On 6 April, Captain Stokes sent this report with
excerpts from the *Westmeath Examiner* of 21 March to the inspector
general, who forwarded it to the under-secretary, who gave it to the
attorney-general. In the absence of documentary evidence of Bishop
Nulty's electoral interference, the chief law officer merely 'noted' the
report, but its political sensitivity is signified by the file's inscription 'not
to be sent out of the office'. The newspaper excerpts referred to Nulty's
'divine right' of nominating guardians in Navan and in Mullingar,
which Stokes said 'has been seldom questioned owing to the influences
which are always used against those who are independent enough to
exercise their civic rights. For instance, in Navan those who have had
the hardihood to put forward candidates in opposition to three out of
the five nominated by Dr Nulty were denounced in fierce language at
the three Masses in Navan on Sunday last.' This was despite the fact
that 'in most districts throughout the country the ratepayers are
deemed the proper people to make the selection of guardians. The
deputation, consisting of ten of the most respectable and prominent
businessmen of Navan, were denounced for lecturing his lordship
(and) for disrespect to him.' Thus ended the Navan men's well-
intentioned though ill-prepared attempt to head off a row which their
bishop and parish priest was determined to engage in.

Bishop Nulty's second letter, which would have interested the
authorities as evidence of his interference in the election, is the only
manuscript for this period to survive, tattered and partly illegible, in the
Meath diocesan archive in Mullingar, where it was probably placed after
Fr Woods died as parish priest of Trim in 1920, thus avoiding the
destruction of 1909.[64] Addressed to Fr Woods and dated Mullingar, 13
March 1891, it testifies to the bishop's direct involvement: Dr Nulty
ordered that if the Parnellites did not withdraw their nominations, 'then
you have nothing for it but to warn the people against them and to call
on all to vote for the men I nominated. Let all the priests . . . make a
house to house canvass vigorously besides.' He pointed out his
difficulty in getting men 'willing to undertake the care of the poor',
rather than, like William Lawlor, attending meetings merely 'to advance
the interests of their own faction'. Also, if he were now to withdraw his
nominations, he would 'practically declare myself a Parnellite'. The
bishop complained of the Navan deputation not giving him proper
notice and in particular of 'Christopher Quinn lecturing me in my own

house on my duties as a bishop'. To cap it all, some of them had availed of the hospitality of his enemy, John P. Hayden, editor of the *Westmeath Examiner*. He emphasised that the issue was 'not a political but a purely religious question', yet then added that 'their whole malice was directed against Francis Sheridan. If they could only oust him they would be satisfied, but they never will.' Noting that 'Smyth, Nugent, Jones, McNamara and Spicer were the only men that behaved themselves even decently', Dr Nulty concluded that he had 'made not a single concession . . . the three opposition candidates said they would not go on against me, and I think they won't, but you can't depend on them so if they don't withdraw before Sunday then let *all speak publicly against* [bishop's emphasis] them and canvass the people afterwards earnestly against them also. It is my firm belief that they would and will go on if they thought they had a chance of winning and they would not come here if they thought they had.'

Ignoring the fact that they had held their own against such clerical opposition, the *Drogheda Independent* rejoiced that the Navan Parnellites had failed to oust their opponents from the board of guardians. In what would become a recurrent anti-Parnellite accusation, it added 'almost the entire support of the ex-officio [landlord] and Tory electors was thrown solid for the Parnellite candidates'.[65] The new anti-Parnellite daily, the *National Press*, maintained that Bishop Nulty had nominated the two Parnellites in order to avoid a contest.[66] The bishop meanwhile had written approvingly from Mullingar on 9 March to the chairman of the Irish Party majority, Justin McCarthy, who presided at a meeting in Dublin to establish the National Federation to oppose the National League, which the Parnellites had taken over.[67] But this direct, public declaration of the bishop's anti-Parnellite stance did not prevent Fr Mullen from writing to the *Freeman* that at least 40 priests in the Meath diocese supported Parnell.[68] This, along with the massive turn-out for Parnell's meeting in Navan and local Parnellites' defiance of his election instructions, finally forced Bishop Nulty to break his four months' silence and speak publicly on the split. But it was in a moderate tone that, at mass in Mullingar, he regretted the disunity and intolerance of both sides.[69]

Bishop Nulty on Parnellism

The bishop said he was afraid the Healyites were a little intolerant too. There were business men, sensible men, patriotic men who loved their country, on both sides. Calling for patience, he said he had not spoken strongly on this matter, but he would in time to come. There had been no national movement without the bishops and priests at its head. It was remarkable that not a single priest now followed Parnell. At the recent meeting in Navan not a single priest attended. Parnell was isolated from the ministers of the church and then he turned rebellious. He would follow Parnell to the ends of the earth, were it not for his crime. It was through him that Parnell became a politician. If he and his followers began to suspect the bishops and priests on matters political, they would begin to suspect them on matters theological. Irishmen could not live without their priests; their position would be endangered without their assistance. The end of the Parnellite movement would be failure. 'We would ask the people to have patience and although they might be accused of being cowards, let them not talk loudly or uncharitably.' He asked everybody to join the federation to oppose the Parnellite party at the next general election. 'If we are compelled to elect Whig or Tory, we will do so in preference to these men.' After Parnell contested Co. Dublin and his estate was mortgaged for £13,000, he put him forward to represent Meath. He was proud of Parnell all along, but could not now think it possible to recognise his stewardship any longer. No one would have heard of Parnell were it not for the active influence used by him. Where would himself and his party be if not supported by the bishops and priests? 'Later on, these men may return to the fold, when the same harmony will exist as before this unhappy crisis', concluded the bishop who, like many anti-Parnellites, believed that Parnellism would be only a temporary phenomenon.

Following a two-hour meeting with Bishop Nulty,[70] after which Fr Behan of Trim, as he would later reveal, announced that he was no longer a Parnellite, the priests of the deanery of Navan, at their Easter conference, condemned Parnell's leadership on political grounds. As the action of the two Meath MPs in supporting Parnell against the majority of the party was unconstitutional and subversive, they had 'forfeited our confidence'. And Fr Mullen's letter to the *Freeman* 'grievously misrepresented the priests of Meath'.[71] But it would be July before Fr P.J. Skelly, Fr Behan's curate in Trim, joined his fellow priests in subscribing £1 to the federation, though not, he said, 'from any new-born zeal or desire to curry favour'.[72] The primate, Archbishop Logue, also had to exert control of his clergy in the adjoining diocese of Armagh, writing to Bishop Kirby in the Irish College, Rome, on 15 April:[73] 'If the priests are united we could manage the people . . . A week ago at the Drogheda conference a resolution condemning Parnell was brought forward. Seeing signs of lack of unanimity, I insisted on a division. One parish priest, two curates and the Franciscan and Augustinian superiors refused to support it. I gave them fair warning that if they took any public action I would not overlook it.'

Meanwhile, Francis Sheridan, on being unanimously re-elected chairman of Navan guardians, acknowledged that bitterness had been imported into the Poor Law election in the Navan division.[74] But William Lawlor withdrew his pro-Parnell motion, so 'the matter fell through' at last.[75] The *Drogheda Independent* maintained that the Parnellites had intended to contest the chairmanship, replacing Sheridan with either Robert Metge or Luke Smyth.[76] The *National Press* reported that 23 guardians were present for the election to the chair, 'it being an open secret that there was to be "a deal" between the Parnellites and the ex-officios [landlords] to put forward a Parnellite ex-officio' in opposition to Sheridan.[77] Evidently, the numbers on the day did not favour either the Parnellite motion or the manoeuvre against the chairman, confirming Bishop Nulty's assessment that they could not oust Sheridan. More significantly, the mooted 'deal' indicated the beginning of a Parnellite/Tory alliance to oppose the anti-Parnellite/clerical combination, but which the latter would use as an effective political weapon against the Parnellites. By May, Rowan was already criticising Parnellite support for the Tory Irish secretary, Arthur Balfour's, land purchase measures, which many regarded as inadequate. He lamented that £90 had been subscribed in Navan for this 'nefarious . . . conspiracy' and only £20 for the evicted tenants, for whom they should have had a joint collection, as in Drogheda.[78]

Having reined in his clergy, the bishop next 'spoke strongly in Navan cathedral' at Sunday mass in early April to condemn local Parnellites.[79] He did not see how any Catholic could now follow Parnell, who had shown such an utter disregard for the law of God and the principles of morality. During the elections, local Parnellites had cast insults on their priests. Although some of them had sought an interview with himself and then agreed to withdraw from the contest, still, at the instigation of one of their own body, they continued to the bitter end. These Parnellites had been making it their boast that they did not care about the priests, that they could do without them. But they would find that the priests could also do without them. Bishop Nulty was quick to prove his point. By mid-April, James Lawlor, who was also secretary of Navan's Parnell leadership committee, was writing to the *Freeman* on behalf of 28 members, deploring Nulty's 'denouncing from the altar in our parish chapel Luke Smyth, Thomas Nugent and Christopher Quinn, having returned the offerings made by Luke Smyth and Thomas Nugent, because of their exercising a civil right . . . [not] a religious one, namely, offering themselves as candidates for guardians.'[80]

Lawlor demanded 'that we be treated in the same manner', but was careful to point out that they were 'prepared, as Roman Catholics, to accept every religious teaching from his lordship, with all the respect due to his exalted position'. However, 'we are not prepared to surrender any of our civil rights'. Lawlor's classic definition of the Parnellite position as not being anti-Catholic but anti-clerical — because priests opposed them politically — was one which their opponents in Meath would continually fudge into anti-Catholicism, in order to gain political advantage. Explaining the origins of anti-clerical feeling in Navan, James Lawlor recalled that ten years previously, three 'respectable men' who were nominated for election as guardians were denounced from the altar, 'which aroused feelings at the time that are still rankling in the hearts of the people'. He also recalled an effort around the same time to deprive them of a say in nominating an MP for Meath, 'a right which they are determined to maintain at all hazards'. Lawlor was referring to a row in 1881 over the disqualification of Fr Dermot Cole's (Bishop Nulty's administrator) three nominees for election as Navan guardians and to the bishop's nomination in 1880 of *The Nation* editor and uncle of Healy, A.M. Sullivan, to replace Parnell (who had opted to sit for Cork, to the disappointment of his Meath electors), after prominent locals had opted for none other than Healy.[81] On that occasion, Fr Duncan, parish priest of Trim, had said that nobody would grudge Dr Nulty assembling his priests to ask them 'what are the feelings of my people' and the bishop's advice to his priests was 'follow the people if they are right at all and if they are wrong, teach them to be right'.

The bishop's response to 'the 28 just men of Navan' came in a scornful *Drogheda Independent* editorial.[82] Dr Nulty for years had seen it as his duty to nominate the guardians for Navan parish, but this time the Parnellite 'ecumenical council of Navan' had decided 'to fight the bishop'. They tried to and were beaten badly. The bishop spoke strongly of some of them, not because they were Parnellites, but because they had defied him and denied his right to nominate those who would care for the spiritual as well as the temporal welfare of the poor of his parish and diocese. Two of the ringleaders had boasted so loudly that they could do without the priests that he had returned their dues. Then the 28 rushed to the rescue of the injured innocence of these two with a manifesto, 'so Catholic in tone, so Irish in sentiment', which showed what to expect of the new Parnellism: 'The privileges of his lordship as a Bishop of the universal Church and a successor of the Apostles . . . as the guardian of the faith and morals of his people, are as nothing to these eight and twenty apostles of the new Parnellism as compared with what they claim as their civil rights.'

Within a week, the clerical machine began to move against its former allies. A meeting to form a branch of the anti-Parnellite national federation in Navan was attended by six priests and only twice as many local men.[83] Fr Grehan presided at a similar meeting in Oldcastle and Fr Flood did so in Kingscourt. Opening a second front, Francis Sheridan (chairman) condemned at Navan guardians a 'scandalous' editorial in the Parnellite *Meath Reporter* (published weekly in Trim, surviving files of which are unfortunately very incomplete). He said that it had insulted the bishop's administrator, Fr Woods, and the Navan curates 'in their political capacity as priests'.[84] He was present at one of the masses during the recent election and the sermon was purely on moral matters.[85] But the *Meath Reporter* had said

> . . . the Catholic altar of Navan was turned into a political platform and invectives delivered there sufficient . . . to bring the blush of shame to the cheeks of every self-respecting female of the congregation. Such statements made on a public platform . . . would be received with derision as the ravings of an eccentric character. But coming from the altar, under the protection of the sacrifice of the mass, they were received in angry silence by the sympathisers of those against whom they were hurled and by a fiendish joy by those for whom they were made.[86]

Sheridan asked them 'as Catholics, throwing out politics altogether', whether they wished this paper's representative to continue to report board meetings or to give it advertising. M.H. Thunder, J.P., said, as a Catholic, they should treat the article 'with silent contempt', but there was no seconder. Laurence Rowan, supporting Sheridan, said the editor 'was at one time a very great friend', but they should not allow their priests to be maligned — the editor had also called board members 'village tyrants'. P. Austin, J.P., observed that the bishop had surrounded himself with sycophants and 'the ridiculous conduct of his anti-Parnellite priests' was unsurprising. Luke Smyth defensively said he had nothing to do with the article and did not approve of it, but most members of the board, including himself, had in the past been denounced from the altar for their political opinions. The chairman put the resolution to black the newspaper and declared it carried unanimously, thereby undermining the *Meath Reporter* as the main local medium of Parnellite opinion. Most Navan guardians' deference to the bishop was demonstrated further when Robert Metge walked out of a meeting in protest at a farm labourer's cottage being given to a quarry worker who did occasional work for Dr Nulty, instead of to a canal boat 'captain' whose children slept in one room. Despite a medical report that the latter's house was too small, Sheridan maintained that the board could do nothing.[87]

Navan anti-Parnellites, led by their priests, now began a series of ploys designed to undermine their local opponents and which would ultimately topple Pierce Mahony. They alleged a threat of violence when they denounced the town commissioners' refusal of the use of the town hall to 'priests and rate-payers' on the grounds of peace and the safety of their property.[88] Fr Woods, on his election as president of the local federation, repeated that this was 'a direct incentive to attack our meetings'. The Parnellites had called on people to frustrate them 'by every means', but 'the working men of Navan refused to take the cue'. He also condemned alleged attempts 'to boycott and intimidate anyone who joined the federation'. If they continued, he would 'make public the record, political and otherwise, of some of the would-be leaders'.[89]

But it was Laurence Rowan who in May, with Francis Sheridan's support, commenced a deadly attack on Pierce Mahony — made all the more effective by the MP's hesitant and contradictory response to it.[90] The energetically devout guardian said Mahony had told Halley Stewart, an English Home Rule Liberal MP, 'if you knew the Irish priests as well as I do, you would sooner cut off your right hand before you would associate with a party to whom they are connected'.[91] Stewart had already denied Mahony's claim that these remarks were reported inaccurately.[92] Rowan recalled that Mahony had told the Navan convention in November that, although a Protestant, he was honoured to be associated with such priests as Frs Woods and Behan. But anti-clerical divisions in Navan had begun after Luke Smyth and Michael

Denning contacted Tim Harrington, MP, the league's secretary, and Denning had declared he was 'no priest's man'. He proposed a resolution calling on 'the Catholics of North Meath' to ditch Mahony at the next election.

Replying that he too would call for Mahony's resignation if he believed the accusation, Luke Smyth said the people of Navan, 'instead of being anti-clerical, are anti-Francis Sheridan. There is not a more priest-obeying people.' Local animosities began only after the chairman (Sheridan) unfairly allowed an anti-Parnell resolution to be tabled without notice the week before the leader's visit to Navan. Smyth moved an amendment, which William Lawlor seconded, that the issue be reconsidered in six months, with Mahony being asked for an explanation in the meantime. When Smyth objected to Rowan speaking of him 'taking off his coat to fight the priests', the latter replied that his authority was 'an announcement from the altar at Navan'. The chairman said that none of the many errors since this unfortunate crisis arose was uttered so repeatedly as 'down with the priests' and 'clerical dictation'. This cry had even invaded the sanctuary and even the priests were questioned as to their moral right to speak to the people from the altar. He would be surprised if Mahony escaped this contagion and, being a Protestant, he had his own anti-Catholic prejudices. The MP had got into position on the very shoulders of the priests and now he turned round and attacked them. All Mahony complained of was that a private conversation was repeated, thus admitting the accuracy of the report. The resolution condemning the MP was passed by 10 votes to 7. Oldcastle guardians also condemned Mahony's remarks about Irish priests.[93]

Parnell claims Bishop Nulty supported him

In contrast to Navan, Mullingar town commissioners 'disapproved' of a visit by Parnell on 10 May as 'it is calculated to provoke a breach of the peace and is insulting to our beloved and patriotic bishop'.[94] At that meeting, Tim Harrington, MP, sought to embarrass Bishop Nulty by revealing that the bishop had told Tim Healy, MP, two days after the divorce court verdict that Parnell was 'the only man for Ireland'.[95] Harrington challenged either the bishop or Healy to deny it, but when a *National Press* reporter called to Healy, he did deny it, adding that the bishop 'expressed his great grief at the disgrace Mr Parnell had brought upon Ireland'. Fewer than five hundred attended the Mullingar meeting, according to Fr Thomas Drum, Bishop Nulty's administrator.[96] The local federation thanked 'those who, in consonance with our venerated and patriotic bishop's advice, abstained from coming to hear the hero of the divorce court'.[97]

But the Meath priests' support at the Navan convention of 20 November and Harrington's revelation of Bishop Nulty's support became a national issue when Parnell himself referred to them in a speech in Belfast on 22 May, where he said the hierarchy had failed to take any action for 17 days after the divorce court verdict, until it had been made a political question by Gladstone's letter.[98] 'The Bishop of Meath on the same day informed Mr T. Healy that in his judgement my political position and leadership must be upheld. That was the act of commission on the part of the Lord Bishop of Meath which put him out of court' with regard to the hierarchy's condemnation, on moral grounds, of him as leader, Parnell declared. Fr Woods immediately wrote from Navan to the *National Press*, straining credulity by denying that Bishop Nulty knew, let alone approved, until 'long after' the hierarchy's condemnation, of the pro-Parnell resolution at the Navan convention.[99] When informed of it, the bishop had expressed surprise and had told him and other priests that he approved of the refusal of the priests present to support the resolution. Fr Woods also denied Parnell's statement that Healy saw the bishop on the day of the convention. His interview was on a previous day 'and therefore Mr Parnell's proof that Dr Nulty approved of the resolution in support of his leadership falls to the ground'. Fr Woods said he was present during the entire interview and could testify that 'the bishop made no such statement . . . [He] was staying here at the time the verdict of the divorce court became known . . . He regarded Mr Parnell from that moment as ipso facto disqualified from retaining the leadership on moral grounds alone. He felt the greatest sorrow for the man whom he himself brought into public life, but he considered him, unless he succeeded in establishing his innocence, as an irretrievably fallen man' and feared that he would involve the country in his own inevitable ruin.

As secretary to the Navan convention, Fr Woods made much of the fact that its resolution supported 'the *political* [his emphasis] honesty and sagacity of Mr Parnell and the members of the Irish Party'. But he not unreasonably went on to point out that 'last November no question about Mr Parnell's leadership existed. No split had occurred in the Irish Party'. He complained of how anxious the Parnellites were to obtain even the apparent support of the priests for their views, but 'when the Irish priesthood . . . have spoken out against his pretensions, their opinions are . . . to be regarded as of no consequence. They are requested not to interfere in politics and the dishonest cry of clerical dictation is immediately raised.' The Meath convention had been summoned by him some days before the divorce trial began, solely to organise a county collection for the Tenants' Defence Association. The resolutions had been drawn up at headquarters in Dublin 'and sent down to me cut and dry on the morning of the convention . . . insidiously drafted with a view doubtless to future manipulation'. At a private meeting in Kelly's hotel before the convention, Fr Woods recalled saying 'no priest could touch that resolution'. At the convention, Fr Flood, parish priest of Kingscourt, exclaimed 'this is a terrible scandal' and other priests made similar observations. No priest proposed, seconded or supported the resolution, although it was passed without dissent.

> But recollect how matters stood at that crucial moment. The convention met on Thursday, 20th November, with an interval of one day after the publication of the divorce decree . . . We had strong reasons for believing in Mr Parnell's innocence. One of our priests, Fr Ledwith, who had been staying in the same hotel at Glengariff with Mr [William] O'Brien [MP] some months previously, had seen in Mr O'Brien's hand a letter from Mr Parnell in which he solemnly assured Mr O'Brien that he would come out of the trial without a stain . . . Mr Parnell had not yet spoken. We knew that he was to meet his party on the following Tuesday before the opening of parliament . . . Would it not have been in the highest degree criminal precipitancy and unpardonable temerity for a county convention — in fact for any assembly of Irishmen — to pass a sentence of condemnation on our hitherto tried and trusted leader . . . We remembered the infamous Pigott forgeries from which he had just triumphantly vindicated himself . . . [after] for years refusing the offers to clear himself in an English court of law and we clung to what vestige of hope remained . . . For these reasons we allowed the resolution to pass unchallenged and [therefore] . . . we are dishonestly quoted as supporting the outrageous pretensions to the leadership of the virtuous Irish race of a . . . fully convicted and confessed adulterer.

Bishop Nulty himself followed up with a letter to the *National Press* about Harrington's 'wanton and irritating attack upon my reputation and character', when 'I am comparatively helpless for want of time to defend myself' at 'the busiest season of the whole year for an Irish bishop' (administering confirmation).[100] Healy never honoured him as a dinner guest. 'I do not remember having ever made such a statement and with the proceedings of the divorce court fully before me I am quite certain I never made such a statement', the bishop weakly asserted before going on the attack. Because few people had regard for or much belief in what Harrington said and because Healy 'indignantly denied the truth of such statement, I did not believe it required or called for a public contradiction from me'. But following Parnell's reiteration of 'this same defamatory statement', he could not remain silent. Healy was not at that convention, nor in Navan at all on the day. 'That I felt disposed to disbelieve the truth of Mr Parnell's guilt as long as I could, I freely acknowledge.' Because of the Pigott forgeries case, the letter to O'Brien at Glengarriff

> and my own personal knowledge of his character and disposition . . . the proceedings of the divorce court, when I had fully realised them, simply stunned, stupefied and bewildered me. When I further saw that he made no efforts . . . to clear himself of the guilt . . . that he had not the manliness humbly and honestly to acknowledge his guilt and offer voluntarily to go into penitential retirement in atonement for it, I felt it would be treason to the . . . principles of Christian and Catholic morality to acknowledge him as leader of my countrymen any longer. As I had taken a rather prominent part in the creation of Mr Parnell's political existence, I had no desire to have any hand in hastening its extinction . . . but . . . I feel myself under no personal obligation to him any longer.

In a letter in the *Argus*, stating that Parnell's political extinction was 'inevitable and merely a matter of time', Bishop Nulty warned that as he had 'with very little discernment and delicacy of feeling, wantonly assailed me before what I may suppose was a largely Orange audience in Belfast, I felt myself under no personal obligation to him any longer.[101] I have then to request that . . . while "putting me out of court" he will listen to the case . . . which, as soon as I have gained the necessary leisure time, I feel myself bound to make against him . . . for the enlightenment and guidance of my countrymen.'

Harrington swiftly denied in the *Freeman* making any attack on Bishop Nulty.[102] At the Mullingar meeting,

I said that Mr Healy informed the committee of gentlemen who were assisting him in preparing the Leinster Hall resolutions that he had had an interview with the Bishop of Meath on that day and that the bishop told him the Irish Party had no other course open to them but to support Mr Parnell. I never . . . insinuated that I believed Mr Healy's statement and of course if Dr Nulty reports that no such conversation took place it will be to me only more proof of the absolute unreliability of the creature who attempts to rival Mr Parnell in the leadership of the Irish race. The Bishop of Meath is very strong in his denial of the fact that Mr Healy was in Navan on the day of the convention there, or that he dined with him. But it is quite true that Mr Healy was in Navan the day preceding the convention and it is also true that he had a conversation with Dr Nulty on that day. It matters very little whether the meal at which the conversation took place was a dinner or a simple luncheon. The question is — Did Mr Healy assert on his return from Navan that Dr Nulty approved of the determination of the Irish Party to hold by Mr Parnell's leadership; were the members of the committee encouraged in their proceedings by that assurance; and was it true or was it false? Now, it is unnecessary to point out that I was not present at the meeting of that committee; I was away in America at the time. But I make the statement on the authority of Mr John Redmond, MP, Dr J.E. Kenny MP, and Ald. V.B. Dillon, who were present — three gentlemen, either of whose word will have more weight with the Irish people than any denial of Mr Healy's, however solemn. So far as I am personally concerned, I can afford to pass by Dr Nulty's comment upon the accuracy of any statement made by me. Those who have watched the course of the present political controversy know that I have made no statement the truth of which I have not been able to establish beyond all question of doubt.

Pierce Mahony also replied in the *Freeman* from Kilmorna, his home in Kerry, refuting Fr Woods's claim by recalling Fr Behan's speech, which was cheered.[103] Fr Woods lamely replied on the 'difference between supporting a resolution and uttering a solitary, detached expression in the course of a speech on quite a different subject'.[104] Mahony could not adduce more proof of positive support of Parnell by the priests 'than a strong expression dropped without a moment's reflection'. Fr Woods added that he had nominated Mahony when he was first returned for Meath, acted as his election agent 'without legal or other assistance' and had continued to support him until he violated the fundamental principle of the Irish Party by refusing to abide by the decision of the majority. Mahony replied from the House of Commons that the Navan convention gave him an ovation when he expressed his support for Parnell.[105] The 35 priests present allowed the resolution of confidence in Parnell to pass without dissent, as they did Fr Behan's similarly distinct expression. That conveyed to him and to everyone at the meeting that the priests heartily concurred. 'It is true that he [Fr Woods] and my constituents accepted me in '86, unknown and untried, solely on the recommendation of Mr Parnell. I hope to come before them again, supported by a similar recommendation from the same leader.'

Support for Mahony's view of the Navan convention is provided in a letter to the Parnellite *Irish Daily Independent* eighteen months later from R.J. Heeney, Gaffrey, Bellewstown, referring to a report of his evidence at the North Meath election petition that 'Fr Behan and all the Meath priests and delegates were Parnellites till after the convention':[106]

> What I did say was 'I was an anti-Parnellite going to the Navan convention, three days after the divorce court, as far as advocating Parnell's nominal retirement for, say, six months, in view of the moral errors just exposed. But when I went there and found all the clergy and delegates were unanimously supporting and calling for the re-election of Mr Parnell and totally ignoring the moral question, I decided that was good enough for me as far as the moral grounds were concerned. This was strengthened further of course by Mr Healy, Mr Sullivan and all the members in the National League meeting and Leinster Hall.' Fr Woods and nearly all the priests at the meeting on that day and Mr Fulham deliberately discussed the whole matter in the presbytery before the meeting and concluded to support Mr Parnell as indispensable and we did so. All this plainly shows the hollowness of the cry as to the moral question and that the material interests of the country are being sacrificed to selfish party and class purposes.

Navan rally calls for clerical moderation

The absence of Pierce Mahony at a Parnellite rally in Navan in mid-June 1891 'had a depressing effect', according to the *Argus*.[107] Luke Smyth, who presided, read a letter saying that the MP had to remain in the Commons 'until the land purchase bill is through'. Smyth said Halley Stewart belonged to 'the same tail as Healy', while Charles Fenwick, the other Home Rule Liberal MP to whom Mahony had spoken, declined to support Stewart's charges that Mahony had insulted Irish priests. They must wait until they got the full explanation from Mahony. Denying that Mahony could be 'disrespectful to the office of bishop or priest', Tim Harrington, MP, said that because the MP was a Protestant did not mean that he should not say what he had seen in the Kilkenny and Sligo by-elections. He himself had witnessed scenes that made him blush for some of the priesthood of Ireland. Surely, Mahony 'or any other man may condemn the policy which would introduce the blackthorn in an election'.

Christopher Quinn (who, as we saw, had annoyed Bishop Nulty by lecturing him on his duty) said 'as a humble Irish Catholic' if the bishops and priests told him 'you must follow us in order to destroy for ever Mr Parnell', he could not in conscience do so. The patriotic priests of Meath had 'failed to stem the torrent of eviction that has swept 89,000 out of Meath and scattered them over the earth. But Mr Parnell succeeded.' Quoting John Mitchel, he said 'hatred of England led to the option of violence against it, forcing young men to join secret societies, leaving them in the power of spies and informers. The bishops and priests of Ireland were unable to prevent this, but Mr Parnell succeeded.'

Harrington denied as a Catholic any suggestion that they had come to Navan to sow discord or lessen the people's respect for their priests, earned by their devotion to the people's cause in times of persecution. They deplored priests being divorced from their people. But they would discover that everything that was good, both from a nationalist and Catholic point of view, was to be found on the side of those who held by Parnell, who acknowledged that 'due deference should be given to the legitimate interests of the Catholic priesthood'. As we shall see, such acknowledgement of a role for priests in politics — but not a dominant one — would be repeatedly made by Parnellites, as well as by their moderate opponents.

Andrew Kettle, Parnell's ally from Land League days, said that it was Isaac Butt, the then leader of the Irish Party, who wrote to Parnell asking him to stand for Meath in the 1875 by-election, so Bishop Nulty had no right to boast of starting Parnell in public life. He was glad to learn that the interference of the priests with the political sympathies of their people had somewhat eased off and he hoped that the clergy of the district would now start to give lessons of toleration, moderation and Christian charity. Harrington appealed to the townspeople to continue to have the courage of their convictions. They could claim credit for never faltering in their practical allegiance to the church whenever a demand was made on them or their help was required. They were presided over by a prelate who had done great service in the national cause, especially for the people of Meath. He appealed to the bishop to have no quarrel or misunderstanding with his people and not to estrange them from him.

Next day's *Freeman* reported the Cannicetown and Kells bands playing national airs at the Navan rally.[108] It reminded readers that Luke Smyth 'is as good a Catholic, though a humble one, as any prelate in his palace' and that 'the word of Pierce Mahony is more reliable than the whisper of a retailer of lobby gossip and scandal'. But Harrington and Kettle were mistaken to think that Bishop Nulty might heed their advice on moderation. Kells parish priest (and future bishop), Fr Laurence Gaughran, presided at the formation of a federation branch there, of which he was elected president. In the following weeks Navan and Kells branches were chaired and attended by priests, including natives of Navan and former curates in the town, all of whom made anti-Parnellite speeches.[109]

At the beginning of July the Irish Catholic hierarchy, having met for the first time since the crisis began, issued a statement not only unanimously confirming their condemnation of Parnell the previous December but also decrying his followers' 'open hostility to ecclesiastical authority'.[110] However, Navan Parnellites' adherence to Catholicism was demonstrated in mid-July when Bishop Nulty presided at the funeral mass of local Mercy superioress, Sister Agnes Mary Duignan.[111] As almost a hundred priests marched in her funeral procession, 'every shop was shuttered as a mark of respect'. Condoling with the nuns at Navan guardians, William Lawlor said 'it would be hard to get her like again for goodness and kindness'.

But the clergy were already striving to drive a wedge between Navan Parnellites and a major segment of their supporters, the labourers. Fr Woods wrote to Navan guardians confirming his resignation from the district labourers' committee:[112] 'I have done all in my power . . . to get every labouring man in the parish a house and a plot of land — in the face of considerable opposition from both owners and occupiers of proposed sites . . . I now retire and let the labourers' friends come forward.' Laurence Rowan said 'the very parties he was working for now turned round upon him and . . . taught their children to disrespect him'. Proposing that Luke Smyth, William Lawlor, Michael Denning and Robert Metge be added to the committee, he added the 'best they could do was appoint the men that these labourers seemed to have such confidence in . . . It will show whether they are the true friends of the labourers or not.' At the next meeting Smyth said the existing members should continue and Metge wrote in similarly. Lawlor agreed, although 'if it would be of benefit to the labouring classes I would certainly act'.[113] In a row about the labourers' committee at the end of July, the chairman, Francis Sheridan, denied Smyth's accusation that he was in cahoots with Fr Woods and that he used Rowan as a mouthpiece, which Rowan also denied.[114] Smyth added that Sheridan had resigned from the committee 'because the Parnell labourers don't choose to join the federation'. Two months later, Sheridan complained about the labourers' committee's 'gross and scandalous neglect', but Lawlor responded 'we could not do impossibilities'.[115]

After Kells guardians rejected a motion condemning Pierce Mahony for insulting Irish priests, he wrote to them that Benjamin Pickard, another Home Rule Liberal MP who had been present, refused to confirm Halley Stewart's charges.[116] 'I never have and never shall object to that influence which a good priest ought to have and which is well expressed by the use of the word "father", but when priests attempt to use an influence which can only be associated with the word "master", then as an Irishman I have a right to protest', the MP declared. He faced his constituents at last at a major demonstration in Nobber in July, when he apologised for his long absence due to work in England.[117] Bell's report to the Castle put the attendance at 2,000, 'many of them substantial farmers and publicans'.[118] Mahony said that their policy of independent opposition involved resisting dictation inside Ireland, as well as from outside, to prove that they were fit for self-government. Regarding insulting Irish priests: he had always respected them as ministers of religion, but if they chose to descend from their high positions to political platforms, he had a right to criticise them. He had protested against the action of some of the priests at the Kilkenny and Sligo elections and would protest again. When they elected him in 1886, they knew he was a Protestant. They did not take him to represent them in religious matters and the fact that he was proposed by a priest showed that there was a difference between religious and political matters. On religious matters, they could not unite, but it had always been the policy of the national movement that in political matters all classes and creeds should unite. They would not ask a Protestant to agree to that if they were going to take their opinions from the Catholic priests, or perhaps more truthfully, from the bishops. He thanked God they had destroyed and uprooted Protestant ascendancy and he asked them for heaven's sake not to set up another in its stead. The Navan convention in November had unanimously supported Parnell's leadership, 'when they knew everything against Mr Parnell that they know now. Then was the time for them to speak . . . I told them clearly enough what I was going to do that day . . . If they say I am wrong now, I have nothing to explain. It is they who have to explain why they have changed.' Dr J.E. Kenny, MP, urged the men of Meath not to submit to the teaching of some of their priests that it was their duty to follow the priests on everything.

Parnellites attack Navan parochial house

On 30 July 1891, the hitherto neutral MPs, John Dillon and William O'Brien, were released from Galway jail, having served a postponed sentence for Land League activities, and declared against Parnell, following which E. Dwyer Gray, owner of the *Freeman* did likewise.[119] Their release sparked off the first of several episodes of mob violence with which Navan Parnellites would betray their cause. 'Illuminations [the placing of candles or lamps in many windows] were general on the release of Dillon and O'Brien, but in Navan the Parnellites turned out in large numbers and smashed the illuminated windows, among them being those of the parochial house, Bishop Nulty's residence', Bell informed the Castle.[120] The *National Press* described this 'ruffianism':[121]

> A man went round the town ringing a bell, followed by a crowd of ragged children and small boys, calling on the people not to illuminate their houses except for Parnell. The proclamation had not the desired effect and the crowd, then increased considerably by all the roughs and corner-boys of the town, proceeded to break the windows of the houses that were illuminated . . . The windows of the Catholic presbytery also were broken. No attempt was made by the Parnell leadership committee, who were walking about the streets, to check the ruffianism of the mob, who paraded the streets till a late hour,

hooting and yelling and throwing stones at the houses of the 'seceders'.

Navan Catholic Young Men's Society regretted 'that the mob has broken the windows of our priests' and his lordship's house' and condemned the outrage.[122] When John Spicer sensibly proposed that Navan town commissioners do likewise, he was over-ruled by Luke Smyth, who said the parochial house had not been illuminated for the previous 70 years.[123] The local federation condemned 'the condoners as well as the perpetrators of such a disgraceful outrage, hitherto unheard of in Catholic Navan'.[124] Fr Woods, presiding, said Smyth's ruling had revealed the true nature of the town's Parnellite leaders, which would be 'handed down to generations . . . If the Protestant rectory were attacked, an indignation meeting would be called and every decent Catholic in Navan would condemn the outrage.' The Parnellites in turn blamed 'the Whig association of Navan' which 'sent the public bellman through this town directing the people to illuminate . . . thus disturbing the peace of Navan, knowing . . . that the entire population . . . with a few exceptions, are unanimous in support of Mr Parnell's independent policy'.[125]

They denied that 'the extraordinary manifestations of displeasure' originated with them, but were 'the spontaneous action of the entire population'. They recalled that Luke Smyth had prevented the illumination of houses when Parnell visited on 1 March, in order to avoid such confrontation. They had great difficulty in preventing 'counter-illuminations', in anticipation of which 'those Whigs were obliged to have recourse to the authorities for protection, a large force of extra police having been drafted into the town'. Only 18 people in the town illuminated their houses. Fr Woods, who was walking through the streets, 'was utterly unable to restrain the indignation which his party had provoked'. (As well as 'seceder', Parnellites applied 'Whig' as a term of abuse to their opponents. Generally meaning liberal, 'Whig' had denoted members of the Irish Party who, before the rise of Parnell, were promoted by the clergy and became a Catholic fringe of the English Liberals which was detested by the ex-Fenian, Land League and active nationalist supporters of Parnell. The anti-Parnellites retorted with 'factionist' or 'Redmondite'). The *National Press* replied sardonically: 'The ecclesiastical tyranny and intimidation displayed in illuminating the priests' and bishop's house on the occasion of the release by Mr Balfour of two such traitors as Mr John Dillon and Mr William O'Brien fully justified "independent" Parnellism in hiring rowdies to resent it by wholesale window smashing. Parnellism cannot abide intimidation, you observe.'[126]

Parnell in Kells

'Not only the masses of the people but the men in prominent positions, upon whom influence of the most oppressive character was used to keep them away' flocked to Kells when Parnell visited the town in mid-August, the *Freeman* reported.[127] Inspector Bell's RIC report to the Castle described the meeting as 'large and representative . . . in spite of the exertions of the Catholic clergy. It is extraordinary how in Meath the clerical influence has given way before that of Mr Parnell. Branches of the League are being newly established in different parts of the county, while the Federation is not prospering at all.'[128] But the anti-Parnellite *National Press* said the Kells meeting was far smaller than the Navan one six months previously — 'remarkable testimony to the good wane which Parnellism has undergone under the influence of recent events'[129] (the release of Dillon and O'Brien, the bishops' condemnation of Parnell and his marriage to Katharine O'Shea on 25 June). Fr Woods claimed that several local people listed in the press as attending the Kells meeting 'were in Navan that day or at the sea' (in Bettystown).[130] He added that such was Parnell's prestige in 1886 that an unknown Pierce Mahony, then 'engaged in a government job in the west of Ireland . . . was two days member for Meath before he knew anything about the matter'. However, the usually reliable *Argus* reported that 'at Navan the platform was thronged and when [Parnell's] train came in a band played national airs. The deputations from Navan which joined the train were numerous' and the *Irish Times* agreed.[131] At Kells, Mahony recalled the Navan convention yet again, while Parnell again explained the importance of his policy of independence: political expediency was the rule of English statesmen, both Tory and Liberal, coercing Ireland when they could and conceding only when they had to. John Morley (the Liberal MP, who was an important link with Irish Party members and later Irish secretary) had come to see him nine days before the divorce verdict and had left knowing that it would go against him, but Morley's great anxiety had been that he should not retire from his position, no matter what happened at the trial.

Despite the success of his meeting in Kells, Bell reported to the Castle in September that even in Meath, where alone in the Midlands Division Parnell was likely to retain seats at the general election, 'his supporters are falling away'.[132] At the electoral register revision sessions for Trim, about 300 voters did not register themselves because they did not want 'to vote against Parnell, nor disobey their clergy either'. In October, Bell noted that Oldcastle branch of the federation, with Fr Grehan in the chair and Fr Kearney present, condemned the Fenian, James Stephens, for returning to the country to spread secret societies. Bell's reports throughout autumn 1891 mention stirrings of secret societies in several counties, including Westmeath, but not in Meath. In his May report, he had noted that bishops' and priests' denunciations of secret societies were 'simply an electioneering manoeuvre adopted by the clergy to throw discredit on Mr Parnell and his party'. This would become a significant issue in the Meath election petitions in the following year.

Death of Parnell

'The country has done with Mr Parnell, not for a time, but forever. He has gone to his political grave and it is a dishonoured one — the grave of a suicide. And the *Freeman's Journal* forms his appropriate winding sheet.'[133] This grimly prophetic statement was made by Fr Woods to Navan anti-Parnellites on 22 September, five days before Parnell, 'looking frail', addressed his last meeting in Ireland at Creggs on the Galway–Roscommon border and a fortnight before his sudden death in Brighton. Fr Woods had said that Parnell was 'publicly convicted of a career of shameful crimes and [was] an arch traitor'. In stark contrast, Navan town commissioners, at a special meeting on 8 October, expressed 'heartfelt grief' on the death of 'our dear and beloved chief'.[134] They condemned 'those who in their infinite malice and tiger-like thirst for his blood hounded him on to his death and sent a poignard into the heart of Erin' and 'the barbarous conduct of those who even in death are still firing their poisoned arrows at the man . . . for whom the best, most sincere and most loving of Irish hearts are bleeding today, whose name posterity will cherish and revere whilst their names will be remembered, if remembered at all, with disgust and loathing'. James Lawlor wrote to the *Freeman* that 'all that are true and patriotic in Navan' attended Parnell's funeral in Dublin.[135]

A black-ruled editorial in the *Argus* strove to be inclusive: 'Throughout Meath especially, which cradled his fame, which was loyal to him politically to the last, standing by him with a chivalry which resisted forces which it wrung the heart of its splendid people to resist, the wail of regret was intense.[136] The illustrious Bishop of Meath was the first to discern the statesmanlike qualities which the young Wicklow aristocrat brought to the service of Ireland. From the Navan platform rang out the phrase "hold your grip", from which such mighty results to the tenant class sprang.' In a now rare show of unity, Navan guardians passed a vote of sympathy with Parnell's 'mother and relatives', proposed by Laurence Rowan and seconded by Luke Smyth.[137] The chairman, Francis Sheridan, remarked 'there is nothing political in this', Sir John Dillon adding 'I am most happy to join any vote of sympathy to Mr Parnell's widow'. Even Fr Woods, presiding at the federation, proposed a similar vote, saying 'we would wish to draw a veil over the incidents of the last year of his life, if we be allowed to do so by his own followers'.[138]

While many of his enemies assumed that Parnell's death would lead to re-unification of the party, such hopes were quickly scotched by the Parnellite MPs' manifesto of 12 October, confirming their policy of independent opposition, which the majority, by abandoning Parnell at Gladstone's insistence, had sacrificed. It was also reported that Pierce Mahony 'will be elected by the Parnellite members as leader of the party.[139] The choice, it is said, lies between him and Mr John Redmond.' Mahony presided at a meeting in Dublin to expedite the launch of the *Independent* newspaper, which Parnell had been working on since the *Freeman* had switched its support from him two months earlier.[140] Shortly afterwards, he was described as 'the new chief' by an admiring audience at Usher's Quay (Dublin) branch of the league.[141] But the *Irish Times* reported that, while Mahony presided at a private meeting of the Parnellite parliamentary party in Dublin, the question of the leadership was not discussed.[142] 'It is in fact not likely that any chairman or leader of the party will be elected for the present.'

Back in Navan, he attended a meeting in the street of 'less than two hundred, mostly women and children', according to the *Drogheda Independent*, which adopted resolutions of sympathy on the death of Parnell 'to his widow and other members of his family', renewed confidence in their MP and condemned 'the terrible efforts which are being made to suppress our right to hold and express our own political opinions.'[143] This followed a Parnellite convention in the town hall, the use of the CYMS hall having been refused.[144] Mahony explained, as something had been said about his ancestry, that he was educated in England, but that was not his fault, for his blood was Irish and since 1872 he had been a Home Ruler. He had never made any secret of the fact that he did not like Parnell's policy then on the land question. But it was his experience as a land commissioner for three years that convinced him that he was wrong and Parnell was right. The land agitation was not only justifiable but also necessary and that was why he joined Parnell in 1886. He had been taunted with being a land commissioner and that in '82, '83 and '84 he had fixed rack rents which he said were too high in '86. He did say so and his words were thought so important that they were printed specially. William O'Brien knew all that when he asked him to act for some of the tenants on the plan of campaign estates.

The convention appointed Luke Smyth as chairman, Farrell Tully of Kells as treasurer and Christopher Quinn as secretary, to organise the constituency for Mahony. This move and the MP's *apologia*, so soon after Parnell's death and his own prospect of party leadership, would indicate that Mahony now realised that he would be faced with a contest for his seat at the next election, himself and Edward Sheil having been elected unopposed in 1886. As we shall see, Mahony was involved in unsuccessful behind-the-scenes talks between the Parnellites and anti-Parnellites on not contesting seats which either side were likely to win in the coming general election, in the interests of peace. His proposal appears to have been that his North Meath seat would not be contested, in return for the anti-Parnellites obtaining the South Meath seat on the planned resignation of Sheil. But it is apparent from later comments that Bishop Nulty and his clergy were instrumental in rejecting this suggestion. Mahony's reaction may be judged from his remark, after John Redmond failed to hold the dead leader's Cork seat in a by-election marked by violence and clerical intimidation in November 1891, that he would rather be in his coffin beside Parnell than have anything to do with the cowardly gang who had betrayed their leader.[145]

James Dalton, barrister, MP for Donegal West and the Australian brother-in-law of John Redmond, who would replace Sheil as the Parnellite candidate for South Meath, meanwhile suggested ironically that selected curates be sent to Westminster instead of elected MPs.[146] As long as Parnell was alive the priests went around the country saying there was a moral question, but that existed no longer, he said. Now some Catholic priests were rushing forward to try and get back the power they had had for a hundred years and which they appeared now to have got back again. The Irish Party had lost their parliamentary independence and were no longer free or able to return an MP unless he had the imprimatur of the bishop and priests of his diocese. Was

Ireland to be a country where political life was to be open, he asked, where men could call their souls and their consciences their own? He saw very little to choose between despotism from Westminster and despotism from Cashel or Dublin.

Portrait of Thomas Nulty, Bishop of
Meath – No Parnellite 'can remain a
Catholic' (courtesy of the Administrator
of the Cathedral of Christ the King,
Mullingar).

William Lawlor, Navan, Parnellite
town commissioner and Poor Law
guardian – 'Give him [priest] blow for
blow' (photograph courtesy of Philip
Smyth, Ardmulchan, Navan).

Portrait of Fr Michael Woods, Bishop
Nulty's Administrator in Navan, who
ridiculed Navan Parnellites as 'asses'
(photograph courtesy of Fr Pat
McManus, St Columban's, Dalgan,
Navan).

Charles Stewart Parnell – Stood, in
Navan courthouse, 'at the parting of
the ways' (courtesy of the National
Library of Ireland).

St Mary's Church, Navan, and the parochial house where Bishop Nulty partly resided (Lawrence Collection, courtesy of the National Library of Ireland).

Interior of St Mary's Church, Navan, often referred to as a cathedral (Lawrence Collection, courtesy of the National Library of Ireland).

Luke Smyth, chairman of Navan
Town Commissioners and Parnell
leadership committee (photograph
courtesy of Philip Smyth,
Ardmulchan, Navan).

Fr Peter McNamee, Bishop Nulty's
Administrator in Navan, who
knocked down William Mongey
after he struck Michael Davitt and
they both 'rolled in the mud'
(photograph courtesy of Fr Pat
McManus, St Columban's, Dalgan,
Navan).

Laurence Rowan, Stackallen, anti-Parnellite member
of Navan Poor Law guardians, who commenced a
deadly attack on Pierce Mahony (photograph
courtesy of Eva Ryan, Castletown, Navan).

Fr Peter Kelly, parish priest of Slane, in whose house Michael Davitt stayed, as
'he would have been murdered in Navan' (photograph by Richie Brady, Navan,
of Fr Kelly's memorial in Slane church, courtesy of Fr Joe Deegan, PP, Slane).

Chapter 3

A nun for Navan workhouse

The real turning point in Pierce Mahony's career came at the end of October 1891, with the death of Mrs Cowley, who had been matron of Navan workhouse for the previous fifty years.[1] This at last gave his enemies the lever they needed to dislodge the Parnellites from Navan guardians as a necessary prelude to toppling the sitting MP. Within a week, Francis Sheridan read them a letter from Fr Woods, asking them to consider appointing a Mercy nun in her place, to care for the 'Catholic poor, especially in their dying moments'.[2] It was decided to advertise the position, but the *Drogheda Independent* enquired why the Catholic guardians of Navan should not appoint a nun. When a vote at the next meeting resulted in a tie between the nun and a sister of a guardian, it was decided to re-advertise.[3] But the paper protested:

> Eight elected guardians who profess to be Catholics joined in an unholy alliance with the Protestant ex-officios [landlords], made themselves the rump of the Orange bigots in order to inflict defeat and humiliation on the nuns . . . All the Catholic ex-officio guardians . . . attended and voted for the nuns. The Protestant ex-officios never attended in such numbers before . . . although there is not a single Protestant inmate in the workhouse . . . Their action . . . is the outcome of pure, rank, undiluted bigotry. But what explanation can be offered for the conduct of the eight Orange Catholics, as O'Connell would call them.

Bishop Nulty, who the previous week had presided at a 'mission' in Navan with over-flowing congregations,[4] followed this with a vitriolic sermon in Navan cathedral:[5] 'If the sisters are placed there in that poorhouse there will not a pauper die there that will not pass to the enjoyment of God in heaven. Refuse them admittance, and I will not be responsible for their salvation.' The conduct of the Protestant ex-officio guardians was clearly 'a premeditated and organised insult . . . to the sisters [and] a bigoted insult to our old religion.' Pointing out that the Protestant chaplain was receiving £25 a year 'for preaching to and teaching no one', the bishop warned the Protestant ex-officio guardians:

> We have suffered enough at your hands and at the hands of your predecessors. Look at this very county, in which for the past half century your predecessors have banished and exterminated our people. You have reduced them by 100,000 in this county, less than we were half a century ago . . . Now all this is past and gone and we are willing to forget it, but they ought not act as they did. If they have come to the conclusion that either we or they must go, I say we will not go. The chances are against them, that they will go . . . If they persist in their hostility to the Catholic religion and to the sisters, they will irritate the people and excite them to rebellion and revolt against them . . . I will never interfere to stop them . . . Of our own Catholic guardians . . . they certainly have entered into an unholy alliance to oppose the interests of the Catholic, dying poor of God. But I am willing to accept that they did it in ignorance, but some of them manifestly did it for corrupt motives, for their friends and relatives . . . If they persist in it, after what I have explained . . . they are enemies and traitors to their religion. Because the mandate that a Catholic guardian gets is not merely to look after the temporal wants of the poor man but also to look after the wants of his immortal soul. If he fails in it he is a traitor to the trust reposed in him and it ought not to be imposed on him again.

At the next meeting of Navan guardians, Major Everard enquired 'if all the candidates are of the same religious persuasion, how can sectarian feeling be said to enter into the matter at all'.[6] Sheridan ruled him out of order for 'dragging in' the name of the bishop, whose 'action was taken on a purely moral question, which he was perfectly entitled to take'. Captain Roberts: 'I think it was dictation and intimidation.' Pointing out that Fr Woods had sent the bishop's sermon to every member of the board, Major Everard asked 'were not the doors of that institution open to every sister who would enter this dreary refuge to administer the consolations of religion to the sick and dying?' As to organised action, until he entered that room he did not know how a single vote would be cast. The bishop said they were exterminators: there were only three landlords, including himself, 'on the wrong side' and he pleaded not guilty. In the twenty years that he had resided on the property it had never been his misfortune to evict a single tenant. Perhaps his predecessors were the guilty parties? But over a hundred years, the number of his tenants had increased. His lordship threatened that if they were to exercise their civil right he would 'let loose a sea of elements of strife and disorder'. Was that the justice and charity they all expected from one occupying so eminent a position?

Rowan said that Major Everard could not be accused of bigotry and was one of the best employers in the country, but he had not a good many more imitators. Smyth said that a great deal of bad feeling might have been avoided if those who wanted the nuns had not held back for a week: 'None of the parties would have come forward were it intimated that one of the nuns was going to stand for the position.' He would stand by his promise to vote for the other candidate. Sheridan read a letter from Fr Behan of Trim: 'You have an opportunity now of rendering incalculable service to the poor as well as saving the rates by appointing a sister.' Thomas Gerrard said the ex-officios 'are not here to be muzzled'. The *Irish Catholic* reported that 38 guardians turned up to vote following Bishop Nulty's 'strong comments . . . in Navan cathedral'.[7] There had been 18 votes for each candidate, but an ex-officio, G.V. Briscoe, and an elected guardian, Matthew Sheridan, 'who voted for the lay candidate on the last occasion, now gave their vote for the sister of Mercy', who won the post.

The *Drogheda Independent* rebutted the ex-officios' defence, while castigating the elected Catholic guardians who did not vote for the nun, which was a religious question, 'after the clear and convincing explanation of their duties[8] . . . Navan has recently acquired unenviable notoriety . . . degenerate Navan . . . Politics should not have been allowed to touch the sisters of Mercy.' The LGB later approved Navan guardians' appointment of Sister Mary Nelson as matron at £30 per annum, plus rations.[9] But Parnellites and Protestant landlords were not the only casualties of this battle over the nun, as Bell's secret year-end report to the Castle shows:[10]

> In Navan there is a very strong anti-clerical feeling. Fr Woods has been doing all he can to put down Parnellism, but he has been unsuccessful and he has made himself so unpopular with a large body of his parishioners that Bishop Nulty will probably remove him by promotion to parish priest . . . I have heard from an intimate friend of his that the bishop thinks Fr Woods

has shown want of tact and that he will remove him from Navan. The bishop was greatly annoyed at the failure to have the nuns appointed . . . He preached at Navan last Sunday that formerly, when the hounds were stopped because Lord Spencer [the lord lieutenant] was with them, he used all his influence to allay popular feeling but he would not do so now, for certainly these ex-officios did not improve a poor man's land by riding over it. This may have the effect of causing some interference with the hounds near Oristown, but the people about Navan reap so much pecuniary advantage from the hunting that I do not believe there will be serious opposition.

An explanation for Bishop Nulty's outburst may be contained in the census figures which had just been published, showing the population of Meath at 76,987, compared to 87,469 in 1881.[11] Catholics numbered 71,690, a decrease of 10,053 in the decade. The *Freeman* commented on the decrease of well over 100,000 people in Meath in half a century — from 183,823 before the famine:[12] 'Land now given over to grazing and sheepwalks, where once must have stood the happy homestead and smiling village, is certainly a terrible indictment against misrule and bad landlordism.' One in 22 inhabitants of Meath was getting Poor Law relief, the same as in 1881. 'In no county in the whole country has emigration made such havoc', the total during the previous 40 years reaching 60,639. The bishop himself, at a hearing by the Educational Endowments Commissioners in Dublin on the Charlton bequest, had noted that because of the industrial revolution in England in the first half of the previous century and of the effective prohibition of breadstuff imports under the corn laws, agricultural production flourished, in Ireland especially and in Meath in particular, as it was a great tillage county.[13] Some 400,000 acres in Meath were under tillage, compared to 130,000 acres in pasture, at the time of the will (1792). The enormous labour requirement, which led to better wages, had encouraged large groups of migratory workers, called harvestmen, to come to Meath from all over the country.

Towards year's end, the *Freeman* decried 'rampant rowdyism' in the Waterford by-election and mocked Pierce Mahony, whose 'partnership with Mr John Redmond in the leadership of the party of faction . . . will at least give him some notoriety.[14] It is amusing to see Mr Mahony masquerading as an advanced nationalist.' Michael Davitt had opted to stand in the election, probably to pit the weight of his reputation against Redmond's prospect of winning, after getting a severe blow on the head while canvassing — prefiguring what would happen to him in Navan.[15] He attributed his defeat to 'Toryism and terrorism', a cry which would also be repeated in Meath.[16] But a jubilant meeting of Navan Parnellites on Christmas Eve congratulated Redmond, who had proved at last that Parnellism was here to stay:[17] 'We send our Christmas greeting to Messrs Davitt, Dillon and all the other Gladstonian lickspittles and hope the Christmas box which they received from Waterford may not impair their digestion.' Mahony was not as elated, however, revealing in 'a long letter' to his continuing friend on the other side, Davitt (according to the latter's correspondence with Dillon) his 'fears of what may happen at the general election'.[18]

On 20 January 1892, Bishop Nulty wrote to a Westmeath federation convention in Mullingar, chaired by Tim Healy, MP, urging the creation of branches in every parish, involving 'the clergy of the parish and adjoining districts, together with intelligent and patriotic laymen', to revise the parliamentary register in anticipation of the general election expected that year.[19] Parnellism could not survive much longer, as it was 'an unnatural organisation' which aimed at 'no great common good'. Doubtless contemplating its Navan exponents, the bishop wrote that it had no political programme, but reviled the Liberal Party to enter an unpatriotic alliance with the Tories, who had always been the deadly enemies of 'our race, our country and our religion'. He was 'an independent oppositionist long before some of these Parnellites were born and I am so still'. Parnellism was 'no longer guided by reason, justice and truth', but was governed by 'blind, unreasoning and vindictive feeling'. Such 'passion and revenge' made men 'insensible to human suffering'. Significantly, in view of his later nomination of him in Meath, Bishop Nulty praised Davitt's patriotism and criticised the electors of Waterford for rejecting him. 'Unchristian hatred of its old comrades and colleagues' was the hallmark of Parnellism, which had 'an almost maddening sense of the political influence it has lost'. But at the coming general election 'it may make a desperate and expiring effort to ruin the national cause, to prolong the country's agony and to wrest from it its present hopeful prospects of a satisfactory Home Rule bill'.

The bishop again chose mass in Mullingar to blame Navan Parnellites for the rift with his clergy, fudging their position as 'anti-Catholic'.[20] Opposing 'anything a bishop or priest undertakes', Parnellism had created estrangement, 'suspicious jealousies and hatred'. Parnellites had united, with possibly one exception (Patrick Keogan), with 'enemies of their race and creed' to exclude the nuns from the workhouse of Navan, thereby endeavouring to deprive paupers of greater chances of salvation in their last moments. But 'even the Parnellite himself must come to die; even he cannot live forever and in his last illness he who has calumniated and reviled the priests is under the necessity of summoning one of them to his bedside', the bishop threatened.

The *Irish Catholic* reported Bishop Nulty as saying that Parnellism had done more harm in two years than 300 years of persecution.[21] The *Drogheda Independent* thought the bishop's advice about election preparations in Westmeath 'applies equally to the men of Meath, in many portions of which county nothing whatever has been done'.[22] Bell gave the reason in his January report: 'Fr Woods told Mr Denis Kilbride, MP, who visited some districts to arrange a Meath convention, that "it would be useless to try and hold one just now".'[23] The new Parnellite *Irish Daily Independent* criticised Bishop Nulty for on the one hand urging anti-Parnellites 'to conciliate, to enlighten and prudently and patiently to persuade the electors', while on the other condemning Parnellites for their 'vindictive feeling'.[24] And Navan Parnellites condemned the 'misnamed' *Irish Catholic* 'as unfit to be placed in the hand of poor, confiding, country people' and advised 'everyone wishing to understand the political situation not to be misled by its endeavour to mix up the question of religion and the clergy with the present crisis'.[25]

The *Irish Independent* had the further 'painful duty' of castigating Bishop Nulty's 'narrow-minded bigotry and intolerance' in urging the 'Catholic nationalists' of Westmeath to select one of their own as coroner, instead of an 'anti-Catholic' and anti-clerical Parnellite.[26] 'Delivered at the foot of God's altar . . . to an assemblage gathered for divine worship', the bishop's words insulted his flock and gave ammunition to Tories and unionists opposing Home Rule as Rome rule. This did not deter the bishop from telling massgoers in Mullingar that the bishops had spoken on the political crisis and it was the duty of Catholics to obey them.[27] Parnellites were forfeiting their Catholicity. Answering criticism of pronouncing on a political matter, he said it was entirely one of religion and morals and it was his duty to speak on it. Pierce Mahony responded at a league meeting in Dublin that in political matters the people ought to be able to judge and act for themselves.[28] If a priest decided to take part in politics his voice ought to have no more weight than any other sensible, educated man's. They did not seek to deprive the priests of the influence which a good Christian minister must always have. But they objected to a priest trying to use the power of his spiritual position to further a political object. Catholics opposing priests reassured Protestants that Home Rule was not Rome rule and also gave the lie to the Tory cry of 'clerical dictation'.

Navan Parnellites routed in Poor Law elections

As the annual local elections loomed, the *Drogheda Independent* complained that 'rampant Tory bigots' had registered their 'property' votes, 'in order to revenge themselves by unseating the Catholic guardians who voted for the nuns'.[29] A landlord could have as many as 36 votes in the same electoral division, the paper pointed out, so the wishes of its inhabitants might be overcome by a few landlords. Absentee landlords had also been induced to register their votes and to appoint proxies. But all the elected guardians who voted against the nuns were being opposed and 'the outraged Catholic spirit of the ratepayers will pass sentence' on them. If voters thought that no one would oppose retaining the nuns in the workhouse, 'why is Mr [Patrick] Keogan, a strong Parnellite, opposed [by the Parnellites] in the Navan division except that he voted for the nuns?' Bishop Nulty's five candidates in Navan were Sheridan, Keogan, N. Kelly, P. Casey and M. Lightholder. The *Irish Independent* reported that the bishop also had instructed his priests throughout Meath to nominate candidates to oppose Parnellites.[30] At two Sunday masses in Navan, Dr Nulty 'called upon the Parnellites to withdraw from the contest. The latter positively decline to hand their civil rights over to anyone . . . His lordship strongly objects to two', Smyth and Lawlor, because they voted against the nuns.

The Parnellites called on Navan voters to support their candidates — Smyth, Lawlor, Denning, James Everard and Patrick Blake — 'who will uphold the banner of independent opposition', while the *Irish Independent* complained about 'the use of the altar' to oppose Catholic guardians because they had refused to follow the bishop.[31] Bishop Nulty might say that he was acting in the interests of religion, but it was for a political party which any Catholic was free to vote against. However, the *Drogheda Independent* denied that Dr Nulty's nominations in Navan were politically based, citing Keogan's Parnellism, 'so the calumny that the bishop has refused to nominate Messrs Lawlor and Smyth because they are Parnellites is exploded'.[32] Bishop Nulty's objection was based 'on higher and holier grounds than the mere passing political beliefs of either Mr Smyth or Mr Lawlor', who 'joined in an unholy alliance with the Protestant magnates' to deprive the poor of the sisters. As the 'divinely appointed guardian of the poor of Christ', he had to urge people 'to deprive such men of a trust of which they have proved themselves unworthy'. The *Drogheda Independent* would be 'false to our duty as Catholic journalists' if it did not warn 'the Catholic electors of Navan' against Smyth and Lawlor, 'who have for some miserable petty motive proved false to a sacred trust on a memorable occasion . . . doing so again'.

Also denying an *Irish Independent* claim that a contest was forced on the sitting guardians the previous year, the *Drogheda Independent* recalled that Bishop Nulty had nominated every one of them, although two of the five were Parnellites. It was the latter who had nominated opposing candidates and forced a contest. The paper also criticised remarks by Luke Smyth about Rome rule and a statement by James Lawlor that a Poor Law election was not a religious but a political matter: the pope himself had instructed 'that good Catholic men are appointed to take charge of the Catholic poor [but] . . . Mr Lawlor has read a distinguished politico-theological course and knows all about these complicated problems'. Fr Woods also wrote to the *Drogheda Independent* challenging Lawlor and Smyth to say whether W. Donnelly, a fellow guardian, in canvassing for his sister as matron, referred to the nuns also, thereby refuting their claim that they did not know in time that a nun was going for the job.[33] After that election resulted in a tie, providing a fortnight for further consideration, the bishop was 'surprised and deeply pained by the action of the Catholic guardians who opposed the nuns. He took occasion on the Sunday after the election to speak from the pulpit . . . [on] the duties and responsibilities of the Catholic guardians.' Fr Woods enclosed the letter which the bishop had instructed him to send to each guardian (along with a newspaper report of his Navan sermon), which stated: 'As a priest, I . . . ask you as a Catholic guardian to support the election of a sister of Mercy.'

However, Fr Woods continued, 'all these appeals were in vain'. This was 'a purely religious question, where the salvation of souls was at stake. And yet there were Catholic guardians found to turn a deaf ear to the most solemn entreaties of their own bishop and pastor.' Fr Woods then tried to refute a second 'excuse' of the Parnellites: that he himself had approved another candidate, Mrs Timmons, in opposition to the nuns. He admitted that he had told a friend of hers 'that as Miss Donnelly was going to — to use Mr Donnelly's own phrase — "fight the nuns" — she might as well have her chance', but he refused to give her a letter to assist in her canvass. He denied that the selection of guardians, 'who have in their hands the appointment of doctors, nurses and teachers for the poor, is altogether a political question, with which religion or its ministers should have nothing to do. Those who want to give effect to their political opinions can wait until the parliamentary elections and then freely and without fear of losing trade or custom or undue influence in any form record their votes for the party they uphold. But let them not gamble with the most sacred and dearest interests of the poor in an attempt to gain a party advantage.' Implicit in Fr Woods's statement was his assumption that only the clergy had the interests of the poor at heart, so they should have a free rein in Poor Law elections, which would otherwise be open to unfair local pressures, but this would not be the case in secret parliamentary ballots — a conjecture which the priests themselves would shortly disprove.

Fr Woods then preached in Navan that the bishop and his priests' habit of nominating guardians was entirely satisfactory to the community.[34] 'No one seemed to be displeased; if they were, no intimation of it was given.' While the officials of the workhouse were 'most zealous' that the sick poor had a priest to attend them, they all knew what scandals from time to time occurred in public institutions. 'What could the poor ignorant nurse do in those circumstances, without the training, education and piety of the sisters?' Some guardians' rejection of the bishop's appeal to vote for the nuns was 'a clear vindication of the bishop's assertion of his rights in the choosing of guardians'. They had lost the confidence of the bishop and priests. Were a Catholic people going to support the men who would refuse to allow the nuns to assist at the bedside of the dying poor? Those men were not true to their religion. They had proved false to Catholic interests and there was no guarantee they would not do so again. Persons who did not belong to their religion had sent in their votes to be cast for the men who opposed the nuns. Would they as Catholics join with them? If they did, they might have reason to regret having done so.

W. Donnelly wrote to the *Drogheda Independent* correcting Fr Woods's recollection of their conversation.[35] Fr Woods had replied

'she would be a very suitable person for the office, but we are thinking of putting forward the sisters of Mercy', expressing, as he himself admits, a doubt as to their being eligible . . . I did not consider this either 'positive or unequivocal' . . . Had Fr Woods been a little more decided at that time I am certain that she would never have been a candidate. It was only when she found that Mrs Timmons was canvassing with the sanction of Fr Woods that she decided to stand for the appointment . . . Mr Smyth . . . said at once that she should have a very good chance and then and there promised to vote for her . . . Mr Lawlor . . . told me that in case a friend of his own did not come forward he would support my sister . . . When it was decided by a large majority of the board to advertise the appointment, the chairman announced . . . that the nuns would not compete with outsiders, thus leaving everyone under the impression that the contest would be solely between the lay candidates . . . I never used the phrase that Miss Donnelly was 'going to fight the nuns'.

The *Irish Independent,* recalling the previous year's Poor Law election, after which Bishop Nulty had rejected Smyth's Easter offering, said the Parnellites were just 'as violently opposed before this question cropped up at all, although their opposition to the nuns as matrons is considered a good cry to raise against them on the present occasion.'[36] In response to the intense clerical barrage, Smyth and Lawlor merely answered their critics at a public meeting in Navan.[37] They relied on 'the good sense and intelligence of the people' and unwisely eschewed canvassing, despite the priests' canvass being made 'not daily but hourly'. Smyth repeated that the disunity between priests and people originated in the guardians' surprise anti-Parnell resolution before his visit to the town a year earlier. They had no objection to the bishop nominating guardians, but they objected to the men he nominated insulting Parnellites. Complaining of Sheridan's lack of impartiality, Smyth said that after the board passed a resolution condemning Mahony, the chairman asked a member who had voted against 'was he a priest hunter?' He (Smyth) was making no 'excuse' for voting against the nuns. On the day Mrs Cowley was interred, he promised Donnelly he would vote for his sister, whom he knew and also knew that she was qualified. It was open to the clergy that day, when the board was adjourned as a mark of respect, to intimate through the chairman that the nuns were to be put forward, but they did not. Both Mrs Timmons and Mrs Reilly were told to continue canvassing by the clergy. Two of the men who voted for Miss Donnelly on the first occasion changed their minds and voted for the nuns on the second: it was the same priest who induced one of the guardians to vote against Miss Donnelly. 'Were there any nuns twelve months ago, when we were opposed?'

Luke Smyth explains why Patrick Keogan was dropped

Patrick Keogan had broken Parnellite ranks in the vote on the nun, but Smyth omitted to mention this embarrassing fact as the real reason for not re-nominating him for that year's Poor Law election, explaining instead that 'when a fight came on he was not to be had, he was in Dublin or unwell'. He (Smyth) was not ashamed of being a shareholder in the *Irish Independent* and unfortunately he was a shareholder in the *Drogheda Independent* too. Navan was not anti-clerical, 'but anti-Francis Sheridan'. He had not canvassed the Protestant votes but 'there was not a single Protestant vote that was not canvassed by the other side'. He denied that he had said Home Rule would mean Rome rule. As for the charge about the labourers' cottages, all the good sites had been disposed of and it was difficult for the new committee to get a site at all. Some of the labourers looking for cottages were asked would they join the federation 'and to their honour they refused'. He denied the complicity of Parnellites in local disturbances surrounding the release of Dillon and O'Brien. On the necessity of carefully completing voting papers, at the last election 'the chairman of the board would have been the last to be elected but for 28 votes being spoiled, as the clergy subsequently objected to them'. Blaming the priests for starting the whole row a year previously, Smyth remarked 'it would be interesting to know what happened between the chairman [Sheridan] and Fr Woods when the want of confidence motion was brought'.

William Lawlor explained that nothing occurred about the nuns in Donnelly's interview with him three days after Mrs Cowley was buried. He promised he would vote for Miss Donnelly and kept his word and neither priest nor bishop would prevent him giving his vote. The bishops went with Keogh and Sadlier (who were elected MPs on a pledge of independence, but in 1852 accepted government office), with the exception of Bishop McHale. When Gladstone came into power the same would occur, as it occurred also at the time of O'Connell. Positions would be taken and the people would be sold. They had a fine parish priest before the present bishop took Navan (the town in fact became a mensal parish of Bishop Cantwell in 1853).[38] They were not then trusting to curates and administrators, who were only 'birds of passage', telling stories to the bishop when he came to the town and poisoning his mind against them. The five Parnellite candidates would compare favourably as supporters of their priests with the others. This was a question of Parnellism versus McCarthyism and had nothing to do with religion and by supporting them they would end the controversy for ever. Michael Denning said he was only going forward at the insistence of his friends. 'If blame was to be attached, it was to the men who did not bring forward the nuns in time.' John Spicer said he was opposing the bishop on this question as a ratepayer; the men they were putting forward were far superior to the others as representatives.

The *Irish Independent* reported that the Meath clergy 'made violent harangues from the altar and a house-to-house canvass of the electors, using threats and intimidating many electors'.[39] It protested against the efforts of Bishop Nulty and his clergy 'to crush out the spirit of independence' among Meath Parnellites.[40] As the elections progressed, the *Drogheda Independent* reported that in Kells 'the Parnellites gave up the fight and retired from the field before the day of election'.[41] In Oldcastle, anti-Parnellites secured both seats, 'despite the Tory and Parnellite alliance', and won the seat in Killeagh as well. The nominees of the 'unholy alliance' had been beaten in Bective, Donaghpatrick and Ardbraccan and although the results in Navan were not yet declared the paper hoped that those who opposed the nuns would be defeated. It proved correct, the result of the Navan election being almost the reverse of the previous year's, the anti-Parnellites winning by nearly two to one — 2,442 votes to 1,367: a majority of 1,075 in a poll of 3,809 — and Bishop Nulty's five nominees being elected while Smyth and Lawlor were unseated.[42]

Inspector Bell, in his RIC report for March,[43] did not doubt that these victories

> were obtained by the strong pressure used by the bishop and the Catholic clergy. Fr Woods of Navan and other clergy in the Meath diocese used all the influence their profession gave them to compel the people to vote for their nominees. They made the people look on the struggle as a religious one. They claimed for their bishop, Dr Nulty, the *right* [Bell's emphasis] of nominating the guardians and they demanded as a right the obedience of the electors to the bishop's known wishes. The introduction of religion into politics has been recently much

> condemned in some quarters, but the Poor Law elections lately
> held in Meath show how very ready and willing the clergy are
> to use the powers which their sacred calling confers upon them
> to do the thing which has been condemned and they prove . . .
> that the religious question is very near the surface and that it
> is sure to appear at the occurrence of any crisis.

Bell referred to Frs Grehan and Kearney in Oldcastle destroying and
spoiling voting papers against their candidates and denouncing such
parishioners for being in league with 'Protestant bigots'. At the end of
May 1892, an LGB inquiry into the allegations against the two priests
reported to Oldcastle guardians that it had established that in some
cases voting papers were tampered with and that voting in favour of
one of the candidates was deterred, but having considered the
majorities by which guardians were returned, 'the board will not
disturb the return of the election'.[44] Bell also reported Smyth saying to
a crowd of Navan people 'if they did not support independent
opposition by their votes now, they would have, and deserve to have,
Rome rule instead of Home Rule in the future'. In other parts of Meath
'the clergy have stooped to work upon the superstition of the poorer
class of voters. Fr Rafferty, curate, warned one man that if he voted
against the wish of his priest "he would turn him into a stone".
Although when the police tried to get evidence of this no one would
admit having been thus threatened, fearing a prosecution might follow,
it is the common talk of the neighbourhood that the priest did certainly
use the language reported.'

The *Irish Independent* said the result was expected and wondered
how the Parnellites received so many votes 'in face of wholesale
intimidation and terrorism' by the clergy.[45] It mentioned the possibility
of legal proceedings 'to upset the election'. But the *Drogheda
Independent* hailed the anti-Parnellite victory as 'a triumph of Catholic
principles . . . not without political significance'.[46] The Parnellites had
asserted that the issue was a political one and that the result would
predict the outcome in the coming general election in North Meath. 'Be
it so . . . The Navan Poor Law election must have given [Pierce Mahony]
a cold shiver . . . It has written up . . . the doom of faction in Meath.'
Unusually, the *Argus* was partisan, with 'Bravo Navan'.[47] The return of
five anti-Parnellites with nearly 500 votes each and the defeat of five
Parnellites with under 300 votes apiece would disappoint Mahony
'who looked on Navan as his great stronghold'. Patrick Keogan was the

only Parnellite returned in Navan, with the support of anti-Parnellites and opposition of Parnellites, having voted with the majority in the election of a nun as matron. 'Men who have for long years been most attentive guardians have been sent to the right about . . . because the principles they advocate [independent opposition rather than the liberal alliance] . . . would eventually lead to the wilderness and the extension of coercion rule.' Asserting that the Parnellites had 'the support of the landlord property votes', the *Freeman* remarked that personal attacks on the patriot bishop and priests of Meath had provoked 'a healthy revulsion'.[48] Mentioning the possibility of Luke Smyth, despite his defeat, being a Parnellite candidate at the general election, it wished him 'the same good fortune'.[49]

Francis Sheridan was unanimously re-elected chairman of Navan guardians, where Laurence Rowan intimated his intention to continue to comment on 'the political aspect of the struggles the country is passing through'.[50] Later, Sheridan complained about Luke Smyth alleging that the guardians made membership of the federation a condition for giving sites to labourers.[51] Smyth had not replied to his letter asking him to tell the board who these members were. Only nine members attended a meeting of the Navan league, which resolved that because of the clergy's involvement in the Poor Law elections in Navan and elsewhere, 'in the interests of freedom it is absolutely necessary to have the system of open voting changed to that of the [secret] ballot'.[52] They called for branches of the league to be formed in every parish and, applauding the success of the *Irish Independent* and *Evening Herald*, they appealed 'to the labourers and artisans of Navan and elsewhere to form clubs, enabling members to become shareholders by paying small instalments'.

Bell's RIC report for April, noting their call for the secret ballot to be extended to local elections, also recorded that Navan Parnellites were 'highly delighted at the transfer of Fr Woods to Rahan, King's County [Offaly], as he was the principal cause of the bitter feeling which exists between the two parties there'.[53] On Fr Woods's promotion to parish priest, the *Freeman* reported that a leather purse of one hundred gold sovereigns was presented to him by the Young Men's Catholic Society and the Catholic population generally of Navan.[54] The Parnellites had wanted to banish from politics this priest, who 'went to Navan 19 years ago and has been the guiding spirit in turn of the Tenants' Defence Association, the Land League and the National League in his district. He was Mr Parnell's volunteer expense agent when he attacked and defeated the coercionist Harry Bourke, who is now hand in glove with the independents.' Fr Woods's presentation was proof 'of the permanency in unimpaired strength of that bond that has ever united the Irish priests and people', the *Drogheda Independent* remarked.[55]

Meanwhile, Navan guardians further muzzled local media criticism by barring Mr Smith, proprietor of the Parnellite *Meath Reporter*, from future meetings for refusing to reveal the identity of the writer of a published letter alleging that two patients in the workhouse 'were got dead in their beds and where were the good nuns?'[56] Mr Cowley, master of the workhouse, denied this. Amazingly, the guardians voted to continue this ban a decade later.[57] They did not react to Smyth's continued failure to respond to their request to back up his allegation of political bias in awarding labourers' sites in Navan, which Sheridan again denied while Rowan said Smyth was treating them with contempt.[58] Nicholas Kelly, with unwarranted optimism, remarked 'as things are settling down, it would be best to leave it an open question'. In fact, as we shall see, the trouble was only beginning.

Chapter 4

Michael Davitt in the 1892 election

With the Parnellites vanquished in their Navan stronghold, it was time to concentrate on ousting Pierce Mahony in the general election, the *Drogheda Independent* proclaiming that 'such pledge breakers' must be sent 'to the right about'.[1] And who better to do so than a big name like Michael Davitt, who had the added advantage of having been elected for Meath in 1882 as a protest while he was in Portland prison (but was judged by the Commons ineligible to take his seat as a convicted felon)?[2] Bishop Nulty had been intimately involved in his 'old friend's' (as Fr Kelly of Slane would later call him) nomination then, as he would be now. It was no coincidence that both men's names were repeatedly linked by Henry George, the American radical who visited Ireland four times during 1881–84 in a vain attempt to get the Land League to support land nationalisation instead of peasant proprietorship.[3] But Davitt would bitterly regret allowing himself to be cajoled by the bishop and the party into standing again in Meath.

The 'father of the Land League' re-entered Meath politics at a meeting on 24 April 1892 at Slane, where he was accompanied by John Dillon, MP. But the police noted much disappointment at the smallness of his meeting, even though 'it was rumoured' that Davitt was to be named as Pierce Mahony's opponent.[4] Only about 1,400 attended 'and there was none of the old pomp and parade . . . The speeches created no applause and were badly listened to.' The RIC also quoted Mahony's view that the Parnellites 'will be able to secure as many seats as they hold at present at the general election', losses in the midlands being made up by gains in the west. Their May report, however, noting that the Navan league would have a collection to defray his election expenses, warned 'the fight in this county will be particularly bitter, particularly in this (north) division', but it was not expected that they would retain either of their seats in Meath.

Davitt's candidature was not announced at the Slane meeting, which merely pledged to relegate Mahony 'to his original obscurity'.[5] Fr

Woods, who was received with cheers, said his reception was proof that the maligner of the Irish priesthood (Mahony) would get the reward of his treachery at the general election. The Parnellites had said the Poor Law elections in Navan would give a foresight of the general election — and they had. Patrick Keogan was the only Parnellite to be elected, because he 'had seen the error of his ways and abjured Parnellism six months ago' (by voting for the nuns). Every land grabber, bailiff and official and even the militiamen voted for the Parnellites in Navan. Yet all they could say was that their defeat was the result of clerical intimidation. He challenged them to identify a single anti-Parnellite vote that was obtained by undue influence. The intimidation was on the other side and he could give names, if asked. People who owed money were afraid to vote otherwise than as they were told.

The *Drogheda Independent* reported that Fr Kelly presided on the platform outside his parochial house in Slane and it claimed that 2,000 heard Dillon deride Mahony's posturing as an advanced nationalist.[6] Fr Woods remarked 'it is worthwhile getting your windows broken to get that cheer'. He ridiculed as 'asses' the Navan Parnellites who maintained that Poor Law elections were a political and not a religious issue. The paper declared that it was only since the split that the Irish priest was 'dubbed a dictator when he headed his people'. Davitt, it said, was received with cries of 'our next member'. The former opponent of clerical influence raised the possibility of not contesting Parnellite seats, only to discountenance it by saying that they could not have any arrangement with people who did not tolerate priests in politics. He said the Parnellites would have acted wisely after the death of Parnell had they rejoined the Irish Party, thus healing the split. Then, working in harmony for the one cause with the majority, they could have tried to convince the country that Parnell's later policy (independent opposition) would win a better measure of Home Rule than that which a united party had pursued from 1886 to '90 (the Liberal alliance). If the Parnellites had done this, the anti-Parnellites would not oppose their MPs in the coming election (though Davitt failed to specify whether this would have applied to Mahony).

But John Redmond, MP, accompanying Mahony at a meeting in Drogheda shortly afterwards, challenged Dillon to deny in public that he was constantly expressing in private warm approval of a recent suggestion about not contesting Parnellite seats.[7] However, Healy had declared against the proposal, so Dillon was silent on it in Slane, even though the idea had originated with himself; the Parnellites had made no proposals about this at all, being an independent party, said Redmond. Annoyed, Dillon immediately wrote to Tim Harrington complaining about Redmond referring dishonestly to their private conversation about not contesting seats.[8] 'As you know, the first advances in this matter came from Mahony and from another quarter which I am not at liberty to mention' (Sheil?). Redmond's malignancy, 'for the sake of a pitiful point in a speech . . . makes it utterly impossible for me or anyone else to make any effort in the direction of peace'. The *Freeman* taunted 'when the split came, Mahony, having no fixed principles to guide him, calculated only which side would win . . . He made a mistake and is sorry for it.'

Healy, in *Why Ireland Is Not Free* in 1898, recalled that on 22 February 1892 the moderate John Dillon had proposed to the party committee that in the interests of peace he be empowered to open negotiations with the Parnellites on a 'deal' on seats in the next election, Redmond's party then numbering 30.[9] This was opposed by Healy but passed by 7 votes to 2, although no action was taken on the resolution, which William O'Brien revealed in a speech in Cork in May. Also, T.P. O'Connor had 'openly advocated a seats deal' in a speech at Liverpool on 5 April (the 'recent suggestion' which Redmond recalled in Drogheda). Healy complained that the Parnellites were thus encouraged to fight the general election 'with far greater bitterness and determination' and also that the majority party was never consulted about handing over at least 15 seats to them. He added that Dillon on 30 May 1892 secretly began fresh negotiations with the Parnellites, even though the party, in consultation with Davitt, had that day appointed an electoral committee. Over three days (on the last of which, 1 June, Davitt and Patrick Fulham were selected as anti-Parnellite candidates by the Meath clergy in Navan seminary) Dillon and O'Connor, with an un-named Irish-American arbitrator, discussed the 'deal' with Redmond and Harrington in Dublin. But Redmond, said Healy, 'was obliged to reject these overtures' because if the bulk of his MPs were not accommodated those 'left out in the cold' would denounce the arrangement. Healy said that finally in Bradford on 5 June Dillon proposed without optimism an arrangement whereby, if an agreed board believed in a Parnellite MP's ability to retain his seat, 'we will give you the seat'. This would not infringe the rights of constituencies, Dillon had maintained, and would save the country 'manifold injuries'.

Tim Harrington would later claim, as we shall see, that it was the anti-Parnellites who rejected an offer on seats, including dividing the

Meath seats, which the Parnellites had made in order not to give any advantage to conservative candidates. But perhaps Harrington (and Redmond) were deviously trying to gain political advantage by publicly blaming the anti-Parnellites for the failure of what would be the last peace effort between the two sides until nearly the end of the decade. Whatever about a seats offer only encouraging the Parnellites, as Healy maintained, a seats deal would have removed a great deal of bitterness from the 1892 general election campaign, which cemented the divisions among nationalists. In Meath it would have avoided not only the turmoil of the elections, but also the rancour of the subsequent petitions and fresh elections, by giving Mahony his seat uncontested in exchange for that of Sheil, who was about to retire.

Mahony complained at the Drogheda meeting that 'an old and stale lie had been re-circulated against him . . . A little handbill had been sent round at the meeting in Slane', which repeated his alleged remarks about Irish priests to two other MPs at Westminster, which he had denied. Reported in the *Irish Independent* as referring to a priest in Mullingar threatening to ruin the business of local Protestant traders because of their political opinions, Mahony said:[10] 'To the priests of Meath I have nothing but good feeling', because 35 of them cheered him for supporting Parnell 'and if they changed their minds it is for them to make an explanation, I have no need to . . . I appeal to them in this struggle, in which their congregations are divided and in which no question of religion or morals enters, to stand aside and let their congregations exercise their own judgement.' Responding to Dillon's attack in Slane, he said 'I have never been a Fenian, but I have expressed in Meath long before this split and on English platforms my admiration for the courage, devotion and patriotism of the Fenians. The position which Irish nationalism occupies today is in a long measure due to their action.'

The *Freeman's* correspondent, analysing general election prospects in North Meath, which had 6,232 voters in a population of 39,394, mischievously noted the view of an anonymous local Parnellite:[11] 'We have a great part of Navan, most of Kells, the whole of Moynalty and they . . . have only part of Oldcastle and Slane. If Mahony is held up by them as a place-taker, a landlord and a magistrate, that will only get him the Conservative vote and if the people are fairly divided a thousand Conservatives will turn the scale . . . Meath, the first county to send Mr Parnell to parliament, won't have any of the men who brought our chief to his grave.' But in Navan, Francis Sheridan told the

Freeman that the anti-Parnellites, although a minority, were growing. 'In Navan last year there was a strong show of Parnellism. This year the situation is reversed and Mr Lawlor, who polled 518 last year, received last March only 271 votes, while Mr Sheridan increased his votes from 349 to 484 . . . Last year the factionists [Parnellites] secured only about half of the Tory votes in the division. This year every available landlord vote was cast for them, so that the decrease in Mr Lawlor's poll . . . was in spite of an increase in the number of votes given for him by the Tories . . . The utmost interest attached to these elections, as the results were considered a test of what would happen in the more momentous contest later on in the year.' The *Drogheda Independent,* wondering how Meath was so strongly Parnellite, put it down to 'Parnell's early association with the county and the disorganised state the crisis of November found it in', with branches of the league 'almost defunct'.[12]

Having appealed for priestly neutrality, Mahony made an equally unpromising bid for overt clerical support when he told a meeting in Clonmel in May that he knew a number of Parnellite priests who were forbidden by their bishop from supporting them publicly, thus 'depriving them of the rights of citizenship'.[13] Parnellites were fighting 'for the right of private judgement in political matters'. Mahony also appealed to labourers, reminding them that it was Parnell who won the franchise for them and promising to introduce legislation for an eight-hour working day. Later in May, when Fr Davis in Ashbourne exhorted massgoers to vote for Davitt, 'the selected of Meath', the *Irish Independent* remarked that he 'may have been privately selected by himself and his reverend brethren as the proper person to force upon the constituency'.[14]

That paper reported that 4,000 people attended a Mahony rally in Kells in May (the RIC estimated 3,000, amid 'much enthusiasm').[15] William Lawlor who, with his son James, was the most anti-clerical of the Navan Parnellites, sent a letter of apology for his absence due to illness:

> I am with you heart and soul in this fight for freedom of thought and action in political matters. I am an old man now and I have a vivid recollection of the betrayal of the national cause in 1852. Sadlier, Keogh and their colleagues had then the blessing of the bishops and priests of Ireland, with the exception of the Archbishop of Tuam. History is repeating itself. There is another 'defender of the faith' at the front now

[Davitt], a man who has disgraced the public life in Ireland and yet has won the confidence of the bishops and clergy. Everything that has occurred during the past eighteen months is simply a repetition of '52. The Healyite, Dillonite and O'Brienite factionists will find their level soon. A Whig convention is announced to be held in Navan on 1st June to select candidates to carry the national flag to disgrace. We in Navan know nothing about the so-called convention and I may inform you that this game of selecting a candidate without consulting the people was tried here before and defeated. By the help of the independent men of Meath, who will, with an overwhelming voice, reject this selection, it will be again defeated.

Luke Elcock, a leading Drogheda Parnellite, referring to Mahony's Protestantism, said 'the Catholics of Ireland could not hope to win a parliament in College Green unless they could bring the northern Protestants to shake hands with them'. The latter would be watching the fight in Meath to observe whether it was a bigoted one. P. McDermott, chairman of Kells guardians, and Luke Smyth also called for labourers to vote Parnellite. Mahony declared that while they could not trust those who had deserted Parnell 'and therefore we can never again be one party', he thought they could work together for agreed objectives. But their opponents had rejected the suggestion of not contesting Parnellite seats. So 'we will go through this struggle to the bitter end . . . I believe that in North Meath we shall win', but, win or lose, 'it is absolutely necessary for the future that there should be in Ireland an independent party'. He pointed out how a Parnellite-proposed reduction of £1.75 million in Ireland's contribution to the imperial exchequer could fund an Irish old age pension, to avoid people having to go to the workhouse. But the *Drogheda Independent* equated voting against Mahony and Sheil with voting for Home Rule, because it was for unity and against division.[16] Rehearsing a common anti-Parnellite theme, the paper maintained that the present MPs were 'more devoted to a man than a cause'. Whatever the Parnellites' motives — 'personal regard for a once great leader, a feeling of overwhelming loyalty to a fallen man, self-serving deceit, a desire to appear consistent . . . time sufficient has elapsed since his demise to allow any feelings of warmth thereby created to cool'.

Davitt assaulted in Navan

Michael Davitt and Patrick Fulham were selected as candidates for
North and South Meath at an anti-Parnellite convention in the study
hall of St Finian's seminary, Navan, attended by 400 delegates,
including 47 priests, on 1 June 1892.[17] As was normal at the time, the
proceedings were first conducted in the absence of the press. Davitt was
proposed by Fr Gaughran of Kells and seconded by Francis Sheridan.
It was agreed to form an election committee in every parish to canvass
and to collect the expenses of the contest. Davitt and Fulham signed the
party pledge and the press were then admitted. William O'Brien, MP,
who presided, said it was 'farcical' for their opponents to talk of Davitt,
the former prisoner of Portland, as the representative of English
Whiggery and of Mahony (earlier referred to as 'an 18-month
nationalist') as the embodiment of the principles of Emmet and Tone.
Fulham's life, in and out of prison, was worthy of the sacred cause of
Ireland and he was one of the best of the local leaders. The election
would 'test the patriotism and good sense of the Irish people', which
could 'save the cause of Ireland', while 'personal folly or passion could
wreck it'. The emancipation of the Irish race and winning of a national
parliament were 'within the hollow of our hands'. For the first time, it
was not they but their enemies, the landlords and their Orange friends,
who were threatening to face the bullets, the gallows and penal cells to
restrict a British Act of Parliament. The most formidable and almost the
only obstacle to Home Rule now came from those old colleagues who
'reserved all their criticism and cold water' for him (O'Brien) and his
friends and their allies in Britain.

Davitt replied 'the honour is one I have not sought'. He had tried
to convince the Irish Party that he could serve the cause of Ireland
much better outside than inside parliament. He wished they had
selected a local man. The only time the anti-Parnellites were beaten was
when he was put forward in the Waterford by-election the previous
December in preference to a local man. He had committed many
mistakes in his political career and had 'never been much addicted to
making apologies'. But he would try to abide by the decision of the
majority or else resign. He would have as his opponent a man of
considerable ability (Mahony). In a promise which he would soon
break, Davitt said that he would not fight him unfairly or say anything
at which he could take offence. His fight would be for principle, not for
personality. He would rather be beaten than win by 'methods that
would cause Irishmen the world over to blush for their race'.

Landlordism had been the scourge of Meath: 'I will ambition to be the scourge of landlordism.' Fulham said he was well known throughout Meath as an organiser of the old Land League. Fr Woods explained that Edward Sheil, MP, 'not finding himself in agreement with the majority of his colleagues, offered to resign his seat but was persuaded by myself and the bishop to hold his seat until the next general election'. He therefore considered that they could part with him on honourable terms. (The remarkably taciturn Sheil had first been returned unopposed for Meath in 1882, after Davitt's disqualification, having represented Athlone but been defeated there in the previous general election.[18] A 4-hour private meeting of the Meath clergy in Navan, Bishop Nulty presiding, had recommended his election 'in deference to the wishes . . . of Mr Parnell'. But Patrick Egan, the Fenian Land Leaguer who was first offered the Meath nomination in return for his earlier withdrawal to enable Davitt's election,[19] publicly complained that Sheil had never opened his mouth during seven years in parliament and had never done or said anything in support of the land movement).

Afterwards, the *Freeman* reported, as Davitt and O'Brien were walking to the railway station, 'accompanied by some priests and a few friends, they were surrounded by a small crowd who assailed them with hostile cries, indulged in filthy language and threw mud and stones. A fellow named Mongey, employed in a shop in Navan, approached Mr Davitt and when within a few yards flung a stone which struck Mr Davitt on the head, outside his hat, with such force as to cause him to fall. Fr McNamee, Navan, followed the man, caught him and handed him over to some police, who were rather impassive spectators at the scene . . . Several clergymen had their clothes spattered with mud thrown by the mob. The wound which Mr Davitt sustained is not a severe one.' The *Irish Independent* blamed Davitt's assault on 'the aggravating nature of a display of Whig delegates and clergy marching through the streets of a town like Navan . . . It was anything but edifying to see clergymen in soutane and biretta engaged in heated political controversy with their parishioners.' The paper reported that a large hostile crowd had gathered outside the seminary. Fr Behan, fearing disturbance, had advised the delegates to retire by a back gate and escort Davitt and O'Brien across the Fair Green to the parochial house and thence to the station, en route for Dublin. But many of the delegates chose the normal route, through Academy Street, and marched along with a number of clergy, surrounded by a strong opposing element which followed them to the parochial house. After describing the assault on Davitt, the *Irish Independent* said that O'Brien and a number of the clergy and delegates also 'had their clothes bespattered with mud, presenting a gruesome spectacle when they arrived at the station'. Davitt was attended by a doctor in one of the waiting rooms, while an angry crowd gathered on the platform. Those travelling home from the convention were greeted with cries of 'we will have no seceders in Navan' and 'traitors must go elsewhere'. Davitt said he would not prosecute, his injury being 'only a trivial scratch'.

Regretting the incident, the *Irish Independent* said Davitt would not make a good candidate because of his 'notorious crankiness, his incapacity for working in harmony . . . his intolerable vanity and overweening self-esteem, his narrowness of view and his extreme ignorance of the rudiments of many subjects of which he talks glibly[20] . . . He has been converted from Irish nationalism to British radicalism; he thinks less of Home Rule than of the universal brotherhood of man; he is about the most egotistical, testy and self-sufficient politician who ever cursed any nationalist movement by insincere support.' But the *Drogheda Independent* cried 'shame on Navan',[21] while the *Argus* predicted 'in Meath, the coming contest threatens to become one of the stormiest, if not most embittered, that ever took place within its borders . . . The priests of Meath have ever been found in the vanguard of the struggle for Irish liberty . . . but most lamentable is it to see them confronted by any formidable section of their people . . . The after proceedings at Navan cannot be too strongly denounced and deplored.'[22] Captain Stokes's police report for June (which unfairly described Fr Woods as 'a *violent* political agitator') noted that O'Brien and Davitt 'were followed *to* the nomination meeting in the academy by a small crowd calling them names like "jackdaw" and "ticket of leave man".[23] The proprietor of the *Meath Reporter* was turned out of the meeting by order of the clergy.'

Navan Parnellites repudiated a *Drogheda Independent* claim that they had 'hired and imported from Kells, Athboy and Nobber' the mob which 'resented the efforts made by the clergy' to foist Davitt on North Meath.[24] They blamed instead 'those who for eighteen months have thwarted the feelings of the people of this town, both from altar and platform' and whose convention was an insulting 'attempt to foist Whiggery on the county'. The paper responded that this showed that the Parnellites felt that the attack on Davitt was justified: 'They failed to repudiate and condemn it.' It also dismissed a suggestion by Tim

Harrington that Parnellite seats should not be contested in the general election. But Mahony told a meeting at Syddan that he regretted that even a slight injury should have been sustained by Davitt, who should 'be able to pass through North Meath unmolested and untouched . . . I don't want you to fight this election as a personal matter.'[25]

When Mahony was selected at a convention in Trim on 16 June, along with James J. Dalton for South Meath, he repeated his appeal for his opponent's safety, although his residence in England and his interest in *Labour World* made him forget his Irish origin, so that 'he was the first man to point out that noble Irish quarry [Parnell] to the English slaves and the Irish curs'.[26] He also mentioned Tim Harrington offering the anti-Parnellites peace during the general election for the sake of Ireland, but they had rejected it. The *Drogheda Independent* mischievously published a report about South Roscommon Parnellite opposition to the party's agreement to an alleged request by Mahony 'to surrender his chances in Meath' for their safe seat 'because he was at one time so near being himself their leader'.[27] Meanwhile, Fulham wrote to the *Drogheda Independent* complaining that Navan Parnellites had lied that he had opposed John Martin's election for Meath in 1871. Their 'hillside' meeting was presided over by Luke Smyth, who in 1866 had got himself sworn in as a special constable 'to protect the British government against the Fenians', Fulham alleged.[28] Fr P. Clarke, curate in Kingscourt, about whom much more would be heard later, wrote to the *Drogheda Independent* complaining that Parnellite MP, Tom O'Hanlon's taking of notes of his sermon on the conventions in Cavan and Meath and the forthcoming election was 'a scandalous irreverence in the house of God'.[29]

The *Irish Independent* said there was a strong working-class element at a Mahony rally in Navan. Luke Smyth, who presided, urged them to avail of the secret ballot, as he recalled (before the Ballot Act of 1872) shame-faced men being driven by landlords and their bailiffs into the courthouse there to vote against their consciences.[30] Parnellites would not insult their opponents, because they allowed to others the liberty of thought and action they claimed for themselves. Mahony also stressed the right to vote 'without dictation or pressure'. He said he supported the regulation of working hours, votes for all men and land nationalisation — provided it did not interfere with the rights of tenant farmers. He was in favour of compulsory acquisition from landlords, but farmers should be cautious of the price they paid, because tax on land would be increased considerably. He would give the state power to take land from tenant farmers for labourers and to build houses for artisans in the towns. He had got provision in the Land Act for building labourers' cottages with allotments. What practical reform had Davitt ever advocated or passed into law? What practical benefit had he brought to one single workingman in Ireland? Davitt was always on the point of doing something. The difference between the Liberal Party's and the Irish estimate of the imperial charges could be used to pay a 5 shillings a week pension to everyone over 65, without increasing tax. The workingmen of Belfast would not resist such a social reform. The Poor Law system should be changed to enable better care of children. Afterwards, Mahony was conducted to his hotel by a crowd bearing torches. But the *Drogheda Independent* told of Parnellites marching round the town 'booing and yelling' and breaking windows of nationalists' houses: 'Priest's man and seceder have become synonymous terms.' [31]

On 26 June, Parnell's birthday, 5,000 attended a gathering for Mahony and Dalton on the hill of Tara.[32] Mrs Emily Dickinson, a sister of Parnell, was accompanied by Mrs Mahony and veterans of the O'Connell movement were also present. Mahony drove from Navan at the head of a line of cars nearly a mile long, passing under green arches past cheering groups, as Canicetown Band headed the procession. Mahony's friend, barrister George Coffey, said the doctrine was preached in Ireland now that the clergy were the state and the people were nothing. They would never get self-government, nor deserve to get it, if they allowed that spirit to spread over the land. Mahony, referring to O'Connell's monster meeting at Tara in 1843 and to the croppies' grave there, asked why should he be attacked in North Meath — what terms had he broken? Davitt had divided the Irish vote in Glasgow in 1885 when Parnell had wisely asked the Irish in Britain to vote against the Liberals. He went on to quote Davitt criticising the Liberal alliance in the past and his vitriolic description of Parnell after the divorce.

Davitt's scurrilous attack on Mahony

On the same day, Davitt broke his promise of a clean fight by making a scurrilous attack on Mahony at a meeting in Drumconrath. He would later try to justify it by the MP's public befriending of Mongey, but it was probably fear of electoral defeat which made him say[33]

As Mr Mahony traduces me in almost every speech he delivers
. . . I am compelled to handle this gentleman without gloves for

once. He is the one and only man as far as I know who came
into the Irish parliamentary party with the hallmark of Dublin
Castle stamped upon him. That he had been a successful office
hunter before he joined the nationalist movement is generally
known. But the nationalists of North Meath are not aware that
he became their representative upon the recommendation of an
under-secretary of Dublin Castle . . . It sheds considerable light
upon the underhand work of party bossism . . . that the official
. . . could actually wield sufficient influence with the late Mr
Parnell to induce him to admit into the ranks of the Irish Party
an ex-official of this detested system of government in Ireland
. . . He is . . . a Kerry landlord . . . [with] a substantial income,
yet . . . was not ashamed to quarter himself upon the
parliamentary funds and to accept £200–£300 a year . . . He
has traduced the priests of Meath, the men who accepted him
and elected him on trust . . . Among English Liberals, he was
the most active political flunky . . . who for years hob-nobbed
with all the baronets, lords and earls . . . Meath has done
everything for Mahony, Mahony nothing for Meath . . . He has
tried his best to destroy the Home Rule cause by factionism
and folly . . . He tries now to keep the Irish Party permanently
divided . . . Mahony, the patron and backer of Mongey of
Navan . . . Who will the landlords of Meath support . . . the
exterminators of the people of Meath? . . . There is not a land-
grabber, emergency-man, bailiff, landlord's dogman, agent or
understrapper, a Tory, Liberal or Unionist or open or
concealed enemy of the Irish cause . . . who will not . . . vote
for Mahony as readily and as heartily as if he were an open and
avowed foe of Home Rule and Land League principles. Will
the tenant farmers of Meath cast a vote for the man who cries
'more power to Mr Balfour's elbow' and thereby help to keep
the Tory government in power long enough to re-fix the
judicial rents at the expiration of your present statutory leases?
. . . [Or] back the man whose chief supporter is Luke Smyth,
who had himself sworn in as a special constable to arrest the
Fenians in 1867?

In a letter to the *Irish Independent,* Mahony responded from Kells that
he was unaware that the Castle under-secretary, Sir Robert Hamilton,
had anything to do with his nomination for Meath by Parnell.[34] 'I am

not and never have been a landlord . . . Mr Parnell . . . urged me . . . to take money from the parliamentary fund . . . £200 to about £350 a year [for] travelling expenses in . . . Britain. Unlike Mr Timothy Healy, I neither claimed nor received anything for my time . . . My constituents are going to pay the expenses of the present contest, as I am unable to do so.' And at a meeting attended by 3,000 in Nobber, James Lawlor denied that Luke Smyth was sworn in in 1867 to protect the people of Navan from the Fenians.[35] Davitt had neglected to say that the priests, now his only supporters, condemned the Fenians then even more than they condemned independent opposition now. Mahony told the meeting that he would not follow Davitt in making low personal attacks, but mentioned his inconsistencies and betrayals, including his statement of 7 February 1891 that 'a peasant propriety will only take the land from one class to confer its ownership upon another. It will substitute one set of landlords for another set.'

But the onslaught continued at a meeting for Fulham after mass in Skryne, where M.J. Kenny, MP, said Mahony 'was a very mild type of nationalist until after he was dismissed from the sub-commissionership he held under the Land Act. During the years 1883–84, when the country was being scourged with coercion, Mr Mahony begged himself and got his friends to beg that he might be reinstated in his former office and it was only when his efforts were unsuccessful that he became a member of the Home Rule Party.'[36] The *Freeman* had another charge, which would be repeated despite refutation: that Mahony had signed the requisition for the meeting which deposed Parnell.[37] It criticised the *Irish Independent* for defending Mahony, one of its directors, as an 'honest' Castle official and advised Mahony 'to hold his tongue about the British gold he pocketed fixing rack-rents on the Irish people'.

On his way to a meeting at Oldcastle, 'at Kells station, a small section of the crowd which greeted Davitt were Parnellites and they did their best to insult him by booing'.[38] But in Oldcastle itself there were no Parnellites, Fr Grehan, who presided, saying Mahony was a political humbug and a sham. Davitt sounded conciliatory: he knew there were 'honest men, true nationalists and good Irishmen' on the Parnellite side and 'no matter what treatment I receive from mistaken men in this fight, notwithstanding the unjust words that have been spoken about me, I shall not utter one word or sanction one act against an honest opponent which would bring discredit on the Irish cause'. As regards Mahony: 'I wish to speak of my opponent with all kindness and respect. I have absolutely no personal feeling against him at all. He rather amuses me as a politician . . . and I would be sorry to say anything that would be personally offensive to him.' But he accused the MP of misinterpreting his speech in Bandon some months previously to imply that he would be satisfied with any measure of Home Rule, however small, from the Liberals. Trading on his patriotism, Davitt concluded 'when a large section of the Irish race at home and abroad were struggling for a republic, I faced the music, I endured the penalty and I would like to know where Mahony was in those days.' Voice: 'He was minding his Kerry farm.' A mob of about a hundred booed Davitt at Navan station, en route from Oldcastle.[39]

Bishop Nulty's pastoral

As the chief protagonists thus traded insults, Bishop Nulty's pastoral letter, dated Mullingar, 19 June, was read to about 200,000 people in 148 churches in the diocese on Sunday 3 July and printed in the *Drogheda Independent* of the previous day.[40] In it, the bishop claimed a 'divine right' to instruct his flock about the essentially religious question of Parnellism, whose future they would decide in the general election. Having disgraced himself by the events proved in the divorce court, Parnell, whom he had esteemed, was deposed by the clergy and 'all that was great, good and noble in the laity of Catholic Ireland'. But 'I have stronger antipathies to the anti-Catholic and anti-nationalist character of the living organisation or party into which Parnellism has developed'. The Catholic hierarchy

> have solemnly warned and taught their respective flocks that Parnellism was unlawful and unholy, that it was in distinct antagonism with the principles of Christian morality and even dangerous to their faith as Catholics and consequently that they should shun and avoid it. They who refuse to accept that teaching . . . deprive themselves of every rational ground for believing in the truth of any of the other doctrines of their religion . . . Invincible ignorance may undoubtedly excuse many of the misguided . . . but no intelligent or well-informed man can continue to remain a Catholic as long as he elects to cling to Parnellism . . . The dying Parnellite himself will hardly dare to face the justice of his Creator until he has been prepared and anointed by us for the last awful struggle and for the terrible judgement that will immediately follow I

earnestly entreat you, dearly beloved, to stamp out by your votes at the coming election this great moral, social and religious evil which has brought about so much disunion and bad blood amongst a hitherto united people, which has worked so desperately but in vain to break the golden link of love that has bound 'the priests and the people' for centuries inseparably together, which by sowing dissensions in the national parliamentary party weakened its strength and efficiency and which has seriously imperilled on the very eve of victory the claims of our poor country to its legislative independence.

The pastoral also revealed something of the emotion underlying Bishop Nulty's behaviour:

I had a close and intimate personal knowledge of Mr Parnell throughout almost the whole of his public political life. During the whole of that period I respected and esteemed him as a man of high principle, of pure morality and of unblemished honour. I regarded him as the very last of men then living who would stoop to the degrading meanness of defiling and disgracing himself by the vilest and foulest form of sensuality and crime. The irresistible certainty which the divorce court furnished of his guilt created in my mind a painful sense of anguish and agony which were equalled in bitterness and pain only by the sad and deplorable necessity of parting and breaking with him forever.

The *Drogheda Independent,* justifying the pastoral with an editorial headed 'the fight against the priests', asked 'let us have no clerical dictation . . . what do they mean? . . . Freedom of thought and licence of action similar to that which marked the enthronement of the goddess of reason on the high altar of Notre Dame during the days of the French Revolution?'[41] At his meeting in Duleek that Sunday of the pastoral, Davitt referred to the living conditions of labourers in the village as worse than he had ever seen and to the area as epitomising the gulf between idle landlords and the labouring poor.[42] He again contrasted his prison term with Mahony's Castle job and laughed at him for calling himself an advanced nationalist and him (Davitt) a Whig. Fr P. Callary, parish priest of St Mary's, Drogheda, said that the young William Mongey was 'neither a native of Navan nor a voter' and the town's 'respectable inhabitants', whom he had worked among, were 'simply sick' of Parnellism and would vote solid for Davitt. Fr Murray, of the seminary, alleged that both Mahony and Dalton had signed the requisition for another meeting of the party to ask Parnell to resign the chairmanship.[43]

Commencing a sustained attack on Bishop Nulty's pastoral, the *Irish Independent* lamented that Richard Lalor Sheil's description of the clergy at elections as 'colonels in black' still held true.[44] 'In four-fifths of the constituencies of Ireland, the priests are marshalling the timid, the corrupt, the indifferent and the illiterate voters against the policy of independence.' It decried the pastoral as 'unworthy of a Catholic bishop' and regretted that 'no judicious friend was at hand to advise his lordship', as it 'will not be lost upon the stranger and the foes of Home Rule'. The *Irish Independent* also reported from Oldcastle on the reading of the 'extraordinary, electioneering' pastoral, which it described as 'the discharge of this heavy piece of political artillery'. Mahony's alleged disparaging remarks about Irish priests were 'repeated on large placards posted up all over the town and even on the chapel gates'. Fr Grehan said Mahony would be passing through that day to cause disturbance and not to go near him as there might be a riot. Fr Brogan, his curate, said it would be 'political apostasy' for any individual to attend Mahony's meeting. He had described priests as 'scoundrels', in spite of their support after he was 'pitchforked' (the same word as used about Parnell's imposition of Captain O'Shea on Galway constituency the same year) on them six years previously by Parnell, 'who betrayed Ireland for the embraces of a heartless woman'.

At his meeting in Oldcastle, Mahony said that Davitt was 'going around North Meath like a rat walking round a rat trap'. It was 'a nasty place for rats'. He did not think that Meath would return to parliament a man who ratted from the Irish cause and did not even wait to get the order from his English master (being the first to call for Parnell's resignation). The MP's election advertisement in the *Irish Independent* recalled that he had Parnell's recommendation in 1886 and again in Navan on 1 March '91. He highlighted his proposal that a reduced Irish contribution to the imperial exchequer would enable the funding of pensions — 'instead of workingmen and women being driven to spend their last days as paupers in the workhouse, imprisoned there not because they have committed any crime but because they are no longer strong enough to work'. The *Irish Independent,* pointing out that it was 'the poorer voters in the country . . . [who] are subject to the special influence of the partisan clergy', emphasised that 'no moral, religious or spiritual issue whatsoever is involved in the present contest'.[45] Bishop Nulty's attempt to show otherwise outraged common sense and contradicted the archbishop of Cashel's declaration even in Parnell's lifetime that not only the laity but also his priests could take any side they pleased. It differed from Dr Nulty's previous stance in allowing his priests to support a vote of confidence in Parnell between the divorce verdict and Gladstone's letter and it ignored the fact that Parnell's death removed any pretence that his moral offence affected the current political situation.

Navan rowdies awaken Bishop Nulty

On 7 July Davitt was formally nominated in Kells for North Meath by Bishop Nulty, seconded by Patrick Casey, Alexanderaide, Navan. He was also proposed by Rev. Peter McNamee, the bishop's new administrator in Navan, and seconded by Nicholas Kelly.[46] Fr Woods's reading of a letter from Dr Nulty to Fr Gaughran, dated Navan, 7 July, about being awoken the previous night by 'noisy rowdies' under his window 'created the most profound indignation' among Davitt's supporters at his nomination. The bishop wrote of 'a disorderly and drunken mob' who

> hooted, booed and yelled and manifested their hatred, contempt and scorn by the wildest and fiercest screams . . . I cannot understand how wanton and unprovoked insult, outrage and contempt, even of a bishop in one of the principal towns of his own see, can . . . advance the political interests . . . of any parliamentary candidate. Each of Mr Mahony's arrivals in this town since I reached it a few days ago was the occasion of the most terrorising public disorder and of the saddest scenes of crime and sin that I ever witnessed anywhere . . . The plain object of this terrorising rowdyism is to cow and intimidate the electors from voting for the candidate . . . they prefer. Electors of Meath, be men; have the courage of your convictions and do not be deterred from following them by the terror with which these mobs seek to inspire you.

Taking his cue, Davitt denounced

> the abominable outrage perpetrated by Mr Mahony's supporters upon the venerable Bishop of Meath . . . You could

not find in all Ireland, not even among the Orangemen of
Sandy Row in Belfast, a gang of men so low . . . as to offer
deliberate insult to the venerable bishop who has done so
much for the Irish people and for the cause of true land reform
as Dr Nulty has accomplished. Pierce Mahony, the ex-Castle
official . . . the nominee of the Castle under-secretary, the
patron of Mongey of Navan . . . the patron of the
emergencymen and the supporter of Balfour, the grandson of
the Kerry souper, the man who can encourage his rowdy
followers to offer organised insult to the Bishop of Meath.
Electors of Meath, avenge this insult at the polls. Teach this
Castle hack, this successful place-hunter, that North Meath
will not surrender to the forces of landlordism nor to the
menaces of Redmondite ruffianism. Teach this adventurer
from Kerry . . . this factionist renegade, that the nationalists of
the county of Frederick Lucas and John Martin are not going
to insult their record nor to humiliate their manhood by
returning this Kerry shoneen.

'This won't do', the *Argus* said of the incident, which it described as 'a
tactical blunder of the gravest kind'.[47] Parnell had 'not only recognised
the right of the Irish priest to be in politics but saw that in the
circumstances of the country it became a matter of necessity'. All
through the land war, Bishop Nulty had been 'a tower of strength'. But
the bishop's letter would be described as 'artful' by Parnellite counsel in
the later election petition, as it made Mahony responsible for an
incident with which he had nothing to do. It is also a good illustration
of Dr Nulty's circular reasoning, by which he repeatedly cited the
violence which he himself provoked as evidence of the anti-clerical or
anti-Catholic nature of Parnellism, which therefore must be
condemned.

Tim Healy, in his *Letters and Leaders of My Day*, even incorrectly
attributed Bishop Nulty's pastoral to his 'exasperation' at the Navan
boys' awakening him under his window with cries of 'blind Tom'.[48] But
as we have seen, the pastoral was issued the previous weekend and may
well therefore have caused this incident. Perhaps Healy became
embarrassed by the pastoral. The possibility of a genuine mistake is
rendered less likely by the facts that bishops are not wont to dash off
pastorals in pique, Dr Nulty's was dated nearly three weeks earlier than
the incident and Healy was later Davitt's counsel when 'the pastoral lost

us the petitions'. The error reappears elsewhere, including in Mark Tierney's *Croke of Cashel*.[49] As regards Davitt's crude 'souper' insult, a possible explanation — though no excuse — may lie in Mahony's great-grandfather's changing from Catholicism on his second marriage.[50]

The *Freeman* reported 'no demonstration of hostility' in Kells and Albert Meldon, resident magistrate in Navan, wrote on 7 July to the Castle that 'although feeling runs perhaps higher than ever', the nominations there passed off quietly because 'the two sides were kept apart'.[51] The *Drogheda Independent* carried an anonymous, but doubtless clerical, response to a Navan Parnellite pamphlet which quoted an authority of Maynooth college that in an election 'any exercise of authority by a bishop or priest . . . was an abuse of authority':[52] 'Every intelligent Catholic knows . . . that in all matters wherein the bishop commends or prohibits, he is bound to obey.' As Bishop Nulty had pointed out in his pastoral, Parnellism had a religious aspect, having its origins 'in sensuality and sin', defying the hierarchy and trying to bring the authority of priests into disrepute.

The RIC noted Bishop Nulty and his clergy 'working strenuously' to have the anti-Parnellite candidates returned in Meath and Westmeath.[53] In addition to the pastoral, at an anti-Parnellite meeting in Oldcastle, Fr Curry, parish priest of Collinstown, had called on those present to raise their right hands 'in the presence of almighty God and promise to vote for Davitt' and almost all present did so. At Slane, Fr Kelly had told his parishioners to assemble in the square, 'armed with a good blackthorn' to march to Davitt's meeting in Drumconrath, but they did not bring blackthorns. Fr Grehan had told his people in Oldcastle before Davitt's meeting there that if he was assaulted again 'we will defend ourselves'. Noting the public's reluctance to support anti-Parnellite candidates financially, the police reported 'on the other hand, the Parnellites have collected considerable sums in Meath and Kildare' — £160 and £120.

The RIC's Captain Stokes later added: 'on the anti-Parnellite side, the greater portion of the money was subscribed by the clergy and their friends and on the Parnellite side by the shop-keepers in the towns'.[54] Bishop Nulty's pastoral and his references to Parnellites from the altar during the elections had caused deep resentment, 'which was manifested in Navan, Trim and Duleek by a considerable number of Parnellites leaving the chapels'. At Navan, the bishop referred to the Parnellites as non-Catholics, cowards and traitors. Eleven cattle which were being grazed free by farmers for Fr Behan were driven into Trim on 19 July and left standing in the market place until taken away by the parish priest's servant. About 29 of his other cattle were still kept by different farmers, 'but they say that next year they will give him no free grass as, if he was able to guarantee £200 towards defraying Mr Fulham's election expenses he should be able to pay for the grass of his cattle'. An attached return showed £368 collected for Parnellite candidates in Meath and £185 for anti-Parnellites.

The *Irish Catholic* trumpeted that Bishop Nulty's 'splendid pastoral has goaded the Parnellites nearly to madness'.[55] Such 'bold, plain speaking' was needed 'in defence of the principles of religion and morality in connection with politics and to safeguard the right of our clergy to enjoy the most ordinary civic liberties'. But the *Irish Times* carried a letter from H.R. Reichel, Dundrum Castle, Dublin, quoting the pastoral to show that Home Rule would be Rome rule and that by invoking morality the bishops could direct their people on any matter.[56]

As the rival groups planned clashing demonstrations in Navan on the Sunday before the election (10 July), Meldon, the RM, wrote to the Castle that Mahony had informed him that, despite his advice, his followers were determined to meet the main body of the anti-Parnellites outside the town and to prevent their entering.[57] 'I recommend that 130, or if convenient 150, police should be in the town, when I shall prevent the Parnellites leaving.' Captain Stokes minuted tersely that he had 'already made ample arrangements for the preservation of the peace'. First to arrive at Mahony's meeting, according to the *Irish Independent*, was 'a strong body from Ardbraccan, headed by their band and bearing a banner displaying a portrait of the late Irish leader, above which were inscribed the words "murdered" and beneath "revenge" . . . Considerable excitement prevailed.'[58] The 150 extra constables had been drafted in and about 20 of them marched at the head of Davitt's supporters as they entered the Square from the Slane Road, while the rest of the force was drawn up across the Square, separating the townspeople from 'the imported mob'.

Davitt, walking at their head, 'was hooted' as 'several attempts were made by a small portion of the Parnellite meeting to force the cordon of police . . . At the lower end of the Square, Mr Davitt produced a revolver and called on a man who was prominent in hooting him to come on. Again an attempt was made to force the line of police and in the effort the Ardbraccan banner was torn . . . The constables had drawn their staffs before charging, when Mr Mahony succeeded in quelling what had almost developed into a disturbance.' Davitt's meeting on the Fair Green was attended by supporters from Kingscourt and Carrickmacross, according to the *Irish Independent,* while Slane was the only Meath district represented. These contingents did not return through the town but, with Davitt still at their head, marched home by a route which added 4 miles to their journey, while those from Kingscourt were escorted to the train by a large body of police. Meanwhile, Luke Smyth presided at Mahony's meeting on the Square, where the MP remarked that he had not found it necessary 'to carry a revolver or to draw one'. He did not think that Meath voters would be discouraged by election results from other parts of the country (elections then did not take place on the same day), as Dublin was sound.

The *Freeman* admitted that Davitt's supporters would, 'if it was sought to disrupt them, pay the disruptionists back with interest[59] . . . All, prepared for attack with stout blackthorns, would have had little difficulty in disposing of their factionist opponents were it not for the police interfering.' It alleged that Parnellites had assaulted Thomas Keappock and Thomas Sheridan on their way home from Davitt's meeting, at which, on the motion of Fr Behan, Fr McNamee took the chair and congratulated those present on their patriotism. Voice: 'We have not the scum of Navan here anyway.' Fr McNamee referred to Mahony twice as a traitor. Voice: 'We won't go to him for a bowl of soup anyway.' Alluding to the Parnellite cry of 'no priests in politics', Fr McNamee said that before the divorce verdict, they were very glad to have the support and influence of the *soggart aroon.* He asked for votes for faith and fatherland. Davitt told the meeting that their great demonstration for free speech and order contrasted with the rowdyism and blackguardism of the corner-boys of the town. Voice: 'They had plenty of cheap porter today.' Davitt said their opponents had broken an agreement about no cheering and booing. Every landlord, bailiff and 'planter' would vote for Mahony: that was his message to the tenants and labourers of North Meath. Fulham said their meeting was 'not one that had to be summoned by taking the bung out of the porter barrels' and it was the best answer by the Catholic people of the county to those who had struck Davitt in Navan and to the insult sought to be put upon Bishop Nulty the previous Wednesday. M.J. Flavin of Listowel claimed that when Mahony got his recommendation to Parnell from the Castle, nationalists of Listowel intended to send a delegation to North Meath to expose the man who was being foisted on the constituency, but in the interests of unity they refrained. Mahony postured as the labourers' friend, but he paid his own labourers 6 to 8 shillings a week, while the surrounding farmers paid from 10 to 12.

The *Drogheda Independent* exaggerated that 10,000 attended Davitt's meeting, where it highlighted Fr Behan's contribution. Trim's parish priest said it was commonly stated that the priests of Meath went wrong at the time of John Martin's election in 1871 and therefore they were going wrong now.[60] But Martin's candidature was sprung on the people of Meath and there was scarcely any opposition to him, the people electing him of their own free will and the priests interfering in no way. In January 1891 he (Fr Behan, who on his later admission was then still a Parnellite) had come to Navan to see Luke Smyth, who had sought his advice on a requisition being signed around the town, asking Parnell to come there to a public meeting. He had told Smyth not to have anything to do with it, that the priests and people in Navan were always united and that nothing should be done that would cause dissension. Perhaps in a moment of weakness, Smyth yielded to some of the irresponsible, unthinking young men of the town. Parnell was brought there and that was the beginning of the disunion. He (Fr Behan) was accused of being a Parnellite himself: at the Navan convention, it was publicly stated that Parnell was innocent and would not subject himself to a packed English jury, that he would come out of the divorce trouble as he came out of the Pigott forgeries. He (Fr Behan) believed that Parnell would come out clear, as most people did, until his guilt became apparent. They were now face to face with a contest between themselves.

Meldon's report to the Castle numbered the two crowds at the Navan meeting as 4,000 and 5,000 for Davitt and Mahony, respectively.[61] 'The latter were bent on fighting, as they regarded the other as an invasion of the town.' He re-routed their return 'as otherwise, except by the use of firearms, a general conflict could not have been avoided'. Enclosing press reports that Davitt produced a revolver, Meldon noted he 'produced nothing more deadly than a knuckle-duster', while 'Mahony did what he could to prevent a general conflict'. Davitt, whose papers are preserved in the manuscript library of Trinity College Dublin, printed a handbill for the North Meath election, stressing that even an illiterate man could vote in secret and urging support 'for Davitt, Home Rule, Land League principles and labour rights'.[62] He also wrote from Slane to his old friend, Richard McGhee, before polling day:[63] 'Come on to Navan on Wednesday and call on Fr McNamee of the parochial house. He will look after you. Navan is my weakest point and it is the largest polling district. Mahony is to have the services of some Belfast "experts" and your duty will be to match these and assist all round . . . Navan is simply *a hell* [Davitt's emphasis] of landlords and prostitutes and bastards. If you do not identify yourself with my side on Wednesday, you may pick up information which will be useful.'

An *Irish Independent* editorial on clerical interference in the general election did not mention Meath, but East Wicklow, West Kerry, Tyrone, North Galway and North Roscommon.[64] The paper remarked on Mahony being opposed by Davitt and the priests as 'a very unnatural alliance . . . If [Davitt] was sour and cross-grained against Parnell, he was also a persistent denouncer of the priests.'[65] Mahony's election 'as a Protestant gentleman' would prove to the English the absence of religious bigotry. But Mahony, declaring in Kells the 'absolute falsehood' of Davitt's slur that he was the grandson of a Kerry souper, said that it was intended to stir up feelings against him because he was a Protestant.[66]

When Fulham won South Meath by 2,207 votes to Dalton's 2,126, a majority of 81, Dr J.E. Kenny, MP — speaking at an eve of poll rally which Mahony's supporters braved in their opponents' heartland of Slane — made the first reference to an election petition, predicting that Fulham would 'never sit for parliament'.[67] Within a short time, a petition would be lodged, claiming the seat for Dalton and the seceders would have to answer in court for illegal practices and clerical terrorism. Irishmen should not be lied to or threatened with 'punishment here and hereafter to terrify voters' into violating their consciences. The police separated the opposing crowds at Slane, where the priests ordered their supporters out of earshot of the Parnellite meeting while Fr Kelly 'got a chair and listened in stealthy ease from the midst of a group of policemen'. Mahony said they were not fighting against the tyranny of the English government merely to change it for a worse tyranny. As citizens they were the equals of the clergy and capable of exercising their own political judgement. They had been told it was a sin to vote for him, just because he had refused to break the promise he gave in Navan, which 35 of the clergy of Meath cheered him for making. The Navan contingent, led by Mahony, returned by Beauparc. 'Along the road into Navan the people turned out with candles and lanterns and cheered.' Mahony, Dalton and Dr Kenny then addressed the crowd, mainly on the practicalities of voting and the secrecy of the ballot.

The *Irish Independent* reported that a petition would in fact be lodged against the election in South Meath:[68] 'Intimidation used by the priests . . . probably cannot be beaten in any other constituency. Last Sunday the chapel gates in Clonard were closed against the Parnellites. Last Wednesday the bishop said he would rather attend the bedside of an adulterer or a drunkard than the bedside of a Parnellite and that women with Parnellite sympathies are worse than abandoned women . . . Priests in the last few days . . . [tried] to pledge people in the confessional . . . to vote against the Parnellite candidate.' Dalton, after the count in Trim, said that Fulham was not the member for South Meath, but simply a member for the bishop's palace in Mullingar. He (Dalton) had been denounced from the altars and, not content with issuing a pastoral against himself and Mahony, the bishop had supplemented it everywhere he went by violent political sermons. His information would upset a dozen elections.

Election rioting in Navan

The *Irish Independent* also reported serious violence on polling day in North Meath:[69] 'In Navan, a few clergymen were to be seen on the streets', but 'they filled the polling stations . . . The first violent act of today was committed by a priest.' People were cheering and booing around the town hall polling station in Trimgate Street, when Fr Christopher Casey, curate in nearby Dunderry, struck a young man named Pat Byrne with his blackthorn stick and knocked him down, breaking his hat and drawing blood. 'A scene of the wildest excitement ensued.' Fr Gilsenan of Navan withdrew to the other side of the street with Fr Casey and together they 'assumed a most aggressive attitude'. When William Lawlor suggested that the clergymen should be deprived of their weapons, Fr Gilsenan remarked that he was 'an old rascal . . . A crowd shivered the windows of a man named Allen. Mr Meldon, RM, who held the town with 60 policemen, had the Riot Act read [which gave police special powers of arrest after warning a crowd to disperse], but the only persons who availed of this delay were the clergy, who scuttled off rapidly and did not reappear for some hours. As the police charged, the crowd made smithereens of the large glass front of an ironmongery establishment owned by Mr [Francis] Sheridan, while a portion of the gathering directed their missiles on the advancing constables. When close quarters were reached, several heads were broken.'

At Moynalty, Mahony had been met by Fr Mullen, many men and the local band. He returned by train from Kells to Navan a little before

8 p.m., to find 'the people most excited over the incidents of the day'. He addressed them in two different places and entreated them not to copy the example set by some of their opponents. He assured them that the assaults committed by the clergymen that day would be investigated and asked everyone to remain at home, to show the men who had forgotten their position an example of peace. Dalton assured them that a petition would be filed against the South Meath election. 'When nightfall came, a few stones were thrown and the police, who had been strengthened by a draft of forty constables from the surrounding districts and the men who had been relieved from the care of polling stations, spread themselves right across the principal streets and proceeded to charge every one of the thoroughfares.' Up to 50 people sustained head wounds from baton charges. One chemist dressed the wounds of 25 people during the day, 9 were treated at the hospital and 3 were detained. Mahony and Dalton went into the streets persuading people to go home, 'but the clergy were not to be seen acting as peace-makers'.

Meldon wired the Castle:[70] 'Serious election riot here yesterday. Mob attacked houses of Davitt supporters, then rescued prisoners from police, who at once charged and dispersed mob, which resisted. Read Riot Act at 2 o'clock and had town well in hand till dark, when stone throwing again commenced. Then charged up and down the various streets and had town cleared by [9] o'clock. [Had] but 60 men and one officer till four o'clock, when county inspector and more arrived. Several police struck but none seriously injured. Necessarily, many of crowd got baton wounds.'

The *Irish Independent* reprinted a graphic report by Bennett Burleigh, 'the well-known war correspondent', whom the *Daily Telegraph* sent over to cover the election in North Meath.[71] In Navan, Nobber, Moynalty, Kells and Crossakiel, 'strong contingents of priests . . . stood on the roadway canvassing the voters . . . [or] marched up to the booths followed by bands of [Davitt] supporters . . . In every polling station, two or more local priests had been sworn in . . . as personation agents' for Davitt. Between 9 and 10 a.m., Mahony, accompanied by his wife, toured the polling places in Navan, a large crowd cheering them good-humouredly, people being 'mostly of one way of thinking there'. But in Nobber, where Davitt spoke cheerfully of his chances of winning, 'reverence for the cloth' saved Fr P. Clarke, curate in Kingscourt, from being struck by onlookers after he assaulted Owen Reilly, aged 73, from Rahood, Burleigh continued. The local magistrate, Mr Walker, told him it would be useless for the police to attempt to arrest a priest with safety on a polling day. In Kells, there were general fights and brawls in the town that night. In Navan, from 7 p.m. the police had been busy trying to clear the streets. Meldon had told him that a few minutes after Fr Casey's assault on Pat Byrne around midday, a well-known anti-Parnellite was hotly pursued by a mob, but escaped with the assistance of Inspector Small. 'Crowds of rough men then began promenading the street, shouting and brandishing sticks.' At 1.30 some of the mob commenced throwing stones and smashing the windows of a local boot-maker named Allen who was a supporter of Davitt. 'A dozen constables thereupon arrested several of the rowdies, but their friends, rushing in with their sticks, rescued them . . . A reserve of thirty constables . . . marched rapidly up and down the main street. The mob, however, got close to the shop of Mr Sheridan, ironmonger . . . and began to wreck the premises . . . The police effected several arrests, but . . . the mob, which by that time numbered 3,000 persons, set upon them and again released the prisoners.' Meldon thereupon had the Riot Act read and the police, once more reinforced, drew their batons and charged into the crowd, scattering it. 'It required several charges to completely break up the mob and for some time it was feared that a firing party of six riflemen would have to be brought out to clear the streets.'

In contrast to the grim prospect of the Navan mob being fired upon, the *Freeman* merely reported that at Navan and other polling stations, 'despite factionist rowdyism and intimidation, the electorate steadily recorded their votes for the father of the Land League'.[72] Next day it rejoiced: 'No defeat during the elections has caused so much heartfelt satisfaction as that of the hypocritical placeman who poses as a latter-day hillsider.'[73] The result in North Meath was: Davitt 2,549, Mahony 2,146, a majority of 403 for Davitt. Now the *Freeman* alleged 'a large number of voters were prevented from supporting Davitt at Navan, owing to the rowdyism and intimidation of the factionist mob, who were provided with drink. Few votes were recorded after 1 o'clock. Voters who came in from country districts were . . . compelled to seek refuge in the houses of shopkeepers.' The *Freeman* also reported that Mullingar town commissioners telegraphed congratulations to Bishop Nulty 'on the victories gained in the two divisions of Meath over the combined forces of factionism and Toryism'. Next day the paper remarked 'Redmond need now fear no rival' (Mahony).[74]

The *Irish Independent* was despondent at the 'absurd' idea that

Fulham and Davitt represented anyone other than the Meath clergy.[75] Mahony was present, but not Davitt, at the count in Kells courthouse, along with Dalton and Fulham — Fr Gaughran of Kells thanking the sheriff on behalf of Davitt. Mahony addressed his supporters from the town hall in Kells. They had 'been defeated today by the Bishop and priests of Meath', who, he wrongly predicted, would 'bitterly regret the cost of this victory'. Bishop Nulty had told them it was a sin to vote for him 'because I am not a recreant and backslider like Fr Behan . . . I have acted as an honourable man . . . they have disgraced their cloth.' The Parnellites had 'made a good fight . . . [but] the Catholic church in Meath — I speak plainly — has been turned during this election into a political organisation . . . You will have to consider how best to organise yourselves to oppose this . . . You will have, as good Catholics, to teach these reverend gentlemen that it is not by knocking men down outside polling booths that they will show their flocks the spirit of Christ, their Master.'

But, in one of his noblest speeches, Mahony acknowledged that some Meath priests had 'won for themselves, under circumstances of enormous difficulty, the hearty respect of all members of their congregation, because they have refused to turn the altar of the Most High into a political platform'. For Parnellites, it was imperative to begin the revision of the electoral register immediately 'and work like men who mean to win . . . If at a future time you require my services . . . I shall be at your disposal. If you select a man amongst yourselves or anywhere else to do the work, it will be an honour and a privilege to me, if possible, to come down here and support him.' Appealing to his supporters 'not to let your ardour grow cool and your courage diminish', Mahony promised to 'fight on', because 'you will never get any Home Rule worthy of the nation . . . until you show yourselves to be all independent people. The majority of the voters of Meath, North and South, have unfortunately shown themselves not fit for freedom, but for slavery.' This situation would be reversed if every man had the vote, but even in advance of that, if they revised the register, the Parnellites could win the next election in Meath. While they might feel disappointed, they could be congratulated for polling 2,146 men 'in spite of the forces that were working against us . . . Many a cause has been won on much smaller beginnings.'

Speaking later from the town hall in Navan, Mahony remarked that Parnellites had not been guilty of dishonourable acts or low personal attacks. They had to decide whether the bishops and priests were in future to elect their MPs. On the voters as Catholics was thrown the duty of saving their church — and it was the people and not the priests who made the Catholic church. The people should decide whether their money was to be used to fight against them and in Navan the people would soon teach the clergy that they were not going to be their slaves. But he warned them not to allow their zeal to lead them into excesses, nor to forget that the priest had a sacred office. He valued the kindness he had received in North Meath, but among the working men of Navan he felt more at home than anywhere else. He would rather get the 2,146 votes given freely by the people than the votes of a whole constituency dragged out of the people by the priests. The priests had done their worst, using every power they could against him, and their worst was only 400. In Navan alone they had enough men who could have votes to turn the tide of the next election and he asked them to work with light hearts to achieve that. He cherished every vote cast for him and considered it a high honour to have polled more than 2,000 under such circumstances. 'God bless Meath and God bless Navan.'

But the *Drogheda Independent* said that Meath, asked to endorse 'the priest-hunting clique who pose as patriots', had instead voted in the interests of country, religion, 'the purity of home and the sanctity of public pledges'.[76] The paper took a predictably different view of the election riots in Navan: at midday, 'small knots of the individuals constituting the lowest and roughest element in the town were observed to collect at the corners'. About one o'clock, over a hundred of them, armed with sticks, marched along the streets, 'visited the shop of a well-known nationalist and demanded drink, but met with a refusal. Their reply was a simultaneous onslaught with sticks and stones on the shopfront, which they shivered to atoms.' For the three hours that the ensuing reign of terror lasted, voters suspected of nationalist tendencies dared not show themselves in the streets and Davitt supporters who had not voted early in the morning were effectively prevented from doing so. 'Thus hundreds of voters were lost' to him. Late in the evening an attempt was made to renew the rioting, so 'orders were at once given to close the public houses'. After the count in Kells, Mahony's supporters 'took their beating like men', though at Navan station, a few prominent Parnellites' greeting of the defeated candidate 'was very affecting, but as far as could be seen no tears were shed'.

A Trim correspondent, writing in the *Irish Independent* about 'how the South Meath election was won', claimed that Fr Behan abused many voters whom he canvassed and, if they were absent, 'the fears of their wives were worked upon.[77] They were told they would have no luck if they voted for Dalton, that their substance would melt and they were asked, if their husbands died, who would anoint them?' In Summerhill, Fr John Fay, of whom much more would shortly be learned, worked up his anti-Parnellite parishioners, who surrounded the home of a Parnellite named Fagan, setting fire to his shed and burning a horsetrap in it. The *Drogheda Independent* reprinted a letter from Fr Clarke to the *London Evening Standard.*[78] Admitting that he gave Reilly 'a slight stroke of my hand' for saying it was 'a shame and a disgrace for me, a priest, to be there', Fr Clarke asked 'had I not a perfect right as a citizen to come to Nobber, apart from my duty as a priest, to counsel these poor people? Why should I be insulted by a violent old brawler egged on . . . by a bitter and designing clique of pothouse politicians who seek by every means to cast insult on their priests . . . We shall assert our rights in spite of all the stuff and claptrap about priestly intimidation.'

Fr Kelly of Slane asked the *Freeman* to insert a letter, dated 16 July (also reprinted in the *Argus*),[79] addressed by Davitt to him as 'chairman of the central county committee', congratulating the anti-Parnellites of Meath on their triumph 'over combined factionism and landlordism'.[80] Davitt, doubtless preparing both a counter-claim to an anticipated election petition and an excuse for his small majority, singled out his 'supporters in Navan, who had to submit . . . unflinchingly to outrage and insult at the hands of organised rowdyism'. Learning on arriving back from England of how 'large numbers' of them were prevented from voting for him, he was 'astonished, after the experience of similar illegality in Trim, that the returning officer did not . . . [ensure] free access to the polling booths at Navan'. The *Drogheda Independent* again used evidence of mob intimidation of anti-Parnellite voters by Mahony's supporters, especially in Navan, to counter Parnellite accusations of clerical intimidation.[81] The *Freeman* also reprinted a letter from Davitt, dated 19 July, to the *Daily Telegraph,* denying that he drew a revolver in Navan: 'Your correspondent doubtless read it [in] an obscure Parnellite organ.'[82] A *Freeman* analysis showed a total Parnellite vote in the whole country of 68,013, which, minus the last Tory poll of 8,498, gave a Parnellite strength of 59,515 against an anti-Parnellite vote of 279,509, yet the Parnellites won only 9 seats, to their opponents' 71, in the first-past-the-post system of election.[83]

Courts adjudicate on election violence

In the aftermath of the election, seven Parnellites who assaulted an anti-Parnellite voter named Brien at Rushwee near Slane were jailed for from three to six weeks.[84] Reporting on two malicious fires on farms in Meath during July, Captain Stokes noted that the wife of one of the farmers, a Parnellite, asked Fr Fay, of Dangan (Summerhill), to request people to cease interfering with them and that the parish priest replied they 'were only getting what they deserved'.[85] In the rioting in Navan on polling day, 'a good many houses were wrecked'. Fifteen of the principal defendants there had been returned for trial on bail, as had two priests. 'There can be no doubt that, but for the decisive action of the RC bishop and his clergy, both Mr Dalton and Mr Mahony would have been returned for Meath. A very large number of Catholic voters in the county resent the action of the bishop and his clergy.' Captain Stokes also reported that in Tullamore church the curate, Fr Murphy, condemned the people of Navan for crying out 'down with the tall hats' and 'clerical rule' and attending meetings got up by Mahony, a Protestant souper from Kerry, the object of which was to starve and boycott the clergy. Referring to the turning of Fr Behan's cattle off land in Trim, Fr Murphy had said it was a wonder the Parnellites did not tar and burn them. On 10 July, when Dr Nulty said Mass in Navan chapel and referred to the Parnellites as non-Catholics, cowards and traitors, a number of Parnellites walked out. The same thing happened at Duleek chapel on 3 July and at Trim chapel on the same date during the reading of Dr Nulty's pastoral, Captain Stokes noted.

Fr Christopher Casey, curate in Dunderry, was prosecuted at Navan court 'before a bench [of] . . . Protestants and conservatives', according to the *Freeman,* for assaulting Patrick Byrne of Knockumber, Navan, on polling day.[86] Matthias Bodkin, the anti-Parnellite MP and former acting editor of *United Ireland*, defending, said Fr Casey was protecting an aged voter named McDermott and his son, who had been so badly maltreated by the Parnellite crowd that there was difficulty in getting them to come to court in Navan. But Byrne said the priest had struck him violently with a stick for no reason. He saw a crowd of about thirty pull about an old man whose face was blackened. Witness caught hold of a whip which a young man had. Witness had been fined 5 shillings before for being drunk and had fled to America to avoid a charge of assaulting the police. The evening of the day he was struck, he went to the parochial house with stones in his hand to ask the name of Fr Casey. He threw down the stones when asked by Fr Woods. Later he was knocked down when the police charged a peaceful crowd and he got a scratch on the head. He was not a voter, but came to Navan to walk around.

District Inspector Duff said the police were scarcely able to deal with the violence of the mob. A prisoner they took was rescued by the mob, whom the police repeatedly charged. Windows were broken by stones and ultimately Mr Meldon had to read the Riot Act. Sergeant Dobbyn said the crowd was 200, not 30. The number of police was not sufficient to cope with the crowd or maintain law and order. James McDermott, aged over 70, said when he was going to the booth a young man rushed up and daubed his face with black stuff. The mob then raised a cry that he was a Healyite and he got a blow on the ear. He heard a man say 'drag him up the lane and kill him'. His son came up and struck one of those with a whip. He was greatly frightened. James McDermott, junior, said he saw the crowd dragging his father about. He saw one man strike his father on the ear and he struck that man with his whip. Witness was struck a blow from behind with a stick which broke his hat. Fr Casey struck the man who had struck witness and knocked him down. Fr Casey's hat was knocked off before this. Witness had to fly for his life. Rev. Thomas Gilsenan said he had asked Fr Casey to go to the protection of the old voter. There was a great deal of confusion and violence. After Byrne was struck he made a violent attempt to wrench witness's walking stick out of his hand. The court decided it had no option but to send the case forward for trial.

Reporting on prosecutions for rioting in Navan on polling day, the *Freeman* named the defendants as John Coyle, John White, Bartle Cronin, John Curran, Bernard McKevitt, Thomas Parker, Patrick Coogan, John Cullen, Peter Reilly, Jospeh Casey, John Kavanagh, Robert Cooke, Thomas Nolan, Bridget Cahill and Thomas Murray.[87] The paper said the town 'seems to have been almost entirely given over to mob law'. Anti-Parnellite voters had 'their faces smeared with tar. They were beaten and hunted through the town like wild animals.' The police themselves were stoned and beaten. 'A mob of about a thousand occupied the streets during the day and attacked every person whom they believed to be anti-Parnellite.' They attacked and wrecked the shops of at least two of Davitt's supporters. Those charged with riot and assault were only the ringleaders.

Head Constable Carty said people supposed to be anti-Parnellites were 'pelted with small bags of flour and rotten eggs and their faces were smeared with tar'. During a baton charge about 2 p.m. he saw Cahill throw stones at the police. She was the worst of all the women who were gathered at Corn Market. Some of the constables were struck. Later in the evening he saw Murray with an open knife in his hand on Market Square. At intervals during the day he saw Cullen heading riotous mobs, including that which chased James McDermott from the town hall booth to James Sheridan's yard. There were at least three hundred men after McDermott and their conduct was most threatening. He saw Cullen and Cronin, with sticks in their hands, at the head of a mob of at least a thousand in Trimgate Street, surrounding Sheridan's shop. At about 11 p.m., Cullen and a squad of them were marched out of the CYMS hall by Pierce Mahony. The police had been stoned from the hall a few minutes previously. Several times McKevitt forced his way through the cordon of police at Sheridan's shop and assaulted the constables who arrested him. At 9 p.m. the police were stoned by a crowd in Trimgate Street and some of them were seriously hurt. All day the streets were occupied by violent mobs.

Constable Bergin said he saw Coogan smash Sheridan's window in Trimgate Street with a stick. At 9 a.m. he saw Cronin smearing tar on the faces of three voters as they were going into the polling booth and the crowd shouted 'kick them out, they are seceders'. Witness was protecting voters and was struck six times with rotten eggs. Sergeant Gernon, Batterstown, said Cullen's hands were covered with tar. Sergeant Daniel Murphy, Navan, said that people whom he put out of Sheridan's shop seemed to be looking for someone. Those inside and outside were greatly excited. After being put out of Sheridan's, Cullen and Reilly headed the mob across the Square to Rothery's public house and he put them out of there also. Reilly then said to the crowd 'come down to Pat Allen's and we'll put him out'. Witness ran there first and kept him out. Reilly asked the crowd were they cowards, would they not follow him. When three or four constables came up, witness arrested Reilly. The crowd then stoned the four policemen and Allen's house, breaking windows. Witness, hit with stones, gave Reilly to the other constables and faced the crowd. They closed in and rescued the prisoner and went back to Sheridan's, smashing the windows of his house. The mob was then charged by a force of police and dispersed.

About 8 p.m. the police were escorting Thomas McNally, one of Davitt's agents, when Parker came out from a crowd at the corner of the Square and threw a stone at him, Sergeant Murphy continued. Witness caught him and struck him when he was throwing another stone: 'I hit him a box with my fist and I also hit him with my baton.' Constable Maguire said Casey, a militiaman, struck him on the right arm with a stone in Trimgate Street. When Casey tried to pull the baton from his hand witness fell to his knees. While down he was kicked and received several more blows from stones. Casey then pulled the baton from him and ran away with it. Sergeant Carroll said he saw Murray rushing into the Square with a knife in his hand, shouting 'it is time to use the knife now'. The police were charging a stone-throwing mob at the time. Witness hit him with his baton as he was about to stab a constable. Acting Sergeant Corry said he saw Daniel Kane and his son drive past the CYMS hall in a trap. The mob booed at them and after they passed the chapel eggs were thrown at them. They drove into the yard of Loughran's house and the crowd followed them. Witness and Sergeant Martin succeeded in getting the old man into Mr Loughran's house. He saw young Mr Kane run, bleeding from the head, out of a shed in the yard, pursued by others whom he did not know. They got him into Loughran's house along with his father. Sergeant Martin identified McKevitt as the leader of the mob who pursued old Mr Kane, whose face was bleeding. The mob was howling and yelling at Mr Kane. All the prisoners were returned for trial to the next assizes on bail.

The *Irish Independent* reported, however, that barrister Edward Murphy, prosecuting Fr Casey, said Byrne had a right to be on the street.[88] How the priest allowed himself to be carried away by his feelings he could not understand. Sergeant Dobbyn said someone cried out 'down with Healy and Davitt' and some women laughed before Fr Casey struck Byrne. He was about to use the stick again but the constable rushed forward and told him to desist at once or he would arrest him. He advised Fr Casey to go into the booth, which he did. Fr Gilsenan was waving a stick over his head, preparing to strike other people but witness desired him to desist. To Bodkin: 'There were two parties. Both were violent. There was no assault committed until the Rev. Mr Casey committed the assault on Mr Byrne.' Charles Meek, an assistant in Diamond's apothecary shop, said Byrne's wound was almost an inch long, penetrating to the bone. Bodkin said there was an attempt to make this a state trial because a priest was concerned. Fr Gilsenan, called by the defence, said he saw Fr Casey strike Byrne with a stick. He could not say if Byrne struck him. To Murphy: he had a stick himself that day. It was after the blow was struck and the blood drawn that the attitude of the crowd became hostile. Murphy said the prosecution was brought to show that neither clergymen nor laymen could take the law into their own hands. The bench sent Fr Casey on bail for trial to the next assizes.

Under the heading 'Coercion prosecution of a priest — mountains out of molehills — factionist falsehoods refuted', the *Freeman* reported that at the petty sessions at George's Cross, Fr P. Clarke was prosecuted for assaulting Owen Reilly.[89] 'The court consisted of Mr Removable Meldon, Mr C.F. Slator, a coercionist land agent in the district and Major Everard, who so unsuccessfully contested . . . the division of Cavan in which Fr Clarke resides. The case excited considerable interest owing to the wild and malicious stories that had been circulated in reference to it both in Ireland and England.' Referring to 'lurid accounts' of the doings of Fr Casey at Navan and Fr Clarke at Nobber, the *Freeman* added 'fortunately, the Castle, in its over-eagerness to score any point against a priest, was betrayed into coercion prosecutions with the result, certainly never intended, of completely exposing the malignant fabrications . . . [It was] conclusively proved some days since at Navan, that Fr Casey . . . had merely interposed, with great courage and self devotion, to rescue an aged and inoffensive voter . . . who had been tarred and was being violently maltreated by a gang of Redmondite ruffians [including Patrick Byrne] . . . The case of Fr Clarke . . . will be summarily tried on the evidence before the great court of public opinion.'

The *Irish Independent* reported on Fr Clarke's case that Murphy, acting again for the prosecution, said that about 200 people were on the streets of Nobber at 11 a.m. when both candidates visited the town.[90] 'Feeling was running high and Owen Reilly . . . apparently in infirm health, used some expressions in favour of one of the candidates. The Rev. Mr Clarke took it as a personal insult and struck the old man a blow on the head with his clenched fist and knocked him down on the road . . . Such violence might very easily have led to a riot in Nobber on that day.' Sergeant Patrick Reilly, Dean Hill, said Fr Clarke 'had something like a list of voters in his hand'. He heard Reilly abusing Fr Clarke, saying 'I want no instructions or directions from you'. He cautioned Reilly, whom some persons clapped on the back, before defendant said to Fr Clarke 'it is a shame for you to come here'. Fr Clarke said he had been insulted, asked for an apology, which was refused, and then struck Reilly on the face, saying 'take that'. When Reilly fell to the ground, people cried out 'you have murdered the man'. They tried to strike Fr Clarke with sticks, but the police prevented them. Head Constable Hanna said the police surrounded Fr Clarke until Fr Everett of Nobber took him away. Owen Reilly, leaning on a stick, said he had told Fr Clarke 'it was bad gratitude to forget the two

men who had done so much for the country and it was a shame for the
priests to head mobs against them . . . I then got a blow on the right
ear, not a hard blow, and I fell with my left ear on a stone. It was easy
to take me down as I am nervous on one of my legs . . . I don't think
Fr Clarke meant to do me any harm . . . I did make a claim but I think
I won't follow it any further because I believe I was partly at fault
myself . . . I had taken two halfs of whiskey, which I think helped me
to have bad manners . . . I am not a whit the worst of it now.' Bodkin
said he was instructed to say that Fr Clarke regretted that, even under
the provocation which the constable said was sufficient to provoke a
breach of the peace, he was tempted to the very slight act by which he
resented it. Meldon sent Fr Clarke forward for trial on bail. There
would be further court cases arising from the bitterness of the general
election, but none more important than the South and North Meath
election petitions.

Chapter 5

South and North Meath election petitions

Before the end of July 1892, William Redmond, MP (brother of John) confirmed that James Dalton was preparing a case against the South Meath result and 'rule by clerical blackthorns'.[1] At the league in Dublin, he referred to priests 'knocking down old men, stating that it was sinful to vote for an independent candidate and insinuating that people who so voted would not be attended to in their dying moments'.[2] John Redmond, MP, attended a meeting in Trim town hall, where Dalton said he was confident of winning the petition, gave £100 himself, asked for subscriptions and collections and said the money was safe.[3] Redmond said he would not go as far as Dalton, his brother-in-law, but 'an overwhelming mass of evidence has been collected — I have never seen a stronger case than this'. Both men then addressed an enthusiastic meeting from a window of Mrs Grogan's house. Redmond confirmed that his much reduced party of 9 independents nevertheless formed part of Gladstone's majority of 40 and they would do their utmost for Home Rule, the evicted tenants and political prisoners. Calling Fulham 'a political omadhaun [fool]', he warned that 'everyone connected with the petition will have to bear much abuse, but let every man stick to his guns'.

Redmond then chaired a special meeting of the league in Dublin, attended by Mahony and Dalton, which formally decided to lodge court petitions against the return of Davitt as well as Fulham.[4] Redmond instanced cases of 'terrible intimidation and undue influence' by priests in many counties, but especially in North and South Meath. There were good grounds for petitions against the members returned for Cork, Kerry and other places, but as the people of Meath had taken the initiative in subscribing the necessary funds, 'the assistance of nationalists throughout the entire country should be concentrated on their aid'. Bishop Nulty's pastoral also marked the Meath elections with 'a special feature'. The *Irish Independent* declared that clerical 'white terror' in Meath had 'turned the ballot into a farce'.[5] It repeated

Courtesy of the National Library of Ireland.

Redmond's call for country-wide support for the Meath petitions, the people of Trim having already subscribed £350. Opening a subscription list, the paper said that £1,000 security had to be lodged for each petition and much more was required to carry them on. As the beaten party would have to pay costs, it was hoped 'that at the end the money subscribed will be either returned to the donors or applied to some other national purpose'.

The *Irish Independent* also maintained that most anti-Parnellite MPs could not have been elected without clerical intimidation, but cost prevented petitions being taken in all cases.[6] James Lawlor, among the first to subscribe £1 to the petition fund, wrote 'could I afford it, [I] would send £100 as freely[7] . . . If there was not another man in Ireland to protest against the latter-day methods of carrying parliamentary and Poor Law elections, I would do so, publicly as well as privately.' *United Ireland* remarked 'the practices which were carried on successfully and with impunity in Kilkenny [by-election 18 months previously] and other counties have been tried in Meath with the result that they have roused its sturdy sons[8] . . . [Parnellites] will never forget that "the people of Ireland" include over a million non-Catholics' and the bishops would not succeed 'in the attempt they have been making for the past 18 months to become the arbiters of the destinies of Ireland and the masters of its political fortunes'.

When the new parliament met in August 1892, the 80 Irish Home Rule members, who now held the balance of power, joined with the Liberals to turn out the Conservatives. Gladstone, aged 83, formed a government committed to Home Rule and parliament was prorogued until January to enable him to prepare this and other measures. Ridiculing Michael Davitt for taking the oath of allegiance at Westminster which he had declared that he would never take, the *Irish Independent* quoted him responding in 1888 to the Bishop of Limerick's attack on the plan of campaign:[9] 'Clerical dictation, which has worked such manifest injury to the Catholic church on the continent . . . would shatter to its foundations the Catholic church of this country . . . To obtain some liberty for the church in Ireland, the infamous Act of Union was countenanced by Irish bishops . . . and it was only through the determined opposition of O'Connell at a later period that Rome was prevented from handing over the independence of all Irish Catholic bishops into the hands of men like Mr Balfour. We are not going to exchange the servitude of Westminster for that of the Inquisition.' But in Meath, Davitt had allowed his chief patron, Bishop Nulty, to call on his flock to stamp out Pierce Mahony and his supporters as 'a great moral, social and religious evil'. Davitt had failed to protest against the action of the bishop, who followed his lead in describing Mahony as 'a Kerry souper'. Thus was North Meath won, said the *Irish Independent*.

That Bishop Nulty did use the offensive phrase is confirmed by a *Drogheda Independent* report of his return to a hero's welcome in Mullingar, where an address from the town commissioners complained that the bishop had benefited Navan by maintaining the diocesan seminary as well as two convents there.[10] Bishop Nulty replied that he 'ought to remain in Mullingar always'. He would never leave that town except sorely against his will. Some men forgot themselves completely when in the contest in North Meath they put Michael Davitt on an equality with Pierce Mahony, the souper from Kerry (a term of even more opprobrium then, within living memory of the famine, and which the bishop neither subsequently denied nor withdrew). Notwithstanding the disgraceful scenes that took place, notably in Trim, Navan and Athboy, said Dr Nulty, the heart of Meath was sound. Although nefarious deeds were done in Navan, the real old natives were a good, pious, moral people. It was the newcomers and an imported mob that created the whole trouble and disorder.

In a flight of fancy, he claimed that at Davitt's meeting in Navan on the Sunday before polling, the Parnellites, 'who were armed with bludgeons, fell upon them and battered and beat hundreds of the poor people. When news of this outrage spread to the country, fully 2,000 able men, farmers and farmers' sons, came into Navan armed with sound blackthorns and if they were let at the factionists they would have smashed them all.' On polling day in Navan, claimed the bishop, 'mad with drink, they went about, some 1,200 of them, and beat anyone and everyone they thought was a nationalist. They broke the windows of several respectable shop-keepers and in my own hearing they shouted "to hell with the priests" [and] . . ."down with the tall hats" . . . The mob was determined to murder Mr Davitt . . . and when they heard he was travelling by train from Kells . . . they even searched under the carriage seats.' Judging Parnellism by its fruits, it was impious for any Catholic to support it. He did not wish to put these (Meath) people on an equality with the people of Westmeath. Fr O'Reilly maintained that it was the people and not the priests who had organised the demonstration in Mullingar, which concluded with the town being illuminated, including the two convents and the college, where a fireworks display took place.

The *Drogheda Independent* also maintained that the purpose of the Mullingar reception was to demonstrate 'the people's anger against the Navan mob 'and their more miserable prompters', who had dared to insult Bishop Nulty.[11] These 'new-blown patriots' had made the name Navan 'odious to Irish Catholic ears' and their insults to their bishop 'have only recoiled upon themselves'. In response, William Lawlor presided at the Navan league to condemn 'the scurrilous attack on the people of Navan by the clerical organ'.[12] Local Parnellites should start their own newspaper, as 'falsehoods will be swallowed wholesale by our country friends, who are not aware of the real facts . . . in this struggle for freedom of thought'. They denied insulting Bishop Nulty, in whose hands rested the future unity of priests and people in Navan. The fight was entirely a political one and would continue 'until priests and people can agree as to the right man to represent them in parliament'. While never saying 'no priests in politics', they would 'continue to protest against the absurd idea that the clergy are to be supreme in political matters'. They were sorry that the bishop 'has so far forgotten his exalted position as to refer to Mr Mahony as . . . "a souper from Kerry".' If he was so now, was he not one when Dr Nulty and his priests adopted him for Meath years previously? Repudiating each of the bishop's characterisations of Mahony's pre-election Sunday meeting in Navan, the local Parnellites maintained 'our meeting was composed of men from all parts of Meath and Meath only, invited by public notice . . . who were not armed with stick nor bludgeon, nor in the slightest degree under the influence of drink . . . Did not the Whigs import men from Cavan, Louth and Monaghan, armed with bludgeons.'

The *Irish Independent* sympathised with the people of Navan on being misrepresented by Bishop Nulty and commended the idea of a local Parnellite newspaper.[13] The *Drogheda Independent*, founded largely by their money, had been turned against them. But that paper defended the bishop: 'The windows of his house were broken . . . In his church when addressing his flock, a Navan man [James Lawlor, as we shall see] stood forth before the congregation and told Dr Nulty he was a liar . . . A crowd of Navan men and women gathered outside the bishop's house at night and hooted and booed . . . The Navan mob, nor stick or bludgeon had they; a sober crowd too, who would not loot a seceder's house, nor tar a voter nor try to murder a mere Whig or Michael Davitt, nor insult a priest and would only knock down a policeman out of mere frolic.'[14]

Petitions lodged

The South Meath petition was lodged on 8 August 1892 against the election of Patrick Fulham because of undue influence and intimidation by Catholic clergymen acting for him by addresses from the altar and other means and by the bishop's pastoral letter, as well as the corrupt practices of bribery and of treating (buying drinks for voters).[15] The next day the North Meath petition was lodged against Davitt's return on the same grounds, along with hiring carriages and horses and paying railway fares for electors.[16] The following day £1,000 sureties were lodged for both Meath petitions.[17] The *Drogheda Independent* charged Mahony and Dalton with using 'English law . . . [as] a superior tribunal to the people's suffrages'.[18] The petitions would inflame sectarian hatred, insult the priests and especially the aged bishop, and were a skilful attempt to distract attention from Parnellite mob violence. Their lack of good faith was 'strikingly exemplified in the fact that they do not claim the seats [for which they would have to prove that the number of votes they lost through clerical influence exceeded the anti-Parnellite majorities], but ask merely that the holders be unseated'.

In September an unsigned article in the *Drogheda Independent* skilfully set out the clerical defence.[19] It declared that Davitt had been elected by a considerable majority with 'no clerical intimidation whatever', Bishop Nulty's pastoral being not 'even remotely suggestive of intimidation'. For ten years the Catholic bishops and clergy had supported Parnell, whose most ardent friends and active helpers had been Dr Nulty and his clergy. There was no talk of 'clerical intimidation' then or when, by Parnell's decision, Catholic clergy were admitted to constituency selection conventions. So why should it now be made a crime for a priest to exercise his citizen's rights? A charge of 'clerical intimidation' came badly from a Protestant nationalist like Mahony, because the few of his co-religionists who were patriotic Irishmen had experienced none of it. But now, because the bishop and clergy of Meath would not condone treason to Ireland, they were to be dragged into the dock as criminals. The petitions would come before a Dublin Castle judge, who would be delighted at the chance of inflicting any indignity on Davitt. Even though Mahony would not be able to present any evidence of clerical intimidation, 'the judge will be his friend and from the judge's decree in an election petition there is no appeal. Possibly Michael Davitt may be unseated and possibly there will be a Castle judge-made member for North Meath, but all Ireland will know what it means.'

At the end of August Patrick Fulham was reported to be considering resigning his seat.[20] But Fr Kelly of Slane presided at a meeting of the North and South Meath election committee at the parochial house, Kells, in the beginning of September to organise the revision of the electoral register in case of fresh elections and to reject the petitions' charges against their new MPs.[21] A letter from Michael Davitt urged them not to relax 'piloting their claims and objections through the revision courts', which, a resolution said, was 'sure to result in a substantial diminution of the forces of the factionists'. The *Freeman* complained, however, that nearly three-quarters of the electors of Slane and Monknewtown, 'which were solid for Davitt', had to meet official objections in the revision courts.[22] But the Parnellite *Meath Reporter* said that 300 objections in Navan to Parnellite voters on the register were 'proof that the priests do not want peace, but are determined to master the people', disgracefully 'expending the money subscribed for their support under pain of disobeying a commandment of the Church to the disadvantage of those who subscribed'.[23]

William Lawlor presided at a meeting of the Navan league to engage a solicitor because of such 'serving wholesale of notices of objection in this district'.[24] The *Freeman* described the outcome of the revision court in Navan as 'exceptionally favourable' to the anti-Parnellites, over 60 of their objections being sustained on one of the three days and only 1 against them.[25] In one case, James Lawlor proved that Fr James Concannon, diocesan catechist, came to Navan only once every three years.[26] Asked by the solicitor for the anti-Parnellites 'is it not your objection that he is a priest?' Lawlor replied 'we do not object to him as a priest, but as a politician'. The case was adjourned for the production of evidence that the bishop resided in the parochial house, Judge Curran remarking there was 'no foundation for that opinion of Fr Concannon that he was objected to because he was a priest'. After a compromise, Fr Concannon remained on the list, the judge appealing, because the election had created ill-feeling, to people on both sides to 'go home and be friends in the future', as they had been in the past. The *Drogheda Independent* put the net gains for the anti-Parnellites at 370 votes in Navan, Slane, Wilkinstown and Drumconrath combined.[27]

Meanwhile, in the ongoing aftermath of the general election, James Brien, building contractor, Stackallen, at Kells court before Judge Curran, sued Peter Harding, police pensioner, John Healy and Patrick Goodwin, all of the same locality, for £50 damages each for assault as he was returning from Slane on polling day.[28] The three defendants had been imprisoned for three weeks for the offence. Brien described being beaten unconscious by the group of Parnellites, who left him on the side of the road. He received the last sacraments some days later. Asked for a reason for the assault, he replied 'the time Mr Davitt was struck in Navan, I helped to arrest Mongey . . . it was well known'. Judge Curran said a man who chose to vote for either Davitt or Mahony had a right to do so without fear of being attacked. He had to see that they would conduct themselves and not behave like savages. He gave a decree for £10 against the ex-constable and for £2 and 10 shillings against each of the other two defendants.

Laurence Rowan, Stackallen, the Navan guardian, sued John Ball, Boylestown, Co. Meath, for damages for assault at the polling in Trim.[29] Rowan, represented by Bodkin, said he was walking towards the courthouse with an acquaintance, Thomas McCullagh, when he heard 'that's the seceder, Rowan — mark him'. He went to the house of Mrs Plunkett to put up his horse and car. A crowd gathered around the house, calling him abusive names and asking that he be thrown out until they murder him. Mrs Plunkett said he had to leave a back way, but Ball came to the window, pointed a stick at him and said 'there he is, there is Rowan the seceder'. Two police came and he left the house as Mrs Plunkett feared it would be broken. He was followed by the crowd, who beat and kicked him and tore his clothes. The police with drawn batons did their best to protect him, but he had to run for his life. Ball raised a stick over his head and witness said 'Ball, you coward, what do you mean? Do you want to kill me? One man against 20.' He later escaped. Asked by Judge Curran to apologise, Ball refused. Saying that every man was entitled to hold his opinion without molestation, the judge gave damages of £10, with costs. The *Freeman* commented 'This of course is not an isolated, but a typical instance . . . Yet forsooth the defeated factionists are whining about the intimidation to which they, poor innocent lambs, were subjected in the district.'[30]

However, the *Irish Independent* depicted the plight of Parnellites in rural areas, whom it urged to organise against powerful clerical oppression along the lines of the old Land League, which 12 years previously had beaten the landlords, entrenched as they were behind the law and all the resources of the English government.[31] The *Irish Independent* returned in October to this theme of 'a black terror' to which 'bishops, by their silence, give their consent'.[32] It said that at the summer retreats of the clergy a plan was tacitly agreed to crush Parnellism. These men were not the church and were abusing their position. The paper later echoed Pierce Mahony's call for priests to be allowed by their bishops to express their Parnellite sympathies openly.[33] And public display of Parnellite affiliation was advocated by William Lawlor when he presided at the Navan league to arrange a local contingent for the first Parnell commemoration in Dublin. He asked 'followers of the dead chief to wear an ivy leaf on 6th October, as an emblem of the tenacity with which they purpose clinging to the principles for which he died'.[34]

Luke Smyth, who presided at a convention in Trim at the end of October, when Pierce Mahony re-appeared to re-organise the league in Meath, felt their position had improved.[35] The anti-Parnellites were falling out over Healy and if there was another election in the county soon, the Parnellites would win it. But he appealed 'specifically to the men of influence in the country districts'. The towns were sound, as the argument was kept up there, but in the country, where it was much more needed, they should do their utmost to bring their scattered forces to a head in local organisation. Christopher Quinn said the prediction at the time of the split that Parnellism would be dead within a year was far from being verified. But Mahony said that during the general election there were districts of North Meath in which they had never been able to hold a meeting. Increased support was also necessary for the *Irish Independent*.

At a later meeting in Syddan, Mahony said that re-organising the league in Meath was necessary to keep independent principles alive until a majority of Irish MPs subscribed to them, even though they had been beaten in the general election and had now only 9 MPs instead of 30.[36] James Dalton said they were not cowed by their temporary defeat: 'We did not use the same methods as our opponents.' At a Parnellite gathering in Bohermeen in November, it was stated that without organisation, in a country district like that, where the homes were so far apart, where men seldom met except on Sundays in their place of worship and on fair days in the neighbouring towns, it was very difficult for them to maintain their independence when terrific forces were at work against them.[37] Dublin was strongly Parnellite, but it was quite easy there, for they had their associations to go to every evening. Among the resolutions was one calling for rent reductions, as agricultural prices were so low 'in this calamitous year'.

The *Irish Independent* again ridiculed Davitt's new clerical affinities by reproducing 'without his permission' his letter to a Meath priest asking him to write to other priests in the county requesting them to

send Davitt details of 'laymen who ought to be justices of the peace . . .
representing popular feeling . . . respectable . . . intelligent . . . No
publican is eligible'.[38] Then the newspaper announced 'Mr Austin
Cowley of Navan has been exalted to magisterial dignity through the
interposition on his behalf of Mr Davitt, MP — pro tem . . . the ex-
Fenian acting as the political pander of the right honourable Samuel
Walker, Lord Chancellor'.[39] Citing Davitt delegating to the clergy
powers of nominating as magistrates 'his prominent bottle holders', the
Irish Independent described as 'too grotesque' the spectacle of 'the ex-
revolutionist, ex-rebel and so forth checking the list of candidates for
the J.P.ship, as prepared by the curates of Meath'. He was posing before
the lord chancellor as a gentleman 'who would keep the lower classes
in their place and posing before the same lower classes as a labour
representative'.[40] Meath priests, compelled by their bishop, had
opposed the Parnellites, whose policy was to lift up poor Catholics who
had long been trodden down by the 'respectable classes' whom Davitt
'wants to be rubbing skirts with in private'. Any attempt to perpetuate
the idea of class inferiority, by intimating covertly that a man was not
fit to be a magistrate because of his social or business standing, would
be opposed by Parnellites. The publicans of Meath had partially helped
to make Davitt an MP, by defeating the independent candidate. In his
defence, the *Drogheda Independent* reprinted a letter from Davitt to a
Derry publican:[41] 'I have not recommended a single person for a JP-ship
. . . I have not written to the Lord Chancellor . . . But I do intend to
make the magistracy of Meath as representative of popular and national
feeling as it is at present of landlord and anti-Irish sentiment.'

Imprisonment of Fr Fay

As preparations for the petitions continued, it emerged that some
priests were trying to influence their parishioners against giving
evidence. On 28 October, when Davitt and Fulham, the respondents,
served notices on Mahony and Dalton, plaintiffs, to deliver 'particulars
of the matters relied upon' in the petitions against them, the *Irish
Independent* said the court action would be resisted.[42] Explaining the
reason, P.J. McCann, solicitor, who had been collecting evidence for the
Parnellites, told the court that the same clerical intimidation which had
prevailed at the election was still being used 'to deter persons . . . from
coming forward to give evidence or assist the inquiry[43] . . . To disclose
the names of the persons whose evidence has been obtained would
subject them to similar intimidation, which would defeat the ends of

justice.' Christopher Friery, another solicitor for the Parnellites, said certain Meath priests had tried to obtain promises from people 'that they would not give evidence at the trial of this petition'.[44] He intended to subpoena those priests, but he also did not want Parnellite witnesses to be identified beforehand as 'the same spiritual influence is now being exercised to defeat the investigation sought'. Accepting the Parnellite submissions, the judges held that the petitioners should furnish the respondents only with the names of the persons practising undue influence and awarded costs against Fulham and Davitt.

Fulham protested at a meeting in Clonard that 'these miserable factionists' were lying.[45] Although they had got a sound thrashing in Meath, they were 'blue mouldy' for another beating and they were trying to get the judges of the courts in Dublin to run himself and his friend Davitt out of the county. He did not expect to go out. He thought that when they put a course of factionists through the witness box in Trim courthouse, with his friend, Tim Healy 'cross hackling them for an hour or two', they would let a little light in on the factionists of Meath. These men talked of intimidation, while the voters dared not go into Trim or Athboy except in fear of their lives and some of them were nearly murdered. 'When we go to Trim next time we will draw a ring of fire round it . . . Navan factionists thought they would keep us out too, but we went in in our thousands and held our meetings in spite of them.' Fr Behan said if there was another contest in South Meath the Parnellites 'will get a licking they will never forget'. What had the priests ever done to forfeit their confidence? It was no harm that neither bishop, priest nor layman was afraid of them. They had done nothing behind doors that a priest or layman need be ashamed of.

Dalton next brought the *Freeman* to court for contempt in stating on 29 October (quoting Talleyrand) 'Let the assassins commence.[46] Let the patriot Catholics who in a fortnight's time will be holding up at the Meath election trial the pastoral of patriotic Dr Nulty and the action of the priests to the horror of Exeter Hall in sheer malice to hurt Home Rule in England and without any hope of ultimate success at the polls . . .' Dalton said he was a Catholic and a nationalist and this malicious libel against him would deter and intimidate people from giving evidence at the petition. His barrister, T. O'Shaughnessy, said 'sending down quotations of this kind to the peasants of Meath — they will take it in its literal sense. We all know the enormous difficulties in getting evidence of this spiritual intimidation from the altar. If once it goes out . . . that they can denounce the people who appealed to law as assassins, as priest-hunters, and state that their sole objective is to hold up to horror and execration their own priests, it is an easy way of getting rid of these petitions.' Ruling that the words used were a contempt, the three-judge court said they could unduly influence witnesses against coming forward, 'because they were told that the petition was really a sham'. Accusing the *Freeman* of 'a sinister motive in reference to the election petitions pending', the court suspended any penalty but ordered the newspaper to pay the costs of the action. O'Shaughnessy made a similar application in relation to the North Meath petition.[47] Mahony said he had never since the date of the petition written an article in the *Irish Independent*, of which he was a director and shareholder, nor had he written anything in an attempt to interfere with the hearing of the petition, nor had he ever attacked the character of the Catholic priesthood. Bishop Nulty had described him in a speech as 'a Kerry souper', although 'my family for at least four generations have been members of the Protestant religion'. The court made a similar ruling in his case.

With much less political astuteness, O'Shaughnessy, on behalf of Dalton, brought Fr John Fay, parish priest of Summerhill, to court for contempt in a sermon at mass in Dangan (Summerhill) chapel on Sunday, 6 November.[48] Dalton's solicitor, P.J. McCann, said on affidavit (from notes which the priest evidently noticed him taking!) that he was at mass when Fr Fay said

> I shall be on my trial in Trim with the other priests of the diocese and the bishop and I am glad of the opportunity of showing up the character of these men who are giving evidence against me. We will expose again the scandal of the divorce court. These people, imbued with the devil, will pursue me to the end. I expect that, I am prepared for it. I tell you the devil will attack me and they are possessed with the devil of impurity, the most frightful of all passions. Now this is pure Parnellism. Is it not a glorious thing to put our bishop like a common criminal in the box after 29 years of service and trial and devotion for you? Now report every word of this accurately and put it in your *Independent*. Don't leave out a single word, for I'll be there and I will prove that every witness that comes up against me is a black-dyed scamp. I never intimidated you. I never said that I would kill you or break your neck or said you would go to hell. You may go there if you like. We will

resume this in Trim . . . but I suppose they will put an end to me on the petition in Trim next week . . . The priest is the ambassador of Jesus Christ . . . They carry their Lord and Master about with them and when a priest is with the people almighty God is with them.

Counsel asked the court 'to throw its shield over the persons who were subjected to intimidation so terrible, blasphemous and infamous'. Fr Fay said the affidavit was inaccurate and he denied trying to intimidate anyone. He had 'no idea' he was contravening the rules of the court and if he had done so he apologised. Parnellites were 'a mere handful' in his parish and 'I sought merely to warn my flock that politics should not be used as an excuse for immorality, as I believe Parnellism is very often'. Counsel said Fr Fay was saying 'that the petitioner, who is an avowed Parnellite, is an immoral and an impure person . . . He does not pretend that he did not use this language — and more horrible, dreadful language it would be hard to conceive . . . [It] is a violation of his duty as a priest . . . of the canons of his church and of decency and propriety.'

Lord Chief Justice Harrison (who sat with Judges Holmes and Madden) said 'We read [Fr Fay's language] with extreme pain . . . He does not state in what respect [McCann's affidavit] was inaccurate . . . These words are clearly contempt of court . . . I ask, with great pain and sorrow, is this not calculated to deter witnesses from coming up? What does it convey? That this proceeding by petition is a polluted thing, that every connection with it is a contamination and an endeavour to support it is merely a crime . . . We know with what reverence the humble Catholic regards his pastor . . . Never in the history of this country was language — and I say so with the bitterest pain — more reprehensible proved to have been used and we have come reluctantly to the painful conclusion that a fine would be inadequate . . . Were it not that at the last moment Rev. John Fay said some words of apology we would not pass . . . the mild sentence . . . [of] one month's imprisonment, with costs.' The following Saturday, Fr Fay was arrested in his presbytery in Summerhill, conveyed to Fern's Lock halt (train stop), thence by train to Broadstone station and on by car to Kilmainham jail.[49]

The *Freeman* reported that his house was surrounded by 54 police and soon several hundred people had assembled.[50] 'When the moment for departure arrived, the grief of the people was redoubled and a most touching scene ensued as they pressed round the car begging for their priest's blessing, invoking blessings on him in return and struggling to grasp his hand . . . A procession of fifty vehicles followed in their wake . . . As the train moved off, every hat was raised.' But the *Irish Catholic* recorded that as a result of the intervention of the visiting committee, Fr Fay was allowed to say mass in the prison chapel, wear his own clothes, receive books and papers and one visitor a day 'as well as to be provided with other fare than that supplied to ordinary prisoners'.[51] Tim Healy obtained a writ of *habeas corpus* to have Fr Fay at the South Meath petition in Trim.[52] On the opening day, he appeared 'in custody of the governor of Kilmainham jail and a small escort of constabulary'[53] while, the *Drogheda Independent* noted, 'those sought to be arraigned [Bishop Nulty and his clergy] await the issue of the trial with the most imperturbable equanimity'.[54] The following week, to coincide with the petition, it reprinted, instead of an editorial, an article from the Catholic *Lyceum* on 'the bishops and political morality', which argued that they were justified in taking sides and telling their flocks who to vote for or against.[55]

South Meath petition

The *Freeman* reported the opening of the South Meath election petition in Trim courthouse on 16 November 1892.[56] It listed the priests present, along with Mahony and his wife 'in a dress with bright green sleeves'. Eighty extra policemen aided the 20 local ones, with a mounted escort for Judges Andrews and O'Brien from the train station. 'There was a large crowd in the town but the general public was not admitted to the court', for which 150 special tickets were issued. Twenty pressmen attended, with 2 shorthand note-takers from London reporting to the Speaker of the Commons. The petition 'commenced with counsel for Dalton making allegations against the Bishop of Meath and the priests of the division, of whom 51 were charged with corrupt practices'. Fr Fay was brought back to Kilmainham in the evening. On the second day, Michael Aloysius Casey, editor of the *Drogheda Independent*, said laymen outnumbered clergy by 10 to 1 at the convention in the seminary, Navan, on 1 June when Davitt and Fulham were adopted without pressure or coercion.[57] After the convention, they went down to the presbytery, followed by a hooting crowd. While waiting there for the train, a howling mob at the gates burned an effigy of Davitt. On their way to the station, women and children cursed and blasphemed the priests. One woman told a priest that if he were in the same position as Parnell he would have committed adultery too.

When T. O'Shaughnessy, QC, objected on behalf of Dalton that this was 'an effort to get in this as evidence in the other [North Meath] petition', D.B. Sullivan, QC for Fulham, replied that the charge of clerical intimidation was largely founded on the fact that the priests were active in organising this election. 'We propose to show . . . that such was the state of terror and intimidation prevailing here against the members of the anti-Parnellite party that no one except a clergyman could be found with sufficient nerve to face it.' Secondly, they wanted to show the basis for the bishop's observation in his incriminated pastoral that Parnellism was 'not merely a political movement, but a revolt against the authority of the church'. Dalton's other QC, M. Drummond, said it was unfair on his client to introduce evidence as to a matter in which he was not present, when he had not even been selected as a candidate and which took place outside his constituency. 'It is sought to make my client responsible for the language of a drunken woman of the streets. Will your lordships hold that evidence as to the acts of a common prostitute will be given against my client?' Mr Justice O'Brien: 'No, oh no.'

Tim Healy, MP, junior counsel for Fulham, quoted from the pastoral about Parnellism bringing the priests into disrepute with their flocks, which thereby would eradicate the Catholic religion from the country. He said their use of clergymen was a case of repelling aggression against them. Re-examined by Drummond for Dalton, Casey said that about 30 people, including priests, went to the station with Davitt and Fulham. Up to half of the mob of over a hundred were women and children of the streets. He saw Davitt on his knees, with a bloodied handkerchief around his head, a couple of hundred yards from the railway station. On the third day, Sullivan said Bishop Nulty was 'in feeble health' and O'Shaughnessy replied that he would get 'ample notice' of being called to prove his pastoral.[58] Matthew Brogan, a Parnellite aged 76, gave evidence of the gates of Clonard church being closed against him and held by a howling mob.

Bishop Nulty was in court 'at counsel's elbow', as Sullivan began Fulham's response:[59] As Parnell resisted efforts to depose him,

> secret societies were soon in baleful activity. Money was
> lavished among the dissolute and drink flowed freely. Secret
> meetings and night meetings were held and there was swearing
> in going on rapidly . . . The basest means were being adopted
> to injure the Catholic church . . . Under the guise of . . .

Parnellism . . . all the elements of disorder in their respective parishes were being arrayed against them . . . Priests were insulted on the roads, in the streets and at their chapel gates. Meetings were held for the purpose of inducing their parishioners to withhold their dues . . . The teaching was impressed upon the young that what Parnell described as 'his fault' was no disqualification for the leader of the Catholic people of Ireland. When those who insisted that a grave moral question was involved in the retention of that leadership, they were assailed as spiritual tyrants and despots . . . The bishop and the priest was pursued by the speaker on the platform, the organisers of the midnight meeting and by writers in the press . . . [Dalton] carried the banner which had risen up in defiance of the authority of the Catholic religion.

Therefore, Sullivan continued, the bishop felt compelled to defend his clergy, but he wrote his pastoral by himself, neither for nor against any political party. His advice related only to the moral issues raised in the general election, knowing that Parnellism was dangerous to the faith, purity and salvation of his people and was a defiance of church authority. Dr Nulty would not question the right of anyone to vote for political independence, self-government or agrarian and social reform. Quoting from the pastoral about the bishop's pain in breaking with Parnell, Sullivan concluded 'it was impossible to read these words . . . and not feel, as it were, the throbs of heart within his bosom. He did indeed love Mr Parnell . . . He [counsel] asked if in this Christian land . . . a bishop of the Catholic church, recognising a danger to the morality of his flock, was not free to address himself to that subject.'

Bishop Nulty was also in court for the next two days, but he was not called.[60] The following day, Healy 'surprised everyone by beginning his summing up'.[61] In response, Drummond, for Dalton, said the election should be voided because of the pastoral, general intimidation and undue influence, the pastoral being sufficient.[62] 'He was listened to with fixed attention by their lordships, both of whom had before them a copy of the now famous production of Dr Nulty.' Drummond agreed with Healy that 'this is one of the most important election petitions that has ever been tried in this country', because it 'may result in limiting or curtailing the power of the clergy of the Catholic church or of every church who interfere in political transactions . . . The real issue is . . . whether or not the Catholic voters of this country can exercise the parliamentary franchise in favour of a member of a political party which may happen to be condemned or disapproved of by the Catholic hierarchy . . . without at the same time ceasing to be members of the Catholic church.' Drummond complained that there was no evidence of the secret societies, night meetings or swearing in that were mentioned. Catholics supporting Dalton were not showing disrespect to the church or disloyalty: 'Whatever the result may be, their loyalty to the church will not be abated and if that loyalty should ever be shaken it will be by the conduct of the bishops and the priests and not by the conduct of the people.'

The court found for the petitioner, James Dalton. Mr Justice O'Brien asked rhetorically 'what was the occasion for the discussion [in the pastoral] of this delicate and dangerous question of personal purity?'[63] He answered by referring to the allegation of the petitioners that

> it was a skilfully constructed wedge to be driven into a political party which would inflame, alarm and excite by appeals to the strongest and deepest feelings of a Catholic population. Mr Parnell was dead. He was dead and 'could do them no more good' to use the expression related by one of the witnesses of the fleeting nature of gratitude for political leadership. In that situation, what was the reason, what was the justice, to dig up the grave, to revive dead and buried shames, to raise the lid of the tomb and again uncover the poor remains of human frailty in order to array a political party in the shroud of departed sin? But the pastoral, which was the great spring to set in motion the whole machinery of ecclesiastical organisation in the diocese, was not the only form of influence which the evidence attributed to Dr Nulty.

In a sermon in Trim on 29 June he said that 'he would approach the death-bed of the heretic and profligate with greater confidence as to his salvation than that of a Parnellite'. His declarations about Parnellite women would have had a powerful impact on his people and priests. The latter were mainly responsible for candidate selection. 'The church became converted for the time being into a vast political agency, a great moral machine moving with resistless influence, united action and a single will . . . The leading idea of the pastoral that Parnellism was sinful, that it was a matter of salvation was in question . . . governed the conduct of the whole election.'

Referring to the closing of the chapel gates at Clonard against Parnellite mass-goers and other evidence of incidents between priests and their parishioners, the judge added that any Catholic would feel 'that he would subject himself to the greatest peril to his soul's salvation . . . if he did not vote as suggested . . . Any person who has to keep an eye on the evidence could not fail to be tremendously impressed by the fact that in this case you have words trembled on the lips of the people as they give their evidence in the presence of the clergy against whom the charges are made.' Regarding the issue of agency, the judge concluded that the clergy 'appear to me to have fulfilled positions of principals, while Mr Fulham was only the agent'.

Widespread reaction to South Meath result

As a result of the case, Fulham's seat would be declared vacant and a writ for a new election would be issued on the resumption of parliament. In addition, Fulham was barred from representing South Meath for seven years and costs against him were expected to amount to £3,000, the *Irish Independent* said.[64] Bishop Nulty was not examined 'and we must conclude he would have been if the reports of the statements attributed to him were not correct'. The news was the 'principal topic of conversation' in Dublin, where 'bands promenaded the streets in the evening'. In Galway there was a torchlight procession, while in Belfast hundreds besieged the offices of the evening papers for the news from South Meath, which 'caused a great sensation' in Cork. In Drogheda, where bets were laid, the result was published in the windows of the local newspaper offices 'when the mill hands were going to dinner and was greeted with applause'. The *Irish Independent* quoted the English press on the judgment:[65] *The Times* assumed that 'a large proportion of the 70 members of the clerical [majority Irish] party owe their seats to influences of the same kind' and noted Dr Nulty's failure to testify. The liberal *Daily News*, referring to the clergy's 'intolerable tyranny', noted that the Parnellites were just as hostile to the political influence of the priests as the Ulster unionist leader, Col. Edward Saunderson, or the anti-Home Rule Liberal, T.W. Russell, and that earlier, 'when the Pope condemned the plan of campaign, Mr Dillon and Mr O'Brien declared that they took their theology and not their politics from Rome'. The left-wing *Daily Chronicle* agreed 'the result may be useful to the Irish Party if it teaches them to curb their priests and to imitate O'Connell in repudiating politics taken from Rome'.

The league in Dublin, discussing their South Meath victory, highlighted once more the need for organisation in 'isolated districts', where Parnellites had been 'afraid and ashamed to lift up their heads'. In Navan, 'there was unbounded rejoicing . . . In the evening a huge bonfire blazed on the Moat.' John Redmond, MP, told a meeting in Wexford that the result marked the end of the worst phase of the controversy and established 'the right of freedom of judgement and political action for every Irishman'.[66] But the *Freeman* disagreed strongly:[67] the attempt to diminish the influence of priests in Ireland had failed because the 'reckless charges' against the bishop and priests of Meath 'turned out on patient investigation to be a tissue of exaggerations'. The election was voided on the pastoral, but if the 'somewhat florid rhetoric of Mr Justice O'Brien' meant that a Catholic bishop was not legally entitled to interpose in an election as the guardian of the morality of his flock, 'then so much the worse for the law'. Were questions of right and wrong to be banished altogether from the mind of a voter? The issue of immorality was not dead and buried with Parnell, because his followers persisted in dividing the country on precisely the question of whether their leader was rightly deposed after the divorce verdict. Evidence in the petition itself proved the bitter anti-Catholic spirit among Catholics, which sprang directly from the Parnellism which Bishop Nulty had condemned. He and his priests had emerged without formal reproach from their trying ordeal; and Parnellite rowdyism would not be permitted by the new Liberal government at the new elections.

The *Irish Times* welcomed the decision as 'proof of the supremacy of the law' over 'threat or sinister intrusion'.[68] While Bishop Nulty and his priests might have reason to fear that Parnellism threatened their authority, it was 'not their place to direct and control the constituency' or even to use their legitimate influence 'to deny to the laity the privilege of differing from them'. The right which had been established of a free vote was 'momentous'. A broad line had been drawn between the clergy's right to counsel and instruct 'and the assumption of a power to master and steer the conscience'. The *Freeman* regretted that Parnellite joy at the result was 'shared by every Orange and coercionist organ'.[69] It quoted *The Times*: 'Englishmen and Scotchmen could not believe . . . that the spiritual influence of the pastor was sometimes prostituted . . . to over-ride the freedom of elections in packing the imperial parliament with nominees of their own'. The *Morning Post* also remarked that Fulham's election 'was typical of that exercise of clerical power which has kept the anti-Parnellite following on their legs and enabled them to bring Mr Gladstone back to office'. The Tory *Daily Telegraph* concluded 'if these are the electoral facts of Ireland today, we can faintly imagine what would be the result of establishing Home Rule and handing over the Irish elector to [Dublin's] Archbishop Walsh'.

However, the Liberal *Manchester Guardian* asserted that, because of the secrecy of confession, several witnesses who said they had been canvassed in the confessional were safe from cross-examination. It was open to priests to believe that Parnellism condoned immoral conduct and perhaps they had reason to think it also meant the growth of secret societies. There was plenty of evidence that Parnellites were in a very aggressive humour and that priests had to defend themselves, their intervention merely balancing Parnellite intimidation. The *Daily Chronicle* did not find anything 'disgraceful' in Bishop Nulty's conduct, which it said was based on conviction. It could not see how to stop spiritual intimidation without curtailing the political rights of priests. *The Speaker*, a leading English Home Rule weekly, agreed that the Irish clergy believed that the new Parnellism tended 'to make light of the sin of adultery, to encourage secret societies' and to undermine the church.[70] The *Irish Catholic* described the petition finding as 'a purely technical over-stepping of the law on the part of a few of the clergy[71] . . . The seat does not go to his Parnellite opponent, who lacked courage to even claim it.' Exonerating Bishop Nulty and his priests from 'religious or sectarian intolerance', the paper declared that they had to defend their flocks from 'a revolt against Catholic discipline'.[72] The *Drogheda Independent* agreed that denunciation of Parnellites' disregard for morality and revolt against church authority was Bishop Nulty's only crime 'against a technical statute[73] . . . The only finding is that what laymen might do with impunity — advice which they could give their followers freely — became a breach of the law when said or done by clergymen.'

Support for the anti-Parnellites also came from John Morley, MP, the Irish secretary, who said at Newcastle:[74]

> The Irish priesthood have acquired their influence by standing up between the Irish peasant and his oppressor . . . [They] have never been powerful in political matters except when they sided with the nationalist cause . . . You cannot show me any Catholic country in Europe in which ecclesiastics have achieved a standing ecclesiastical supremacy . . . Does anybody

deny the part that the Irish Party — who are now to be denounced as slaves of an intolerant priesthood — have played in English politics during the last sixty years? . . . All this about priestly domination, as far as English parties are concerned, take my word for it, is cant.

Welcoming Fr Fay out of prison, the *Drogheda Independent* complained of the impertinence of Parnellites, who denied 'the right of bishop or priest to interfere in what they declare to be a purely political matter. They act themselves up as the judges as to what is and what is not a purely political question.'[75] The *Freeman* noted that Fr Fay's popularity had, 'like that of many another priest in coercion times', been enhanced by imprisonment.[76] Describing the 'touching scenes' at his homecoming, the paper reported Fr Fay telling the crowd at Summerhill that Parnellites who talked about the release of political prisoners were themselves 'putting the priests in jail'. They had dragged him from the altar, showing the real tendency of the movement to attempt to destroy religion. T.D. Sullivan, MP (Healy's uncle and father-in-law) said Irishmen did not have much reverence for British law in this country, so 'Fr Fay went into prison a priest and a patriot and he came out the same'. He (Sullivan) was anxious that priests should continue as the guides of their people and exercise that influence which was due to their traditions and services but, speaking in the presence of priests, he would never consent to the claim of any class to dominate the affairs of the country. But the priests of Ireland made no such claim and had no desire to go outside that sphere to which their services to Ireland entitled them. Referring to the political capital which unionists were making out of Parnellite attacks on priests, the Irish Party and Gladstone, Sullivan appealed to people not to quarrel among themselves. Fulham said that although he was precluded from contesting the seat again, a better man would be found and the contest would be fought under fairer conditions than the last, when Parnellites prevented their opponents voting in several places. In the evening, Summerhill and the houses all round the village were illuminated in honour of Fr Fay.

The *Irish Independent* made the point that Meath 'Catholics who had the courage as witnesses to vindicate the right of the laity to freedom of action in politics' would reassure Protestants and unionists in Ireland and Britain that Home Rule would pose no danger to them.[77] Tim Harrington, MP, told the league in Dublin that the South Meath and

East Clare petitions (in which William Redmond retained his seat)[78] highlighted 'the terrible difficulties against which we had to struggle during the recent election'.[79] He repeated that when doubts were being expressed about the attitude of the bishops in November 1890, Healy, who drafted the Leinster Hall resolutions, silenced them by saying that Bishop Nulty had told him in Navan 'there is nothing for your party to do but to stick to Parnell'. Referring to the 35 Meath priests supporting Parnell's leadership at the Navan convention that November, Harrington said 'the bishop was in the town and they did not go to that convention and declare themselves supporters of Parnell . . . if there was any feeling in the mind of the bishop that it would be contrary to the church or to public morality'.

In an important comment, which he would later amplify, the Parnellite leader, John Redmond, MP, said in Kilkenny that 'if we had money at our disposal we could have done in forty seats what we did in South Meath the other day.[80] What happened in South Meath happened to my own knowledge in the majority of those cases where we were beaten by the anti-Parnellite party . . . We had not at our back any large funds. We had not . . . a nice English Liberal party ready to fill our political pockets . . . We had not, as they had, the machinery in Ireland for collecting money which the priests have at their disposal at the chapel gates.' Davitt meanwhile denied news reports of his resigning his seat in North Meath as 'too previous'.[81] But he wrote to Dillon 'I am convinced I shall soon have plenty of time at my disposal. The case against some of the priests is *absolutely* conclusive' (his emphasis).[82] George William Tully (brother of Jasper Tully, MP, proprietor and editor of the *Roscommon Herald*), proprietor and publisher of the *Westmeath Nationalist and Midland Reporter*, was fined £20 and costs for language of scandalous vilification in an issue of 1 December regarding the South Meath petition which, in Mahony's view, would intimidate witnesses from coming forward at the North Meath petition.[83]

North Meath petition

That petition opened, with the same counsel as in South Meath being heard by Mr Justices Andrews and Johnson, in Trim courthouse on 15 December 1892.[84] Both sides accepted that the allegations were 'exactly similar' to those in the South Meath case. D.B. Sullivan, for Davitt, said he was willing to accept the undue influence ruling of the South Meath case, especially in view of Mr Andrews's judgement. T. O'Shaughnessy, for Mahony, said he too was willing after formal proof of the pastoral to accept the South Meath decision, although he was quite prepared to go on with his case. If his client was permitted to make a personal statement he would then absolve Davitt from the charges of corruption. But Mr Justice Andrews pointed out that an election petition was not a matter concerning individuals alone, it concerned the purity and freedom of election and affected the entire community. The case should therefore proceed. As Mahony and Davitt sat beside their counsel, a number of priests 'proved attentive listeners', reported the *Irish Independent,* but 'the galleries contained comparatively few spectators'.

O'Shaughnessy said Mahony was from an old Protestant family on the borders of Kerry and Limerick, where his great grandfather was a commissioner of the peace and his grandfather, a well-known solicitor, acted for O'Connell. 'Mr Davitt seems to have come into this contest with good intentions [but] to have slung them aside in a very short time.' He called Mahony a souper from Kerry and the bishop then hurled the same insult. For three months before the election, 'it was whispered in the vestries' that Davitt was to be the candidate of Bishop Nulty and his priests, 48 of whom attended the convention which selected Davitt and Fulham. Lay delegates from each parish were selected by local clergymen. 'Undoubtedly Mr Davitt was unpopular in this county; he was, nay, forced on the people of this county by the resistless power of the bishop and clergy.' As well as suggesting that Mahony 'had abandoned the Catholic faith and was a mere souper from Kerry', a document was circulated alleging that he had reviled the Irish priests in a private conversation at Westminster in bitter resentment at their withdrawal of support. This was printed by the *Drogheda Independent*, 'which appears to enjoy the favour of the bishop so much' that it published his pastoral before it was read in the churches.

Instancing the bishop's sermon at Trim on 29 June, O'Shaughnessy stated that he also said that women of Parnellite sympathies were worse than abandoned women. Counsel, quoting the pastoral, said it condemned Parnell's adultery as if the leader were still alive. He refuted the bishop's assertion that the hierarchy condemned Parnellism — they condemned only Parnell. 'No one made a freer or better use of the pastoral than Michael Davitt.' He stayed at Fr Kelly's house in Slane, the priest was chairman of his election committee, 'everywhere he went, 20 to 30 priests stood with him on his platform'. Davitt was the figurehead of the bishop. He appointed no election agent, but personation agents in every booth, which was a direct violation of the law: in Navan, Frs

Peter McNamee, Dermot Cole, John O'Rafferty and Denis Flynn. In two booths only in the constituency there were no clergymen, but in these two, the priests were outside, looking after the voters. Davitt was proposed by Dr Nulty, along with several priests and laymen, but he elected to stand by the bishop's nomination. Fr Corcoran took the chair at his nomination meeting.

O'Shaughnessy said Bishop Nulty's letter about Navan rowdies disturbing his sleep created 'the most profound sensation . . . With that extraordinary incident, which is told in as artful a manner as ever I read, Mr Mahony or his supporters had nothing to do.' After Fr Woods read the letter on nomination day in Kells, Davitt 'denounced the abominable outrage perpetrated on the bishop by Mr Mahony's supporters . . . [calling him] the grandson of the Kerry souper . . . the solicitor who at meeting after meeting of the Protestants of Dublin urged and actually proposed resolutions in favour of Catholic emancipation in 1829'. At Davitt's meeting in Bohermeen on 4 July with Frs Behan, Rafferty, Casey and Dermody, the few of a different view were described as soupers and place-hunters and told to go to 'the Protestant rector of the place'. At a meeting in Duleek on 3 July about 40 priests attended, including Frs Behan, Gaughran, Kelly, Flood, McEntee and McNamee, who spoke along with both Davitt and Fulham, who attended each other's meetings and worked together. At a meeting in Drumconrath on 26 June, Rev. J. Rooney, parish priest, presided and Rev. J. Flood and 25 or 26 other priests attended when Davitt said Mahony had 'traduced the priests of Meath'. Rev. John Boylan and about 30 priests attended a Davitt meeting in Oldcastle on 29 June. Davitt was not present when the poll was declared, Fr Gaughran of Kells thanking the sheriff on his behalf. Frs Grehan and Brogan bought train tickets for meetings and distributed them to supporters. 'In this contest, Mr Davitt and Mr Fulham were not so much the combatants but really the substantial combatant was the Catholic church, as represented by its priests and by a section of the Catholic laity.'

O'Shaughnessy referred to the impropriety of Fr Brogan saying that Parnell 'betrayed Ireland for the embraces of a heartless woman' before he read the pastoral, as 'a priest standing on the altar in his vestments before his Catholic congregation'. He denied that Mahony ever attacked the Catholic church, but recalled Fr Clarke's assault in Nobber and Fr Casey's in Navan and Fr Cole at a mass station in Navan asking for votes for Davitt. There were numerous other examples of priests canvassing for Davitt: Fr Kelly asked people to 'vote for us, for when you're sick and sore and wanting a priest it's to us you'll have to come'. Fr McNamee suggested that voters would have 'no luck nor grace' if they voted for Mahony. Dr Nulty appeared to have preached in Navan on 10 July that the Parnellites were 'cowards and ruffians'. Fr Woods, at a meeting in Navan, 'made the extraordinary suggestion that the Parnellites would some morning find their mouths where their ears ought to be'. Fr McNamee preached 'a very mischievous address from the altar' on the Sunday before the election. He said 'the priests used to be heroes, now they were traitors and children called names at them. They had it on the authority of Our Lord that those who fell on the chief cornerstone of the church would be broken and crushed to dust. Those who had gone against the church had been broken before. They would not have to wait long until those who were going against the church would be examples in the streets of Navan.'

The priests' involvement had continued since the election. At a meeting on 7 December which Fr Kelly attended, a resolution was adopted 'that with a view to meeting the expenses of the North and South Meath election petitions, a levy be made on the parishes of the county'. The bishop had also recently admonished each of his priests: 'The authority of the Catholic clergy, so reflected in religious and political matters, may be as bitterly as possible assailed in the approaching trials wherein the adherents of Parnellism struggle to nullify the two elections . . . It will be the bounden duty of every priest in this county to keep watch diligently so that the enemy may not bring forward false witnesses and that they themselves may be prepared to challenge this doubtful and tainted testimony.' O'Shaughnessy concluded that he was entitled to ask to have the election voided 'upon that pastoral alone', but in addition, Davitt, 'by availing himself of the influence of the priests . . . has made each and every one of them his agents'.

Fr Kelly of Slane said he was present at a meeting on 23 May (1892) in the parochial house, Navan, 'the bishop's [house] . . . he resides partly between Navan and Mullingar'. Fulham was present with about a dozen clergy, but not Davitt. They agreed to recommend Fulham and Davitt to the convention. Afterwards he sent a circular to every priest in North and South Meath, asking them to invite 'prominent nationalist [anti-Parnellite] laymen' to the selection convention on 1 June. Davitt stayed in his house 'on and off'. There were three laymen to each priest on the committee, which met in Navan on 23 May and 17 June. There was a committee to collect expenses: James Everett and Fr McNamee were treasurers. They gave £200 to Davitt to give to Mr Lowry, sub-sheriff, as nomination expenses. A further meeting was held after the election in Fr Gaughran's house in Kells on 9 September to pass resolutions on voter registration and for expenses for these petitions. Davitt stayed in his house 'to save his life — he would have been murdered in Navan'. He heard Davitt say the bishop and he were old friends.

James Lawlor, town clerk, told Miles Kehoe, junior counsel for Mahony, that he heard Bishop Nulty preach at mass in Navan on 10 July that Davitt and his supporters were coming to Navan more in the interests of religion than in a political matter. He said that the number that would come would cow the Parnellites and that the Parnellites were cowards and rowdies. 'I left the chapel at that stage and know nothing further.' There was no application for the use of the town hall by the anti-Parnellites. Cross-examined by Healy, Lawlor 'could not say' if the town hall would have been given if requested. 'After leaving the chapel did you go back again to Mass? No. Have you been there since? Yes.'

Testimony of canvassing in the confessional was given by Patrick Collins, Kells. Patrick Timmons was examined about Fr Darmody canvassing him for his vote. When he refused, his pastor said he would not forget it to him or his. James McCabe gave evidence of assault on himself and a fellow labourer by anti-Parnellites returning from the nomination in Kells, accompanied by a number of priests. Kells station master, James Lavery, said he was paid by Fr Guinan for 150 tickets which were distributed among people for a special train to Navan chartered by Fr Grehan. James Edward Nangle and Peter Mullins said that Fr Guinan, after reading the pastoral in Kells, declared that the people would be judged on it.

Illiterate voter for Davitt

On the second day, 16 December, a witness from Slane, Anne Kelch, said Fr Kelly said in a sermon in the local chapel in June that the Parnellites would be swept into the sea.[85] Fr Kelly had been asked since March of the previous year to say mass in her invalid aunt's house and he had refused. In October 1891, Fr Cassidy, the curate, said he would say mass in their house: 'We had the vestments in the house and kept the breakfast until after ten, when we received a letter from Fr Cassidy saying that he was exceedingly sorry that he had been . . . [interrupted by Healy] I think it was because we are Parnellites.' Her brother, Patrick Kelch, said mass was said in their house four times a year for the previous 50 years. Fr Kelly had ceased to salute him since he began to attend Parnell's meetings in March 1891. He was personation agent for Mahony in the schoolroom booth in Slane when an illiterate voter threw himself on his knees before Fr Kennedy, Davitt's agent, as if he was going to confession, and said in a faltering voice 'I will vote for Mr Davitt'. The presiding officer in the booth was Mr Davis, Navan. Witness chaired Mahony's meeting in Slane on the evening before the election. Margaret Kelch said Fr Kelly told massgoers in Slane on 3 July that 'there was a gang of hired assassins in Navan and they should go prepared and armed to defend themselves'. Mary Caffrey, 'an aged woman', was in her house in Butterstream on 10 July when a crowd of Davitt supporters tore down a flag of Mahony in the street. 'I instantly went down, thinking that they would not meddle with me, but they riz [raised] me up, leaped on me and put my hip out of joint . . . I will be laid up to the end of my life, I am afraid. A priest then said "let her lie there, the old B—" . . . Francis Sheridan . . . called me "a H—".' Cross-examined by Sullivan, who said Davitt saw her thrusting at Fr Kelly with a pitchfork, she replied: 'That I may never get leave to rise from where I am, I never did. Now your honour, don't be putting such talk to me.'

Daniel Lawlor said he was standing at his hall door nearly opposite the town hall about 12 o'clock on polling day with his father (William Lawlor) beside him. He saw Frs Casey and Gilsenan going into a crowd and Fr Gilsenan came over to his house with a stick. His father told him 'they were a disgrace to their religion' and Fr Gilsenan replied 'go along, you old scoundrel'. There was great confusion on the street. He was at first mass on Sunday, 10 July, the day of the meeting in Navan, when the bishop spoke from the altar about the Parnellites and his brother (James Lawlor) got up and left the chapel. Cross-examined by Healy: he did not see the Parnellite crowd on polling day beating anybody, nor any voters tarred. He saw flour thrown on only one person. 'There was no payment for the flour as far as I know.' Healy: 'You sell flour?' 'Yes.' Healy: 'Did you see a combination of flour and tar?' 'I didn't see either one or the other . . . Fr Gilsenan came from the crowd to the wall.' Healy: 'Didn't you hear your father telling them to give the priests blow for blow?' 'Not a word.' Healy: 'Is your father here?' 'He is not.' Healy: 'You left him behind?' 'Yes.' Healy: 'Selling flour?' 'Aye, that's his business.' Healy: 'Didn't you hear that day in Navan that Davitt's voters were tarred and floured?' 'I did not . . . I was never at any of Mahony's meetings . . . in Navan. I was at Oldcastle and at Kells.' Healy: 'To let the father out?' 'Just so.'

George Coffey said he was in Navan cathedral on the Sunday before the election and heard Fr McNamee referring to attacks on the priests. Witness never heard an attack on the priests or the church at any of the Parnellite meetings in Meath before the election. Cross-examined by Sullivan, he agreed that Fr McNamee complained that priests were hooted by the children of their parishioners while parents, instead of using their authority, encouraged their children to attack the priests. He said that if they cast over their clergymen they might as well abandon their religion. 'I thought he was exaggerating . . . I had paid two or three visits to Navan and I had seen no evidence of that disrespect.' Patrick Douglas, a sheep-dealer from Navan aged over 70, said he was canvassed by Fr Behan in Trim and refused to repudiate the principles of Parnell, whereupon Fr Behan called him 'an old reprobate' and 'an old devil' and dragged him into the street, hitting him in the face. Asked if he stood at the door on the day of the convention in Navan and cursed Fr McNamee and other priests, he denied it: 'I never cursed a priest in my life and if Fr McNamee comes upon the table and swears that I did, even without taking an oath, I will agree with him.' A number of witnesses testified to Davitt's supporters driving through the constituency on nomination day and dismounting at intervals to attack individual Parnellites. Margaret Horan, accused of 'throwing stones at the priests', was pushed to the ground by one of them and struck on both cheeks, as was her daughter.

On the third day of the petition, 17 December, James Gannon, Lobinstown, told of Fr Duffy in a sermon describing a Mahony meeting as being held against religion and to sell porter.[86] During the election, Fr Duffy came up to a number of Parnellites who were talking on the street, twirling a stick, and ordered them all home. When they refused, Fr Duffy struck two men on the head with his stick. The crowd rushed at the priest and caught his stick, but witness tried to calm them and said to Fr Duffy 'as bad as you think the people, you won't be hit'. Bernard Clarke, Navan town scavenger, heard Bishop Nulty in Navan chapel tell people to come to Davitt's meeting 'like lambs . . . but to be armed with sticks and if anybody booed or groaned at them to crack their skulls'. Patrick Harding, Rushwee, heard Fr Gallagher preach before the election that those who went to Mahony's meetings were 'scoundrels, ruffians and corner boys'. Casey, the *Drogheda Independent* editor, said the article in which Bishop Nulty called Mahony a Kerry souper was sent from Mullingar by Fr Kearney, a director of the paper. Patrick Fulham was also a director and Fr Woods 'may be a shareholder'. The paper was 'very glad to get the pastoral before anybody else'. James Daly said he met Fr Brady on the road and when he disclosed his political opinions Fr Brady leaped from his car, caught him by the throat, shook him several times, waved a whip over his head and called him a Moynalty scoundrel. As a man he was not afraid of Fr Brady, but he knew that he carried the blessed sacrament with him and on that account he could do nothing. Thomas Evans, station master in Oldcastle, referred to the hiring of a special train by Fr Grehan to convey Davitt's supporters into one of Mahony's strongholds. Bunches of tickets were distributed by Fr Grehan and Fr Grogan. Edward Crowley, station master at Kingscourt, was examined about a similar transaction in which Fr Joseph Flood made himself responsible for £20 for a special to Navan.

On the fourth day of the petition, 19 December,[87] Joseph Collins, a Bohermeen farmer, said there were frequent references from the altar to the Poor Law election, in which he was beaten as a Parnellite. Mass stations in his house for as long as he could remember had been discontinued a year previously. He strongly denied, as a road contractor who placed gravel on the streets of Navan, bringing out broken stones to pelt Davitt supporters on 10 July. Patrick Reilly said he booed, but did not throw stones, when Davitt and a very uproarious procession passed them in Kells on the day of the nomination and asked them to cheer for 'the workman's friend'. Slasher Geraghty of Kells, who was drunk, was being held up by Fr Woods. Patrick Sherlock said that since Parnell's death he heard nothing in Navan cathedral but election matters. He heard Bishop Nulty state that 'any man who voted for Mr Mahony he would stand before the bar of justice and plead against'. He understood the bishop to refer to eternal judgement. At Davitt's meeting in Navan, his supporters carried whips and blackthorn sticks. A priest struck a young girl who stood by him with his umbrella. She was not about to fling a stone at Davitt. James Callan said that when a voter fainted in the booth at Drumconrath the local parish priest, Fr John Rooney, was asked to attend the man, whom some believed was dying. He replied 'go away out of that, I will have nothing to do with yez'. Somebody in the crowd remarked 'he is one of our own, your reverence, and attend him'. Fr Rooney then walked over to the man but, the witness remarked, 'if he was a Parnellite he would be left to die without the priest'. Edward Addy said the same priest advised his congregation that those who attended Mahony's meeting at Syddan would have their names taken.

Francis Doyle, an *Irish Independent* reporter, referred to Fr Grehan preaching in Oldcastle that if they believed in Parnellism they committed a mortal sin, defied the church and were liable to excommunication. Fr Kelly, recalled, said he approved of Davitt calling Mahony a 'souper'. O'Shaughnessy: 'I am sorry you do, for your own character's sake.' Vincent Sheridan, a correspondent for the Parnellite *Meath Reporter*, heard Bishop Nulty say after Mass in Trim on 29 June that Parnellism was moral ruin, that it was improper and unholy. The Parnellites were losing their faith and becoming heretics. If the people did not believe him on this doctrine of Parnellism, how would they believe him on other things, such as confession and communion? In Navan a mob of drunken rowdies and abandoned women had attacked the priests and nearly killed one of the purest Irish patriots living. He was sorry to see Trim the headquarters of Parnellism. Why did they want a new church in Trim when they were sending their subscriptions to help Parnellism? He asked them to give up reading poisonous newspapers or, instead of being the moral people of Meath, they would be a scandal and a reproach to everyone.

Pierce Mahony said that Bishop Nulty spoke to him 'in a friendly way' as they sat beside each other at lunch after the November 1890 convention in Navan. Several supporters 'thought I had not a chance' after the pastoral was issued. On polling day, he saw priests 'everywhere, both inside and outside the booths'. When Sullivan, cross-examining, asked 'who were the rats?' Mahony replied 'well, your friends, Mr Sullivan'. Davitt 'ratted several times . . . oftener than any man I know. I felt the allusion to my grandfather ['Kerry souper'] more bitterly than any personal allusions that could possibly be made.'

On the fifth day of the petition, 20 December, Patrick Clusker, shoemaker, said Bishop Nulty preached in Navan on the Sunday before Davitt's meeting there that his supporters would be 'armed with heavy blackthorn sticks' and 'if you boo, hoot or groan or give them a chance, they will pounce upon you like lions, break your skulls, break your arms and break your legs'.[88] Cross-examined by Healy, witness, who saw only 'pebbles' thrown at Davitt's supporters on the Square on 10 June, said they 'were received with civiller faces than they themselves carried'. James Collins, Trim, was examined about Bishop Nulty's sermon there on 29 June, in which he stated that he would approach the death bed of a profligate or a drunkard with greater confidence as to his salvation than he would that of a Parnellite and that the woman who sympathised with Parnellism was worse than an abandoned woman.

Parnell would still be alive if he had taken Davitt's advice

Opening Davitt's case, Sullivan said that Parnell would probably be still alive if he had acted on Davitt's advice (in his *Labour World*, immediately after the divorce verdict) to retire from public life for a time, after which he might return. The pastoral had been written not in the interests of any political party but for the highest and holiest of motives. The clergy of North Meath were not ashamed of their role in the election. Of the agents appointed, 12 were clergymen, whom Davitt had to ask to take charge of his interests in booths which were manned by experienced officials from Belfast, Dublin and Cork — 'past masters in the art of electioneering'. Davitt's 'souper' jibe was used only after he had been struck in Navan by Mongey, whom Mahony then publicly acknowledged as a friend. The term meant that he was a proselytiser, not one who had abandoned Catholicism. Mahony denied insulting Irish priests at Westminster, but were they to disbelieve the MP, Halley Stewart, merely because Mahony chose to disbelieve him? The sundering of friendships between priests and parishioners in Navan occurred, not in connection with the election, but as far back as March 1891. In the general election of 1882, Davitt had been returned without contest for the entire county of Meath, when in prison. Twice during the recent contest he was struck down and his friends were beaten around him. He won the contest in the teeth of terrorism. The trains on 10 July were arranged to bring his supporters from Kells and Kingscourt to Navan, where they were wanted 'if his life was to be saved' at the counter-demonstration there.

The girl named Lalloway was stoning the procession and was in the act of hurling one at Davitt when a priest shoved her aside. Sullivan said that priests 'had human natures, infirmities and tempers, their patience was not inexhaustible and it had happened, and he regretted it, that in a few instances throughout this electioneering struggle, provoked, insulted and derided, they were betrayed into some acts of violence which he was sure they regretted as sincerely as he did for them'. Owen Reilly was offensive to Fr Clarke in Nobber, Patrick Douglas was under the influence of liquor at the time he alleged being assaulted by Fr Behan, which the priest denied. Likewise, Fr Dermody would assure the court that he never told Patrick Timmons 'I will not forget the refusal to me of your vote to you and yours'. Bishop Nulty's statement that 'Parnellites were cowards and rowdies', deposed to by James Lawlor, was justified by his lordship's experiences in Navan. Fr Casey's advice to anti-Parnellites to 'come prepared' to a meeting, deposed to by Patrick Collins, was justified as a proper precaution in the state of society in North Meath. As to the sermon alleged to have been delivered by Dr Nulty on 3 July, 'out of the hundreds and thousands he addressed, but two witnesses had come forward . . . to ascribe to their bishop the vilest forms of language . . . only two reprobates'. He would not produce his lordship to compete for evidence with those men.

Fr Cassidy denied that any illiterate voter knelt to him in the polling booth in Slane. He was at the Navan convention and afterwards went with one of the priests to walk in the seminary garden, which overlooked the crowd at the parochial house. They saw Davitt getting up from the ground. As well as 'to hell with tall hats', he heard some filthy expressions by women, but he did not believe they were directed at the priests. James O'Brien, recalled, said two illiterate voters whispered to Mr Davis, the presiding officer in the Slane booth, that they would vote for Mahony. But when Mr Davis asked them to declare themselves in the ordinary way they voted for Davitt. They were evidently hiding from Fr Cassidy, who could hear them, but the priest never interfered with either of them. Thomas Morgan said he was at the meeting in Navan parochial house about the middle of June to make arrangements for the election, with about 30 priests and about 40 laymen. This was the bishop's own residence, but he did not see the bishop there and had no communications from him.

On the sixth day of the petition, 21 December, Fr McNamee said he met Davitt at the railway station in Navan on the day of the selection convention, 1 June, and brought him to the parochial house.[89] On the way, small groups of men were 'planted . . . who hissed and groaned and hooted'. As the use of the town hall had been refused and as, under the lease of the CYMS hall, no political meeting could be held in it, there was no other place but the seminary for the convention. Afterwards, 'delegates and priests all walked surrounding Mr Davitt', because of the threatening attitude of the mob and of threats against him in an anonymous letter. About 500 had assembled round the seminary and as soon as the delegates and Davitt came out 'the howling and booing began'. They went to the parochial house for lunch, but the mob was waiting as they left again for the station. An effigy of Davitt 'with one hand' was suspended from a 14-foot pole. It was the 'tremendous loud roar made by the crowd' which made him notice Davitt 'stretched on the ground'. He saw Mongey running away and heard him named by Fr Casey as the one who struck Davitt. He overtook him, knocked him down and they both fell and rolled in the mud. He said 'you murderer, you have killed Davitt' and Mongey replied 'I did not intend to' before being arrested by the police. On polling day, 'from about 9.30 to 11 a.m. almost every one of our men was either blackened or whitened or had eggs thrown on them'. He remonstrated twice with the sheriff about this.

Cross-examined by O'Shaughnessy, Fr McNamee said he did not suggest that the 450 people at the convention could have fitted into the town hall, but it was wrong to suggest 'that because we held the convention in the bishop's place, the thing was a Catholic business'. Refusing the use of the town hall 'was an insult to the clergy' and it was an insult to anti-Parnellites 'to call them Whigs'. He knew that the vast majority in Navan were strongly opposed to Davitt, but denied that he had been selected at a private meeting in Navan parochial house. Frs Kelly, Gaughran and Behan were also at that meeting, which was to start a fund for election expenses. There was no selection meeting until June, although he heard Davitt and Fulham mentioned.

> I maintain that we have permission to speak on elections from the altar by the synod of Maynooth and that we are not prohibited . . . A man who would vote with a false conscience would of course commit a sin . . . An intelligent or well-informed man could vote for Mahony and remain a Catholic . . . The bishop does not mean to say that . . . a person refusing to receive his doctrine will cease to be a Catholic, but . . . he would end in throwing off the faith altogether, little by little, and end in becoming a heretic or an infidel . . . He [Bishop Nulty] is not infallible . . . If they [his flock] have doubt in their minds as to the lawfulness or unlawfulness of Parnellism, they are bound to accept his teaching in settling that doubt . . . He speaks [in the pastoral] upon a religious and moral subject . . . whether public immorality makes any difference in his fitness or unfitness to be a public leader.

O'Shaughnessy: 'But wasn't he in his grave?' 'Yes, but the principles on which that split arose are still disputed . . . To teach his doctrines is calculated to lead to grave consequences against chastity.' Fr McNamee added that he did not believe Parnell's guilt for months after the divorce verdict because of his earlier success in rebutting the forgery-based *Times* charges, which he had left undefended for years.

Cornelius English, clerk of the chapel at Kells, gave evidence of hiring cars on behalf of Fr Guinan for Davitt's meetings. He also paid Slasher Geraghty 5 shillings to go on one of the cars as 'a kind of guard for him'. This amount was also paid to up to 30 men, including Rourke, Bell and Cheevers, because it was 'rumoured about Kells that there was to be an organised attack on Mr Davitt on the day of his arrival in Kells and it was thought necessary that a number of men should be got to protect him . . . They were labouring men and it was not thought fair that they should lose their day for nothing and it was thought to give them a day's wages . . . There was a great deal of risk in it.' All the money was repaid to him by Fr Guinan.

Fr Christopher Casey said he saw Davitt's effigy being burnt on a pole outside the parochial house in Navan while Davitt was inside having lunch after his selection convention. He saw Mongey throwing 'a rough quarry stone' from 7 yards at Davitt 'with both hands'. Navan was 'very disorderly' on polling day. He saw an old man named McDermott from Navan with his face blackened, accompanied by his son, at whom the crowd were yelling and had sticks raised. He faced the crowd, who 'hustled me about and carried me away . . . My hat was knocked off . . . I got a box from this man Byrne . . . I saw Fr Woods himself struck with a stone.' He remembered Mahony's predecessor being selected in the seminary in 1885 and John Redmond 'did not shirk from going into it'. Cross-examined by Drummond, Fr Casey said that Fr Crowley, parish priest of Bohermeen, had asked him to come into Navan to protect voters he was bringing in from that parish. At a meeting in Bohermeen he heard a speaker tell the crowd 'you're a lot of soupers and you may go to . . . the rector . . . There was a souper establishment there some time ago . . . There are some of them Protestants that I understand were Catholics — their ancestors or themselves.' A man from Trim, 'canvassing in our parish . . . was a very notorious fellow and I [said] to the people [at mass] to be cautious, that I knew they were immoral people . . . who were steeped to the lips in the same crime that Parnell was guilty of and my advice to them would be that the next time they canvassed in their houses to keep the females out'.

Richard McGhee said he was a friend of Davitt 'for many years' and a commercial traveller from Lurgan. He arrived in Navan at about 7 p.m. on the day before the election and stayed in Kelly's hotel, Market

Square. He didn't know anyone, but saw a man leading a horse over the bridge who cried out that Davitt was the man for Meath being instantly pounced upon by two or three men who knocked him down and kicked him. Before midnight, Mahony's gathering were 'cheering and shouting going up the street' and the windows of his hotel were barricaded. After 9 a.m. next day he saw 'about a dozen and a half' people at a polling booth, who flung eggs and flour on voters who were recognised as supporters of Davitt. Later on, the crowd grew around the booths and violence against voters increased as they 'cheered and laughed and enjoyed it immensely'. He saw the old man (McDermott) with his face blackened and called on the crowd to let him go. 'I think I heard several people saying "strike him — take his clothes off" . . . I saw Allen's window smashed and Kelly's hotel', as well as Sheridan's. Cross-examined by O'Shaughnessy, McGhee said 'I never saw violence in the way it was used here'. The police 'were too few' and did nothing: 'Any place I have ever been in, the police would clear the crowd at once.' He saw 'about 50, or 60, or 70 voters' with flour on them and 'two or three on the road who would not go to the poll but that I got them'.

Fr Denis Flynn, Navan, told Healy that, returning to Navan on the day of the convention, he met three men standing at the railway gates and said 'good evening'. One replied 'good evening, Fr Flynn, though you are a seceder itself'. Three men coming towards him shouted 'to hell with the priests, to hell with the Pope and hurrah for Parnell'. Whenever Mahony returned to his headquarters in Navan from outlying districts, 'I heard hooting and booing, even opposite the parochial house'. At the pre-election meetings on 10 July, 'I was really frightened'. On the evening of the declaration 'I was reading my office and two or three men shouted after me . . . "to hell with you, you son of a red hat, and your blind-eyed bishop".' Cross-examined by Drummond, Fr Flynn reckoned there were only 200 Navan men among over 5,000 Meath and Cavan people at Davitt's meeting. But he denied that the latter were brought in to over-awe Navan Parnellites: 'It was intended to show Mr Davitt's voters in Navan that they were not a paltry few, as was attempted to be represented by Mr Mahony.' Many of them had sticks, yet all the violence that day was on Mahony's side.

Fr Hugh Behan of Trim said he had served 17 years previously in Navan. He denied striking Patrick Douglas, but said he put him out of Mrs Reilly's lodging house at her request for reviling the priests. Cross-examined by O'Shaughnessy: he believed at the Navan convention in

November 1890 that Parnell was innocent. He said from the altar in Trim on the following Sunday that he did not believe he was guilty and that others, if their consciences were examined, would be a good deal worse. He later explained before his people — when, six months after the divorce court, Parnell had not cleared himself — that now he believed he was not innocent: 'The very same words I used after the bishop left the chair, before my brother priests', at the Navan deanery conference at Easter 1891. But 'there was no recantation'. O'Shaughnessy: 'Were there two other clergymen there at the same time who made the same sort of explanation?' 'I do not remember. I can only account for myself.'

James Lawlor called bishop 'a liar'

Thomas Reilly, relieving officer, Navan, recalled that when the bishop preached in Navan cathedral on 10 July that the Parnellites were cowards, 'James Lawlor, who was sitting beside me, said "you are a liar". There was a commotion in the church and he [the bishop] then said . . . he never thought he would see himself and his priests insulted on the streets . . . that it was evident the people were losing the faith and that on the last day when he would be called upon to account for those people, if any of them would be lost, that he would be there and that he would charge the leaders, who were the worst, with it.' Cross-examined by Drummond: the bishop and priests got him made a relieving officer just after the election. What the bishop's words conveyed to him was that 'anyone of the souls that would be lost, he would hold the leaders accountable for them . . . the leaders of that town'.

Fr Thomas Gilsenan, seminary, Navan, said he was returning to Navan alone on 10 July and 'when the Parnellites saw me in the distance they began to hoot and wave their sticks and jeer at me in a most insulting manner. Two or three came up and cried "down with the tall hats". Mr Meldon . . . told me my presence was exciting the crowd and unless I retired he could not be responsible for the consequences.' On polling day, he called Fr Casey's attention to the attack on McDermott. 'Byrne attempted to pull the stick out of my hand . . . The crowd hooted me in such a way that I thought they were going to take my life . . . In order that the crowd would not strike me I tried to get to the wall. While the crowd was shouting and threatening, Mr [W.] Lawlor passed into his own house and shouted out to the crowd "Give him blow for blow" . . . I didn't strike any person that day . . . not even attempted . . . "Oh", said

I, "you old rascal" after he called on the crowd to kill me.' The conduct of the crowd was beyond description. 'They told Fr Casey and myself to go to our old blind bishop.' O'Shaughnessy: 'You went over to Lawlor's house, to the house of a large trader in the town?' 'I didn't know that until lately; I heard he was a baker.' O'Shaughnessy: 'Keeps a good large bakery in Navan, doesn't he?' 'I suppose so.' O'Shaughnessy: 'Have you any doubt upon that?' 'I have no doubt about it now. I had until . . . I heard him described as a merchant . . . He said that ['Give him blow for blow'] to an excited and infuriated mob.' O'Shaughnessy: 'You had a stick in your hand?' 'Yes.' 'And before that the people wanted to take the stick from you?' 'Byrne did.' 'That is the man whose face was cut by your friend, the other priest?' 'The very same.' O'Shaughnessy: 'So one of the priests cut the man's eye and he was streaming from the blow and he was about to take the stick from you and this man said to give blow for blow?' 'Yes, showing that he was an aggressive fellow, he wanted them to take the stick from my hand.' O'Shaughnessy: 'Didn't all the old seminary boys play [hand]ball at the seminary?' 'Old and young played it.' O'Shaughnessy: 'On your oath, didn't you exclude the sons of Parnellites who had got their education there?' 'I deny that emphatically.'

Michael Davitt, the respondent, told Sullivan that during lunch in Navan parochial house after his selection convention on 1 June, the mob outside 'burned my counterfeit presentment' (effigy). En route to the station the crowd was very savage: 'I was told that the other arm would be cut off me . . . Several epithets were applied — assassin, renegade, traitor and murderer.' Pierce Mahony and he had been fairly good friends, but 'I thought his shaking hands with this person [Mongey] before a public meeting was a direct encouragement and invitation to others'. Fr Kelly had told him in his house in Slane that the bishop intended to issue a pastoral 'and I told him to write at once to Fr McNamee to meet me on the following day . . . I met him at the railway station in Navan.' O'Shaughnessy objected 'he is about to give a private conversation between himself and a priest. This is a public matter, the selection of an MP . . . If you could show in any speech he delivered from a public platform . . . that he repudiated this pastoral I could understand it, but . . . [not] a hole and corner conference by which he is to get advantage in public.'

To Sullivan, Davitt said he understood from Fr Kelly that the pastoral would refer to the election. 'I told Fr McNamee to convey from me to his lordship an earnest request not to issue the pastoral until after the election was over, as I believed it could do me no good but might do me harm.' But he did not know whether his communication was in effect made to the bishop. Cross-examined by O'Shaughnessy, Davitt admitted saying at the Sligo election 'Eight hours at work, eight hours at play and eight hours in company [not 'in bed', he said] with Mrs O'Shea — It was during an election and I had been called a traitor, a renegade, scum and held up to the country as having betrayed the Irish cause. When I am struck I strike back.' Regarding the 'souper' epithet, 'If Mr Mahony's friend, Mr Mongey, had not attempted to kill me, I would have treated Mr Mahony in another way'. He did not know until today that priests had paid for special train tickets and he did not enquire. 'I made [Fr Kelly's] house my central address because it saved me the expense of putting up in the hotel, which I could not afford.' At the meeting in Navan on 10 July, Fr McNamee presided and 34 priests attended. O'Shaughnessy: 'Didn't the priests do their best for you?' 'They did their best for me, as they did for Mr Parnell . . .' 'Did you at any time during this contest draw or produce a revolver?' 'I did nothing of the kind.'

On the seventh day of the petition, 22 December, Healy quoted a precedent 'that if a man were so obnoxious to his fellows that they could not resist the desire to fall on him and do him an injury, he would not be guilty of an illegal practice if he were to pay men to protect him'.[90] Mahony had

> turned Navan into a pandemonium . . . They had to face a general election for the first time where [priests] . . . had up to this unhappy difference a united, sympathetic and respectful population around them. They had that population worked up against them to such a degree that even the official functionary of the corporation of Navan did not hesitate to call his bishop a liar in his own cathedral . . . Never before had the right of the priests of Meath to take an active part upon a political question been disputed . . . [They were] of the people . . . in a little squalid country town, to labour amongst the sicknesses and the sorrows of the poor . . .
>
> One would think . . . Mr Mahony would have spared his lordship, now nearly in the 30th year of his episcopacy and the 75th of his age, the suggestion that, robed with staff and mitre, he told the people of Navan, his own flock amongst whom he had laboured as a curate, as parish priest and as bishop, that their heads and legs and arms and skulls would be smashed by

Mr Davitt's supporters . . . It was thought decent and creditable by those who complain of the epithets of 'souper' and 'priest hunter' to bring forward the leading rowdies and ringleaders to swear away the stainless character of this old man. Even the town clerk, who called the bishop 'a liar', was not asked a question with regard to his sermon and it was the town scavenger who deposed to the threat that their skulls would be broken . . . An amnesty should be given . . . for the one or two priests who alone could be shown to have gone beyond what, as citizens or as clerics, they were entitled to . . . The effort of the Mahony party was to tell the people of Meath that their priests were dishonoured hypocrites, that all was sham about adultery, about Parnellism, about the alcoves of Eltham [Katharine O'Shea's home in Kent]; that all was mere mummery and humbug because everyone, 'mitred prelate and vested priest', had themselves, when the slime of the divorce case reeked filthiest in the land, immersed in its filth . . . Forty priests, he thought it was said, who now made so much of the adultery of the dead man, when he was alive supported him . . . It had been murmured throughout the county that the parish priest of Trim was a Parnellite.

Healy: Suspend Ten Commandments for elections?

Ignoring his own role in drafting the Leinster Hall resolutions and the fact that over 18 months elapsed between the Meath priests' support for Parnell at the Navan convention and Bishop Nulty's pastoral, Healy continued

> They had accepted a resolution of confidence in Mr Parnell and the Irish parliamentary party — sprung upon them, they were told, by the wire-pullers who were in on the secrets of the coming campaign. And therefore, in that county at any rate, there was a necessity that the Bishop of Meath, whose priests had been assailed . . . that their position should be made manifest and vindicated before the country and the world. Dr Nulty . . . had in his view a sacred pastoral duty to discharge. He was told he should have waited until the election was over. He [counsel] did not know that the Ten Commandments were suspended at election time. Had Dr Nulty been a layman, might he have said those things? Might they have been said

from the platform and were they only petitionable matter when they were said within the adjuncts of the altar and the cathedral? . . . He [counsel] denied that any Bishop could make tenets or religion for him, but . . . where doubt arose and until the Catholic could avail of the larger authority of the ecumenical council or of the head of his church, those who were placed over him in teaching authority had the right in their pastorate to give their opinion upon faith and morals. He besought, implored, but he never ordered them. The Bishop . . . chose to consider that this, though a temporal matter, did involve much and affected private life, family domesticity and went to the foundations of the home. So thinking, he issued this pastoral.

M. Drummond, replying for Mahony, said it was the priests' election: 'They did the whole thing themselves and any other person as candidate would have done quite as well as Mr Davitt.' On the question of undue influence, he quoted the judgment of Lord Fitzgerald in the Longford petition of 1870:

> The priest may counsel, advise, recommend, entreat and point out the true line of moral duty and explain why one candidate may be preferred to another and may, if he thinks fit, throw the whole weight of his character into the scale. But he may not appeal to the fears or terrors or superstition of those he addresses. He must not hold out hope of reward here or hereafter and he must not use threats of temporal injury or of disadvantage or of punishment hereafter. He must not, for instance, threaten to excommunicate or to withhold the sacraments or to expose the party to any other religious disability or denounce the voting for any particular candidate as a sin or as an offence involving punishment here or hereafter.

Dealing with the pastoral, Drummond submitted that it was 'absurd' for Dr Nulty or his priests to try to make people believe that a year after the death of Parnell voting for a member of his party was a moral question. The bishops had a right to condemn Parnell, but they had gone too far and were violating the law. This pastoral was published with the aim of crushing the Parnellite party in Meath. After it, Mahony felt that it was 'hopeless' for him to resist its influence. It had come from a bishop who said to 'simple, religious people': 'you can't be saved if you don't obey me. I am the successor of the Apostles.'

The 'friction' testified to was provoked by the clergy, Drummond maintained. He complained of one of his witnesses being called 'a reprobate' for giving evidence of the bishop's 'bitter harangues'. Dr Nulty's characterisation in Trim of Parnellite women as 'worse than abandoned women' was 'almost incredible . . . but it is admitted to be true'. He believed that the bishop and some of his priests had been misled by anti-Parnellites to regard honourable Meath Parnellites as plotting to destroy the Catholic church. For instance, when Davitt's clerical bodyguard caught some of the mud thrown at him in the street, he instanced it as 'disrespect for the priests'.

The bishop's 'skull-cracking sermon' in Navan was 'awful and appalling', but it *was* preached because, said Drummond, if Dr Nulty could contradict it, he would. How could people freely exercise the franchise after the bishop told thousands of people in the cathedral that he would 'appear at the bar of eternal justice and ask the Almighty to condemn' Mahony's supporters? 'You have to go back to the middle ages to find such terrible denunciation as this . . . The Bishop of Meath seems to think that he lives in a time when he could consign a person to be burned at the stake.' Dr Nulty's telling people to carry sticks was an 'awful incitement' during an election.

Drummond said there had been much evidence about the disturbances at Navan and other places, but as Mr Justice O'Brien had said, 'the acts of conflicting mobs are not things that affect an election when they don't result in preventing people going to the poll, unless the candidate has made himself criminally responsible for the acts of the crowd'. When Davitt was selected on 1 June, Mahony was not a candidate, as his convention was not until 16 June. He was the sitting member, but it could not be proved that by word, act or declaration or speech or letter he had communicated his intention of contesting the constituency. Davitt's convention was held in Navan, even though 'they admitted that the town of Navan was Parnellite', and Davitt held an enormous meeting there on 10 July — 'they came in with sticks and so forth . . . The only evidence of any person being injured was among the Parnellites . . . But was any voter prevented from voting? That thing about the blackening of faces was a pure myth [in evidence about election disturbances in Navan], except with respect to the old man, McDermott.' It was to Mahony's credit that when he returned to Navan and saw people about the streets he held a meeting outside the town till the booths closed.

Davitt absent for verdict

As with the counting of votes at Kells, Davitt did not attend the eighth day of the petition, 23 December, when judgment was given against him — nor did his counsel, in a pointed act of discourtesy to the court.[91] As in the South Meath case, as well as being unseated, he was disqualified from representing the constituency for seven years and ordered to pay the costs of the petition. Mr Justice Andrews said that clergy in the election had 'allowed loss of temper to betray them into deplorable acts of personal violence, in some instances . . . against women, which no provocation could justify', but these were not sufficient to void the election. However, he saw no reason to alter the view on the pastoral which he arrived at in the South Meath case. Davitt had made a 'feeble attempt' to repudiate responsibility for it, but 'during the election the respondent was aware of and adopted and availed himself without objection of the action of the bishop and priests . . . The priests were the leaders and Mr Davitt was their nominee, willingly accepting their aid, influence and action on his behalf . . . The result of the election would have been different if [the pastoral] had not been issued.' The sermons of the bishop and clergy were 'little in harmony with the sacred office of the preachers and the temples of religion'. The attack on Davitt in Navan 'was a very disgraceful outrage, but the disorder which existed, though highly censurable and discreditable to those who took part in it', did not void the election.

Media reaction

The *Irish Independent* had, of course, no sympathy for Michael Davitt.[92] The first Irishman to attack Parnell, by his own confession on oath he was the author of a parody against his former leader, 'which no gentleman would utter in the society of a woman'. By his own confession also, he discountenanced the notion of the bishop publishing a pastoral supporting him, but after it had been issued he was happy to profit by it and to be nominated by its author — then he went into the witness box to repudiate it. 'He was a mere tool in the hands of others'. If laymen had committed some of the clergy's acts of violence, they would be sent to jail. Some priests had organised and paid for rowdies to attend meetings. Counsel for the bishop and clergy in the South Meath case had slandered the Catholics of Meath by stating that priests were forced to act against the rise of secret societies in the county, which would go down in infamy to posterity. The paper put it to the other Irish bishops to state whether or not they agreed with

Dr Nulty's position and hinted at an appeal to Rome. The *Freeman* merely said the outcome 'was inevitable' after the result of the South Meath case.[93] However, the separation of morality from voting by both judges 'will not be accepted by voters in Ireland, much less by members of any Christian church', because it was 'absurd' to talk of Parnellism as a purely political cult and 'the law cannot make morality, nor define the duty of a bishop or priest'.

The *Irish Times,* noting that the North Meath decision 'had been anticipated', agreed with Mr Justice Andrews that a free election would have returned Mahony.[94] The *Irish Independent* quoted the English liberal press on the outcome:[95] The *Daily News* did not believe that English judges would have unseated Davitt on the pastoral alone, although 'from the Catholic point of view' it was an injudicious document. The reformist *Daily Chronicle* concerned itself with Davitt's dilemma about the expenses of the petition and correctly predicted 'he may decide to file a petition of his own, this time in bankruptcy, and thus settle the question of another seat for him by becoming disqualified'. It suggested a public subscription, as Davitt was 'much needed in this intensely critical time' in parliament. But the *Irish Independent's* 'London letter' said 'the English radicals feel rather ashamed of their trust in Mr Davitt'. The paper also said that preparations for the fresh contests in Meath would commence after the Christmas holidays. After Christmas it printed a rare drawing of the petition's conclusion in Trim courthouse.[96] The *Drogheda Independent* again minimised the result as an unsurprising 'mere technical finding'.[97] The Parnellites had 'fired their last cartridge against the Bishop and priests of Meath' in seeking 'the aid of a sympathetic legal system to deprive them of their rights'.

Redmond's reaction

The Parnellite leader, John Redmond, conscious of the damage which evidence of clerical interference in Meath could cause to the prospects of the eagerly awaited Home Rule bill, tried to allay British fears by acknowledging the difficulty but pointing to Meath Parnellites' independence as a bulwark against it. In an article entitled 'The Lessons of South Meath' at year's end in the English magazine, *The Fortnightly Review* (reprinted in the *Irish Independent*), Redmond described the petition as 'the most significant event in the public life of Ireland since the inception of the Home Rule movement'.[98] It shows conclusively that but for the undue influence of the clergy the Parnellite party in Ireland at the last general election would have won a clear majority . . . What happened in South Meath happened in every election in the south and west of Ireland . . . The anti-Parnellite party won 71 seats. A very large proportion of their candidates were men completely unknown in the national movement and complete strangers in the constituencies. Were it not for the action of the priests, such men would not have polled as many hundreds as they actually polled thousands.

Redmond maintained that 'had the priests stood aside', Parnell would have won the Kilkenny by-election and gone on to carry 'the entire country'. At the general election, the Parnellites could easily have won over 50 seats. Even if the priests had merely 'abstained from the kind of electioneering disclosed in South Meath', they could have 'trebled our numbers', that is, gained 27 seats. Two-thirds of the elections which Parnellite candidates lost 'would have been upset on petition on precisely the same grounds' as in South Meath. Redmond said the reason more petitions were not taken was lack of money. 'Our party was left after the general election not only penniless but in debt. The machinery for the collection of money in every constituency had passed over with the priests to our opponents.' But the 'Catholic peasants' of Meath — as well as 'swearing against the priests whom, outside the domain of politics, they loved and revered' — provided almost all the money required for the Parnellites to mount the petition and Bishop Nulty's 'sensational' pastoral strengthened their case. 'For the first time in the history of Ireland . . . the petitioner was a Catholic, his counsel and solicitor were Catholics, the necessary funds were subscribed by Catholics and one hundred Catholic peasants, farmers and labourers volunteered their evidence'. Redmond described as 'historically untrue' Morley's assertion in Newcastle that Irish priests had never been able to sway voters except when they were on the nationalist side, quoting successful clerical support for the treacherous Sadlier and Keogh in 1852 and successful clerical opposition to the patriotic John Martin in the Longford elections in 1870. But the South Meath petition 'ought to convince the opponents of Home Rule that the dread of a clerical ascendancy is rapidly becoming an ancient and ridiculous bogey'.

Redmond's need to account for the magnitude of the Parnellites' defeat almost certainly magnified his estimate of their likely gains in the absence of clerical interference. There can be little doubt that voters anticipating a Home Rule bill from Gladstone favoured the anti-Parnellites' continuing alliance with the Liberals over the Parnellites' abandonment of it for their policy of independent opposition. But the first-past-the-post system of election did not do Redmond's party any favours, the Parnellites winning only 9 seats from nearly a quarter as many votes as received by the anti-Parnellites, who gained 71.

The prominent Parnellite, A.J. Kettle, made a novel proposal to disenfranchise Meath in a letter to the *Irish Independent* on 30 December.[99] Kettle pointed out that Bishop Nulty's pastoral 'is still the clerical law in Meath' and the clergy would contest the fresh elections there. 'The whole Catholic hierarchy took up the same political position as Dr Nulty at the general election . . . and many priests in other parts of Ireland pushed their spiritual authority just as far as the priests in Meath.' Since 'the opinions of London are received with due deference at Rome' — because the sacrifices of Irish Catholics had made Catholicism 'free to exercise its spiritual dominion in all the British dependencies' — the best way for Parnellites to influence Rome would be to compel the imperial parliament at Westminister to determine the Irish clerical question. The records of the Meath petitions could be used as 'briefs' in the discussion. The most effective means of raising the question would be for the people of Meath to call on Parnellite MPs to move when parliament met 'that the two constituencies of Meath be disfranchised for a time' on the ground that no free election could be held there until the clergy were 'retired to a safe religious line on secular matters either by the supreme head of the Catholic church or by . . . parliament'.

Davitt on the priest in politics

Davitt, also anxious to soothe British public opinion, tried to minimise the impact of the petitions' revelations of clerical influence in Meath. In an article entitled 'The Priest in Politics', in another English magazine, *Nineteenth Century* (reprinted in the *Freeman*) also at year's end, Davitt said he would not try to excuse the pastoral, nor the words or acts of some Meath priests.[100] But while the judges had 'no alternative but to void the elections . . . neither pastoral nor spiritual pressure induced one single ballot to be cast for Mr Fulham and myself or prevented one vote being given to Messrs Dalton and Mahony'. Nevertheless, 'threats of spiritual punishment or hopes of future rewards should not be introduced into an election' and he hoped 'such practices will never be resorted to again'. He had appointed 88 laymen and 12 priests as personation agents because the Parnellites had brought from Belfast 'notorious electioneering experts' whom 'a young man from the country . . . would be no check upon'. He believed 'that the well deserved political influence of the Irish priest' was best when it was free from suspicion of spiritual pressure. But 'the priest, as a citizen, may reasonably object to being deprived of his political rights because avowed enemies declare it would be better for the church if he were a non-combatant in the political arena . . . The mistake made by Dr Nulty in his pastoral, and by the priests in their interpretation of its contents', Davitt continued, was to treat Parnellites as if they had committed Parnell's sin. Dalton and Mahony 'did not go before the electors of Meath as advocates of immorality. They appealed for an endorsement of Mr Parnell's political programme . . . But unfortunately a number of disreputable persons in some of the towns of Meath, bad characters of both sexes, did identify themselves in the contest with the interests of the Parnellite candidates and by rowdy conduct, by coarse attacks upon the priests and by open insults to them as ministers of religion, gave the Parnellite cause the semblance of . . . an open insurrection against both moral and religious teaching.' Meanwhile

> large numbers of Catholic nationalists, who blamed Mr Parnell in their hearts for the dissensions which he created in the Home Rule movement, adhered to his cause, nevertheless, in protest against the attacks which had been made upon a patriotic, Protestant leader by large bodies of their clergy . . . The chief sin of the clergy of Meath was not their religion, but their politics . . . Those Unionist critics who now assail [them] for having exercised spiritual influence in support of a principle of morality were among the first to attack Mr Parnell after the divorce court proceedings and to reproach the Irish nation for the stained character of its leader . . . The allegation that Bishop Nulty and the priests of Meath were actuated by unworthy motives in their opposition to Mr Parnell from the split to his death and subsequently to his followers, is altogether opposed to facts. It was this very clerical influence which first gave him a seat in parliament. . . . This diocese contributed 2,282 shillings to the Parnell tribute which was condemned by the Pope in 1883, the largest donation from any diocese in Ireland,

with the exception of that of Dublin, and every penny of this sum was collected by the priests . . .

In fact, so devoted were the clergy of Meath to the Parnell leadership that they were among the last of their calling in Ireland to declare in a body against him. This tardiness of repudiation has had a good deal to do with the unusual bitterness displayed between Parnellites and priests in the two elections now voided. The latter were accused of having declared in favour of Mr Parnell even after the divorce court verdict. The plea of moral delinquency lost its force in face of the resolution passed at a convention in support of 'The Chief' and supported by a large body of Meath priests subsequent to the decree *nisi*. On the face of it, this appeared a strong argument against the contention of the clergy that they went against the popular leader on grounds of morality alone and the strength of the position which this circumstance gave to the followers of Dalton and Mahony was such that it could only be assailed, from the point of view of the priests, by that zeal which invariably covers a recantation of opinions or a decision to undo the consequences of a mistake. In justice to the priests of Meath, it must be said that Mr Parnell and his followers had loudly declared that his side of the divorce case was yet to be put before the Irish people. Popular opinion in Ireland was appealed to in this sense and asked to suspend judgement. It was early in this stage of public feeling when some Meath priests gave their assent to a resolution pledging their adherence to the leader whom Meath first elected to Parliament. No such promised exculpation occurred, however, and the Catholic clergy of Meath, with a few exceptions, joined in the agitation against Parnellite factionism.

Davitt maintained that wherever the Catholic clergy 'have taken sides against the popular movement in this generation they have been beaten'. Twenty years previously, the Meath priests' candidate had been defeated by John Martin, a Protestant '48 man, leading the Tory press to believe 'the people of Ireland are tired of priestly dictation'. Priests supplied the place in Irish popular movements 'which members of an intermediate class occupy in other countries where social and political antagonism separate the mass of a population from an aristocracy . . . The venerable bishop who had been held up to public scorn and condemnation in the anti-Home Rule press for a pastoral issued injudiciously . . . is the same Dr Nulty who, twelve years ago — long before any but a very few English progressivists demanded the taxation of ground rents for public purposes' wrote his essay on the land question. (The *Irish Catholic* later took issue with Davitt, stating that a voter did indeed 'place his soul in peril' by 'voting contrary to the advice of bishop, pastoral or priest'.)[101]

Both petition trials were of such public interest that the *Irish Independent* realised a commercial opportunity by publishing verbatim accounts of them immediately afterwards as inexpensive booklets. This, as we shall see, prompted anti-Parnellite denunciations of the Parnellites for depicting Ireland as priest-ridden to a British audience which was about to consider Gladstone's proposals for Irish self-government.

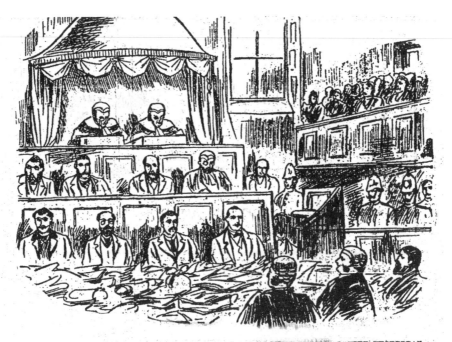

THE NORTH MEATH ELECTION PETITION—THE JUDGES, UNSEATING MR. DAVITT YESTERDAY. From a Drawing made in the Courthouse by the Herald's Special Artist. The portion of the Lawyer's Table set apart for Mr. Davitt's Legal Representatives was Deserted.

Drawing in *Irish Daily Independent*, 26 December 1892,
courtesy of the National Library of Ireland.

Courtesy of the National Library of Ireland.

Courtesy of the National Library of Ireland

Chapter 6

New elections in Meath as Commons debates Home Rule

The new elections campaign in Meath began immediately, with as much bitterness, personal invective — and clerical involvement (later overlooked) — as in the summer, but with a notable absence of political preaching. The *Irish Independent* responded to an attack on Pierce Mahony's ancestry in the *Freeman* that he had never denied that his grandfather was not in favour of repeal of the union, but that he did support Catholic Emancipation.[1] In a hint of renewed clerical activity, the *Freeman* declared that the Meath priests had rights as citizens and would 'use the influence to which even Mr Redmond concedes they are entitled'.[2] It added that Kettle's proposal to have Meath disenfranchised only showed that he recognised 'the certainty of the coming defeat'. But the police reported that the Parnellites, having won the petitions, were free to concentrate on local organisation and hoped to have the benefit of the £2,000 which they had lodged as security.[3] However, the *Irish Catholic* claimed that the petitions had 'produced an extraordinary revulsion' in Meath, especially as 'the chance words of a period of great excitement' were being used in England to defeat the cause of Home Rule.[4] Later the paper wondered whether Meath electors could forgive men who had made Bishop Nulty and his priests 'the targets of the licentious vapourings of hireling lawyers whose harangues have since been utilised to the detriment of the national cause in England'.[5] The *Drogheda Independent* called on 'priests and people' to 'organise and prepare' for victory over 'the anti-clerical party in Meath', whom the petitions had shown to be 'enemies of religion'.[6]

In a characteristically pro-clerical speech at Newcastle, Healy said he was 'opposed to undue clerical influence', but it was 'these priests who stem the tide of local blackguardism, who have influence over their flock and who have on the whole used that influence with splendid zeal for good order and good government'.[7] Hoping the clergy would never allow themselves to be intimidated out of the exercise of their civil rights, he asked why the priests should have taken any other stand? And if a cause was worth adopting 'it was worth putting one's whole soul into it'. Their cause at the recent elections was one of maintaining the party pledge to abide by majority decisions, of putting down dissension and restoring unity to their country. There was no clear issue: he said that 'without any reference to the divorce court at all'. The newly enfranchised voters who had 'to pronounce on these nice questions' knew next to nothing about them and therefore it was right and just that thinking and leading men among the priesthood should have taken the side they did 'and taken it vehemently, vigorously and warmly'. Healy boasted that the anti-Parnellite candidate in Meath, (his phrase, 'however humble he may be', indicating that the unknown James Gibney was in prospect already) would double Davitt's majority.

The *Irish Independent* picked up on Healy's veiled reference to the clergy's opposition to secret societies:[8] His 'gross slander on his entire country' was 'as unfounded as the bogus defence which he was a party to setting up in Meath as an excuse . . . for the priests, viz. that their action was necessitated by their knowledge of the work of secret societies'. It also accused him of abandoning 'his clerical clients' before an English audience:[9] at Trim, he had gone as far as Bishop Nulty in the assertion of the clergy's right to dictate to their flocks on political matters, but in Newcastle Healy's new defence was that the Tories had influenced Rome to interfere in Irish politics and that Presbyterian clergymen in Ulster had exercised undue influence in favour of unionists, therefore clerical influence should not be denounced in Meath.

Influence on Rome was at this point demonstrated by the conferral of the cardinal's hat, not on the politically active Archbishop Walsh of Dublin as expected, but on Archbishop Logue of Armagh. The *Daily Telegraph* noted that its significance would be comprehended especially by 'the electioneering priests of Meath'.[10] As the two immediate predecessors of Dr Walsh, Drs McCabe and Cullen, were both elevated, it was obvious that the Pope had 'deliberately passed over the turbulent and demagogic Dr Walsh to make a prince of the church out of a notoriously peaceful, loyal and self-respecting personage' who was, however, 'a Home Ruler by conviction'. The *Daily Chronicle* said the decision was chiefly influenced by Monsignor Persico, because of Archbishop Walsh's opposition to him in Ireland, where his mission had been to investigate the plan of campaign.[11]

When the League met in Dublin to consider the success of the petitions, they were struck by Davitt's 'extraordinary admission' in *Nineteenth Century* that priests could not be said to rule in Ireland because of the nine seats which Parnellites had won and the 70,000 votes for them.[12] Tim Harrington, MP, praised the 'independent action of men in isolated positions', revealed in the Meath petitions. Mahony's friend, George Coffey, spoke of the courage which 'these cottagers and white-capped old women had displayed'. If Parnellites gave up the fight against clerical intimidation, 'they would be handing back Ireland to the middle ages'. Andrew Kettle, in a further swipe at the clergy, said they would have acted wisely after Parnell's death if they had 'allowed the people a fair field in Irish politics', instead of rushing to lead them in a matter in which they were not competent. Bishop Nulty and his priests had to his own knowledge 'dominated the public life of that county for years' and trampled on every aspect of the public life of their people. But they had been 'met, faced, fought, found out and proved guilty by the humble independent parishioners'. Thomas Henry Webb, 'as a Protestant', admired 'the wonderful independence displayed by the peasantry of Meath'.

Announcing a convention in Trim on 6 January 1893 to select Mahony and Dalton again as Parnellite candidates for the two divisions of Meath, the *Irish Independent* wondered how they could neutralise the 'irresistible ecclesiastical power' which might be used again, 'at least indirectly and subterraneously'.[13] Harrington chaired the public meeting outside the courthouse, reassuring a full Market Square that they had every reason to be proud of the petition hearings, which had not injured Home Rule.[14] Offering to blot out the past, Harrington said all that bitterness could have been avoided if their opponents had accepted the Parnellites' offer to let the fight lapse during the general election, so as not to give any advantage to the conservatives. They had even gone further, offering to divide the Meath seats with the anti-Parnellites, but their proposals had been rejected. Mahony reminded his followers 'the leaders among our opponents are ministers of religion' and should be treated with respect.

John Redmond, MP, said that if Home Rule were to be won by the re-establishment of a religious ascendancy, 'even of the church that I love and believe in, it would be dearly bought . . . While you are voting here in Meath, the English parliament will be discussing Home Rule. If they get it into their heads that Irish Catholics are . . . political slaves, pawns moved about on the chessboard of politics by the bishop . . .

they will never concede Home Rule'. Edmund Leamy, a former Parnellite MP, referred to Davitt's article admitting that the priests and bishop in Meath 'made a mistake', but when the Parnellites stood up against them, Davitt's friends denounced them as enemies of the Catholic church. When Home Rule was being discussed in parliament, English Liberals could point not only to the Independent Party but to the Meath petitions as proof that Irish people could be independent in politics. Long after they and he had passed away, there would be boys and young men about the firesides of Meath telling the traditions of that battle and their proudest boast would be that their fathers were in the fight and were on the right side on the day of the struggle.

Referring to the anti-Parnellites' rejection of the Parnellite offer before the general election to divide the Meath seats between them, the *Irish Independent* declared 'nothing less than the extermination of the Parnellites would satisfy Healy and his backers' (Bishop Nulty and his priests).[15] The offer had been made in the interests of Home Rule and it would have been as well for the clergy if it had been accepted, but the 'same persons who insisted upon war' now accused the Parnellites of being motivated by a 'desire to wreck Home Rule and to assail the priests for the gratification of the Orangemen'. Warning that the Parnellite cause would be damaged by any mob violence, the *Irish Independent* added that 'Gladstone's effort to carry his measure of Home Rule will be vitally affected' by the Meath contests.

The *Freeman* mused that the Trim speeches indicated that attacks on Irish priests would be bitterly continued in the pending contests, but it warned that Parnellite rowdyism would not be tolerated again.[16] This thought also prompted Davitt to write to Dillon:[17] 'Before you leave for London you should see to it that those who have control of the police in Navan are told that no tricks like those played before will be tolerated this time.' Again blaming his low vote on Parnellite violence, he added 'Mahony is sure to enlist the ruffian element again and to resort to intimidation, as this is his only chance of getting the support which enabled him to poll so large a vote in July. Over *200* votes were lost to me in the Navan polling district through the terrorism which *openly* prevailed in the town [Davitt's emphases]. If we win in Meath by a bigger majority than that obtained in July, it will to some extent neutralise the cry about the priests.'

However, the *Irish Independent* reported that 'the very large force of police . . . was not required' at an anti-Parnellite demonstration at Oldcastle, where large numbers came from Cavan and Westmeath.[18]

'The seatless Mr Fulham' apologised for the absence of Davitt, who was 'sick, we believe, at heart'. Fr Grehan, chairing the meeting, said they would give the Parnellites 'such a crushing overthrow that they would never attempt a contest again'. He called on those present 'to vindicate their clergy at the coming election'. Fulham said they had no assistance from the Irish Party the last time because of the general election, but this time MPs would be available to help. 'Although every blackguard in the country was filled full of porter, every rowdy was hired and paid and the whole power of the Tory government was behind the backs of these men, yet . . . we beat them. We beat them then and we will give them a proper threshing the next time . . . In Dublin Castle, Mr John Morley [the new Irish secretary] . . . will see fair play and that is all we want.' The Parnellites said they were friends of Ireland, yet they were publishing in pamphlet form the records of the Meath petitions and spreading them broadcast in England. During the last contest, he and Davitt and their friends fought shoulder to shoulder with their priests and during the coming fight they would do so again. 'Who were the men who during the past 15 or 16 years induced the priests to play an active part in politics? Was it not Tim Harrington and William Redmond and the lot of them, long before Committee Room 15? They were then never satisfied at elections without the priests in the booths and acting as agents.'

Only bishops and priests can lead

In a classic statement of the clergy's position, Fr Boylan, parish priest of Crosserlough, told the Oldcastle meeting the petition pamphlets showed that the Meath priests did their duty as priests and as Irishmen and they had little if anything to be ashamed of. Unfortunately, they were told that they should stand aside and let persons who had more practical experience and patriotism come forward and take up their position. He looked around and he declared fearlessly that he knew no class of people prepared to lead them to victory except the bishops and the priests, in whose hands their liberties were safer. What had they to gain by betraying the people of their kith and kin? Could not the Irish clergy be Irishmen still? If they were to abandon their position they would be betraying the people. Who were the men who had stood between them and their oppressors? Who were the people who could unite them, whom they should obey? It was the priests who felt that they alone could keep the people together and lead them to victory and therefore they would be traitors to their country and to their people if they abandoned them to their enemies in this, the supreme crisis of their faith.

Fulham got a mixed reception in Kells, where he said he hoped they would 'teach the priest hunters and the men who defiled the confessional box that Parnellism was dead in Meath'. All of this prompted Davitt to write to Dillon:[19] 'The campaign in Meath has opened very badly on our side . . . No time should be lost in holding a convention and putting the candidates before the constituency. Some of the priests spoke very like the old mischief yesterday at Oldcastle. If this fight is left to them, a victory by that means would spell a moral defeat so soon after the petitions.'

The *Drogheda Independent* criticised Parnellism yet again for refusing to recognise that priests had the right 'to counsel their people where moral principles were involved'.[20] The following week the paper reprinted a *Lyceum* vindication of Bishop Nulty's pastoral — occupying almost a page, with footnotes in Latin — which criticised Judge O'Brien's ignorance of Catholic doctrine.[21] But former Parnellite MP, John O'Connor, reminded a meeting in London that a devoutly Catholic judge, 'whom Mr Parnell had driven from political life . . . was compelled to condemn in the strongest terms the clerical intimidation exercised over the people'.[22] Meanwhile, the Bishop of Ferns, Dr Browne, answered Parnellite threats of withholding offerings to the clergy, saying it was 'heretical' for them to state that the clergy lived on the charity of the public, as they were bound by the fifth commandment of the church to support their priests.[23]

The *Irish Independent* reported that Oldcastle Parnellites were 'quite jubilant' at this stronghold of their opponents being selected to begin their campaign, which an activist from Waterford, M.A. Manning, would run for Mahony from Kells and Navan.[24] But John Dillon told the federation in Dublin that he regretted that people could find no better occupation for their energies in Meath than dividing the people into camps when there was no political principle to divide them. These contests had been forced on them and would be marked by some of the unhappy scenes of the previous election. The Parnellites, 'who condemn us for truckling to English opinion', themselves appealed to British people to condemn the Irish priests, thereby providing ammunition for those opposed to Irish self-government, said Dillon, ignoring Davitt's article which also criticised the Bishop and priests of Meath. He had never been an advocate of too much power for the priests, but he would always fight for their political liberty. If they were to admit the principle that a small minority should set up a national party and policy of their own, Home Rule would be lost.

John Redmond, MP, told Mahony's inaugural rally at Oldcastle that they had been accused of favouring violence, but 'the petition shows that the hired mobs were not on our side'.[25] Mahony set out his stall as before, promising that a new Dublin parliament 'will do justice to the working man . . . will not squander its resources on fat salaries and appointments, but will try to lift the great mass of our countrymen . . . to bring brightness to the humble homes', especially by the provision of old-age pensions. He welcomed the involvement in the election of 'the first labour member of Dublin Corporation, Mr Leahy'. He rejected a charge by Healy that the Parnellites had 'befouled the surplice of the priests', who had acknowledged the distinction between politics and religion by supporting him previously. Reflecting the anti-Parnellites' difficulties not only in finding a candidate but also in raising funds for an election campaign, Redmond said their opponents were still looking for 'a man with the one qualification of money' to stand in Meath. Echoing Tim Harrington's readiness at Trim to forget the clerical intimidation of the previous election, Redmond repudiated the idea that this was 'a fight against the priests'. As for Dillon accusing him of denouncing Irish priests in an English magazine, all he said was that their spiritual influence should not overbear the liberty of the Catholic peasantry. Davitt, in another English magazine, had taken the same position. Redmond asked did Dillon, in promising to defend the liberty of Irish priests, mean their liberty to threaten excommunication and eternal torments?

Dr Kenny, one of the 9 Parnellite MPs, told a meeting of Dalton's in Longwood that they were 'the real respecters of the priests and of religion'.[26] O'Connell had prevented the English government having a veto on the appointment of Irish bishops and if the latter had stood at Grattan's side in 1800, the infamy of the union would never have been consummated. J.L. Carew, a former Parnellite MP, said that after the petitions Davitt 'had thrown the priests over and that was his gratitude'. Dalton said in Duleek that there was no act of which he was more proud than the petitions, by which they had given confidence to their Protestant fellow countrymen. Tim Harrington told the same meeting that if anti-Parnellites were ashamed of the petition revelations, it was hypocritical to blame Parnellites for taking the cases.

As an indication of the new government's resolve to contain political violence, the *Irish Independent* described how both sides were facilitated in travelling to the Parnellite meeting in Oldcastle and to MP William

O'Brien's opening of the anti-Parnellite campaign in Kells.[27] At Bective, the anti-Parnellites 'left the train. They avoided Navan, which was the next station, and drove some twenty miles over a bleak country to the scene of the Whig demonstration. The special train which went from Navan to Oldcastle was entirely Parnellite.' When they left the train at Oldcastle it was packed with anti-Parnellites, who 'were whirled over the line to Kells, where the train unloaded them and then waited' until the meeting ended and they were taken back to Oldcastle. 'This complication naturally rendered the most elaborate arrangements necessary on the part of the railway officials and the police, who were under the command of Mr Meldon. All the points where any friction was likely to occur were guarded and the Healyite pilgrims . . . had to be let in by a special door and allowed out in a similar way.' There were no disturbances, but the fact that Fr Gaughran presided at the meeting, which was held outside the parochial house, aroused suspicion that 'the tactics of the last election were to be repeated'.

Comparing Parnellites to Orangemen, O'Brien told the anti-Parnellites in Kells that they had portrayed the Irish as priest-ridden, but why hadn't previous bishops and priests in Meath who interfered in politics been 'held up to the horror of English bigots in English reviews?'[28] In darker days, Dr Nulty issued other pastorals which would forever be remembered to his glory, in which 'he held up the extermination of the people of Meath to the execration of the world'. It would take more than 'Mr Mahony's eloquence or the paving stones of Mongey . . . to induce the people of Meath to bring down that venerable old man's grey hairs with insult to the grave'. The priests of Ireland wanted no domination in politics, other than the legitimate influence that their character, intelligence and record as nationalists gave them. The question was whether a majority of the Irish Party was to prevail or whether Home Rule was to be wrecked by Irish hands. His party now represented at least nine-tenths of the Irish race, while their opponents had only 'a programme of vengeance and despair'. It was revolting to think of men of Davitt's record 'being struck down on the streets of an Irish town by some unknown wretch at — I won't say the instigation, but — in the interest of a man who spent as many years in the pay of Dublin Castle almost as Mr Davitt spent in penal servitude for Ireland'. It was on the plea that the people of Drogheda were priest-ridden that Cromwell massacred them at the Tholsel, that the penal laws were enacted.

Implying that Mahony was interested only in personal gain, David

Sheehy, MP, said that during the debate in Committee Room 15 he met Mahony in one of the lobbies and he asked 'Sheehy, if I go to your side, do you think I will be returned for Meath again?' O'Brien closed by saying 'there is no reason why this fight should not be fought out in a rational and good-humoured way. I shall endeavour not to say one unnecessary word of offence to the mass of men who are opposed to us. It is not that I pay the slightest attention to the dirty little street shindies . . . We will have the newspaper correspondents over from England ready to exaggerate and to gloat over every rash word and every discreditable incident.' The *Freeman* tried to steal the Parnellites' thunder by noting 'how Mr Parnell would have loathed their appeal to English bigotry' (by publishing the petition pamphlets).[29] It contrasted Parnell's 'quiet, steady, unflinching co-operation with the statesmen who had undertaken the giant task of reversing England's whole policy towards Ireland' in the Home Rule Bill of 1886 with Redmond's forcing on Meath a contested election during 'the battle for Home Rule at Westminster'.

Anti-Parnellites select James Gibney and Jeremiah Jordan

The people would fight side by side with their priests in this election and win together again, said O'Brien when he presided at the anti-Parnellite selection convention in Navan on 17 January 1893.[30] The *Irish Independent* reported 'stringent' police precautions against a recurrence of the disturbances which marked 'the last Whig conclave in Navan', when Davitt had been struck down. Detachments of constabulary were stationed at all the approaches to the town and at both railway stations (Great Northern and Midland Great Western). O'Brien 'was quietly smuggled over to the seminary', whose students had been granted a half-holiday 'as their reverend professors were employed on business of greater moment'.

At least 60 priests were present as the meeting grappled with finding a replacement candidate for Davitt in North Meath. A majority of delegates opposed the candidature of Major Jameson, a wealthy Irish Protestant Home Ruler, even though he had donated money to the anti-Parnellite cause. And Healy's uncle, A.M. Sullivan, related in his *Old Ireland* how Bishop Nulty and Healy had both asked him to take Davitt's seat, as Davitt himself wished, but he had refused to become a candidate.[31] While unsympathetic to the Parnellites, he reasoned 'it can never be for the benefit of religion that its ministers should trail their robes in the mire of party politics, that members cannot attend its ceremonies without being exposed to insult by the minister who should be the friend and servant of all'. Hence James Gibney being on arrival 'as unaware as that he could catch the man in the moon by the leg', that he would end up as the candidate.

David Sheehy, MP, read a letter from Davitt, still absent through illness, in which he said that their policy of party unity and friendly alliance with the Liberals had been endorsed by the Irish electorate in returning 71 MPs to the Parnellites' 9. The author of 'the priest in politics' accused Redmond and Mahony of 'politically felon-setting Irish priests in English magazines'. While disqualified from standing in Meath again, having 'been found guilty of being the successful candidate', nothing else had been proved against him. No one was to be prosecuted for acts done or words spoken on his behalf. Davitt wrote to his friend, McGhee, that he thought this letter would 'make Mahony, Redmond and co. refuse to pay for a mass for my soul after I die', adding 'McCarthy *insists* on my standing for NE Cork and I cannot see how I can refuse'.[32]

Selected for South and North Meath, respectively, were Jeremiah Jordan, a Methodist shop-keeper from Enniskillen and former Galway MP, and James Gibney, a politically unknown miller and farmer from Crossakiel, near Kells. Jordan, 'as a strong opponent of hero worship', promised to uphold 'the democratic doctrine that the minority must submit to the majority'. Great men did not make principles, principles made great men. Jordan had earlier said at Drumconrath that it was true nationalists like the anti-Parnellites who had stuck to independence and principle by refusing Tim Harrington's offer to divide the Meath seats.[33] Gibney was sorry that they had not selected a more worthy candidate to give Mahony 'plenty of leisure time to again join in the famous Kerry dance'. He would attend parliament regularly, work on the land laws and try to improve the scandalous condition of the labourers.

The *Irish Independent* said nothing occurred in Navan while the procession of delegates was returning to the station: 'Throughout the day the town was perfectly quiet.' The *Freeman* reported 'some women standing in the doors of cottages on the way to the town muttered "murderers" as the delegates passed, but otherwise all was peace and quietness'.[34] The *Drogheda Independent* explained 'the Navan mob had to be on its good behaviour', with no 'infuriated and unwashed viragoes dancing a political wardance'.[35] A large force of police was ready to handle 'the arguments of the paving stone and the overdue egg'.

The *Irish Independent*, claiming a nightly canvass of rural voters by Meath priests already, observed that Gibney, 'a man of generous build and peculiar unreadiness of speech', was well-known as a miller's clerk in Oldcastle and afterwards in Navan before his marriage and move to Crossakiel. Fr Grehan, presiding at a meeting for Gibney in Oldcastle, assured him of the support of the bishop and priests.[36] Gibney said, as a tenant farmer himself, he would represent their interests and those of the labourers. He had supported the candidacy of John Martin in Meath when Luke Smyth did not, a charge later denied by Smyth. After the anti-Parnellite convention, William Lawlor presided at the Navan league, which 'regretted that Whig candidates in whom the people have no confidence are to be forced upon Meath by a ready-made political organisation', the 'tyrannical' clergy.[37]

Expressing confidence in the outcome of the new elections, Tim Healy, MP, told a meeting for Jordan in Summerhill, at which Fr Fay presided, that their opponents had won with the judges in the petitions, but the anti-Parnellites would win with the jury.[38] As John Redmond, MP, addressed a meeting for Dalton at the same venue, 'the entire roadway was lined with constabulary, but there was no disorder', the *Freeman* reported. The constables, including some mounted men, 'did not wear side arms or carry muskets'. Healy said it was through Catholic Emancipation that Mr Justice O'Brien had a salary of £3,000 a year, 'but the priests have only their rosaries . . . Where is the priestly dictation now, when you are asked to return an Ulster Protestant?' Davitt had spent nine years in prison, 'with the bones protruding from his maimed limb . . . while Mahony was drawing £1,000 a year from Dublin Castle'. They had hunted Davitt out of parliament and now they were attempting to have him declared a bankrupt for the costs of the petition. 'Are you going to return honest Jerry Jordan or Donkey Dalton?' Fulham said Jordan had been one of the right-hand men of Isaac Butt, in contrast to Dalton, 'the pudgy patriot from Australia'. P.J. Kennedy, MP, said any voter for them would not be 'on the side of the priest hunters'. Jordan said he was no aristocrat 'like some of the candidates' (Mahony), but 'a simple peasant' who, although defeated in North Fermanagh, had been in public life since 1865. Parnell never understood the North and had no following there. It was only because Parnell was a Protestant that the Catholic clergy supported him 'until they found the empire would not swallow' the divorce proceedings.

Tim Harrington, MP, spoke at a meeting with Mahony in Drumconrath, where 'the curate, Fr Patrick Ballesty, walked up and down to see that no wavering seceders' attended.[39] Pierce Mahony said the priests proved that elections were political and not religious by selecting a Protestant from the North (Jordan) this time. Gibney had ridiculed his proposal for old age pensions, but did he think that the Irish working class 'get from the land even a fair share of their heritage?' It was a disgrace that a man after a life of toil should 'pass his dying moments as a branded pauper in a workhouse, treated like a criminal and separated from his life-long friend, his wife'. Their opponents 'cannot point to Slasher Geraghty on our side. We have not soiled the surplice of the priest.' Harrington said he knew Mahony when he was a land commissioner 'and was not ashamed to walk into the League offices and give me his subscription'. When the split occurred, Mahony stood high with the priests in Meath, with the liberals and with the Irish Party§. 'Was not every opportunity of lifting himself into place, power and position upon the other side? If he has chosen that which is one of difficulty, trial and separation . . . I ask you to conclude that he has chosen the side his conscience dictated.'

Mahony's campaign was now about to get an unexpected shot in the arm from his opponents, whose abuse became even more vitriolic. Fr J. Clavin, curate in Moynalty, presiding at an anti-Parnellite demonstration there, said Mahony, with his 'Orange ascendancy ideas and the bad traditions of his family', would bring them back to the old times, when the majority was subject to the minority.[40] James O'Connor, MP, accused Mahony of being 'a Castle official, a place hunter and a Kerry souper'. They would not, 'at the dictate of Judge O'Brien, surrender the cause of Ireland to Cromwell's stableboys or their offspring'. Matt Kenny, MP and barrister, said Mahony's mother was 'a Hindoo . . . all belonging to him were soupers'. Describing Mahony as 'a shoneen on the shaughraun', Kenny said he 'dared not live in his own county. When he was member for Meath, he spent his time jobbing Kerry cows in England . . . A "cross" between a Kerry souper and a Hindoo woman', they could 'see that cross coming out in the shape of his head'. If they sent Mahony to Westminster they would never catch him again. He would never go back to burrow in Kerry, but in the East Indies. Jasper Tully, MP, described Mahony as 'a mere penniless adventurer from Kerry', while Dalton 'has been all his life nothing but a drunken and degraded bar room loafer'. Denying a claim that he had opposed the building of labourers' cottages by Oldcastle guardians on a farm which he cared for, Gibney merely appealed to the labourers of his own district to say how he treated them.[41] Perhaps

Kenny's crude 'Hindoo' insult had its origin in the fact that Mahony's mother, Jane Gun Cunningham, from Newtownmountkennedy in Co. Wicklow, was a fourth generation descendant in the maternal line of an Indian Maharajah.[42] What must have angered Mahony was the base attempt to dishonour the memory of his mother, who had died in 1868, by digging up a distant connection to hurl as a racist slur.

Mahony assaults barrister MP in Four Courts

There were few people in the Round Hall of the Four Courts in Dublin on the following Tuesday morning when Pierce Mahony accosted Matt Kenny, who was in wig and gown, and said 'how dare you insult my mother'.[43] Kenny made no reply and Mahony struck him in the eye with his fist. 'Why are you assaulting me?' asked Kenny. 'Because of your speech on Sunday', Mahony replied, shaking the member for mid-Tyrone vigorously. As they scuffled, a policeman appeared, who arrested Mahony on Kenny's instructions. Mahony told Kenny 'your speech on Sunday last was a cowardly speech and you are a cowardly and mean fellow'. In court later that day, Tim Healy, MP, for Kenny, asked for a severe penalty as it was a grave offence, committed by an educated gentleman. Q.C., T. O'Shaughnessy said in evidence 'they struck at each other, Mr Kenny having hold of Mr Mahony by the hair of his head'. Cross-examined by Healy: 'Everyone knows I was leading counsel in the Meath petitions and that you were junior counsel on the other side.' He described the encounter as 'a brawl'. John Redmond, MP, in evidence, repeated that he said 'I am very glad; I think that any man who insults a woman ought to be chastised'. Healy: 'Especially if it is a prostitute' (cries of 'shame'). Mahony was sent for trial on bail.

The *Irish Independent* reported that the news was received in Navan 'with the utmost satisfaction', although it was felt that Kenny had 'got off lightly'. The paper blamed the bishops, who had 'practically elected' many MPs and were therefore responsible for their public conduct, for not curtailing the new MPs' Healyite invective. The *Freeman* merely reported Kenny stating that the account in the *Irish Independent* of his Moynalty speech was 'a complete misrepresentation of what I said'.[44] That paper also reported that Joe Devlin of Belfast had arrived in Kells to help Gibney's campaign and that Davitt was expected also. But Davitt, who had by now agreed to be returned unopposed for Cork North East, wrote to Dillon:[45] 'I am getting uneasy about the Meath contests. Mahony's box in the eye to Kenny will not injure his prospects in North Meath. As Healy and Matt are to be in *Trim* next Sunday, there

is sure to be bad work. It is horribly sickening to think of all this at *such
a time* [Davitt's emphases]. I feel almost ashamed to go before an
educated English audience while we are showing ourselves so
unworthy of Home Rule.'

That English audience was also being addressed by what the
Freeman called the 'retrograde Liberal MP', Sir Henry James, who had
issued a pamphlet which used the evidence of the Meath petitions to
show that 'a power has arisen claiming the right to vote for and on
behalf of the electors in 80 constituencies[46] . . . The evil is none the less
because it exists in Ireland, the intimidators are priests and the
intimidated helpless, ignorant peasants . . . Irish members elected by
these votes are now controlling the destinies of the empire.' Michael
Davitt immediately responded to Sir Henry James's claim that 'upwards
of 900' illiterate men had had to declare how they voted in the
presence of their priests in South Meath and that illiterate voters
represented a fifth of the electorate — 1,200 — in North Meath,
ridiculing the suggestion that the priests were able to influence these
voters in his favour.[47]

Davitt said that the illiterate vote in Navan, 'the priestly
headquarters during the election', the largest of the nine polling
districts in North Meath, with 1,200 of the voters, and where a very
large proportion of the illiterate vote was given, was 90 per cent
Parnellite. Some 80 per cent of the many illiterate men in
Wilkinstown voted 'against me', along with 70 per cent in Moynalty,
Crossakiel and Nobber. Most of the illiterate voters in Kells were
'against me'. Only in Slane, Oldcastle and Drumconrath, in which
there was a relatively small illiterate vote compared to Navan and
Wilkinstown, was there a majority of illiterate voters for him. Overall,
over 70 per cent of the illiterate vote was against him. His total vote
was 2,400 against Mahony's 2,000. If all the illiterate votes asserted by
Sir Henry James were eliminated (one-fifth of 6,000), 'I would take
from Mr Mahony 840 and myself 360, leaving me a clear majority of
880 literate votes . . . or more than double the majority by which I was
elected'. Irish secretary, John Morley, later told the Commons that
1,127 illiterate voters exercised the franchise in North Meath and
1,023 in South Meath.[48]

In an effort to damage the Parnellite candidates, the *Freeman* carried
an anonymous letter from Navan stating that Mahony and Dalton had
signed the requisition for a meeting of the Irish Party in the Commons
on 25 November 1890 to consider Gladstone's letter.[49] Dalton had also

signed a resolution two days later condemning the public controversy caused by members of the party, thereby implying that he wanted Parnell to step down as leader. 'But when the meeting assembled and these men found themselves in the presence of The Chief, their patriotism melted.' 'A Meath elector' returned to the issue in the *Freeman*, asking whether Gladstone's letter was the cause of their signing the requisition and, if not, was not the object of the meeting to ask Parnell to reconsider his position?[50] As we have seen in chapter 4 (p. 75), these allegations of disloyalty to Parnell had been raised in the general election campaign the previous summer. Mahony now responded (at a meeting in Moynalty on 5 February 1893) that at the commencement of the Committee Room 15 proceedings he had signed a requisition, but not against Parnell.[51]

'It was chiefly to inquire why, if Mr Gladstone had made a communication, it was not laid before the members . . . Through Mr Justin McCarthy's bungling or otherwise, that letter was never read.' Gladstone heard that in something under a quarter of an hour the Irish Party had met, re-elected Parnell 'and had given to his letter, as he thought, no consideration . . . And in a moment of indignation and temper, he wrote a second letter . . . which has produced such fateful consequences . . . Gladstone publicly telling us that we should expose the man that we had unanimously elected: how could we ever maintain our equality as Irishmen if we had yielded to that dictation? . . . The next thing would have been that these same men would have wanted to dictate to us who was to be our prime minister in an Irish parliament.' Gladstone some months later stated at Dover that although the Liberal Party was ready to give Ireland Home Rule, it was not ready to hand over the government of Ireland to men like Parnell. 'Ah, they would be very glad to do so now . . . They have killed the man who was their best friend. A sham Home Rule of that kind will not satisfy the Irish people.'

Months after the fresh Meath elections, Mahony again addressed the issue of his allegiance to Parnell, in the context of the latter's duplicitous offer to resign if the Irish Party could in exchange get a good deal on Home Rule from Gladstone. Mahony wrote in the *Weekly Independent* that on the Friday following his unanimous re-election as party chairman and before the debate in Committee Room 15, a small number of them had sent a message asking Parnell to consider temporarily retiring from the chairmanship to preserve party unity, 'but we added that, come what might, we would be true to our profession at the Leinster Hall and to our vote at the commencement of the session'.[52] (Barry O'Brien, in his biography of Parnell, who at that stage was telling his party to ensure a good price from the Liberals for his proposed retirement as leader, quoted Mahony on Parnell's response:[53] 'He then saw us all at the Westminster Palace Hotel. Mr Justin McCarthy was present. Parnell said: "I will retire if Gladstone says in writing that he will give the Irish Parliament control of the police and of the land, unless the English Parliament settles it first. Now, I don't want him to write that letter to me; let him write it to Justin McCarthy." And then he turned to Justin and said, with a grim smile, "and Justin, when you get the letter, I advise you to put it in a glass case".')

Luke Smyth, who presided at a public meeting in Navan for Mahony, again reminded voters of the secrecy of the ballot, which he claimed Parnell had achieved, 'but now the clergy want to deprive the people of what they have won'.[54] At the revision of the electoral register, 'didn't the clergy sit in court all day and, if a poor labourer had been ill and forced to apply for a little outdoor relief, get him struck off the list?' Mahony, after reading a letter of support from the old Fenian, James Stephens, repeated that he had never posed as a Fenian, 'but we all owe a deep debt of gratitude to those men of '67'. As in the summer election, he answered charges that as a land commissioner the rents he fixed were too high. 'I said that myself in the Commons . . . rents were of course too high after the fall in prices, which we didn't foresee. The Tory government reduced those rents, due to some extent to my statement.' Again welcoming Leahy, labour member of Dublin Corporation, Mahony firmed up his proposal on pensions: savings from a correct Irish contribution to the imperial fund would enable 80,000 people over 65 to be given 5 shillings a week.

John Redmond, MP, said he believed that the success of the Home Rule bill about to be introduced by Gladstone 'will depend in my opinion largely upon the result of this election'. If Gibney went to parliament 'he will sit there as a dumb dog', whereas Mahony was highly regarded by all English politicians. M.A. Manning, Mahony's constituency organiser, said Gibney had brought an action against Navan's only industry, Clayton's woollen mills, which circulated £35,000 a year in the district. Although he lost the action, the mills had not recovered. But the *Freeman* defended Gibney, who, after he had subscribed for shares in the Navan tweed factory, 'thought that the prospectus did not reveal the true condition of the enterprise.[55] He took an action for the recovery of his money, but was defeated. He accepted the decision and remains a large shareholder to this day . . . Although Navan derives the advantage of the expending of thousands of pounds in wages . . . that great Parnellite stronghold does not own £100 worth of shares in this Irish industry.'

Tim Harrington, MP, held a meeting in front of the courthouse in Trim, where 'nearly everyone wore a sprig of evergreen in his hat', while an anti-Parnellite demonstration took place under the Wellington monument.[56] Targeting Bishop Nulty once more, he stated that on the previous Sunday in Moynalty, a meeting of Parnellites had been called by the parish priest (Fr Mullen), 'who is a Parnellite notwithstanding what the bishop may say'. But his curate (Fr Clavin) assembled a hostile meeting of 'the most foul mouthed men he could gather . . . The parish priest was flouted, set aside and eight or nine curates and parish priests came in', which was only possible 'by permission of the bishop'. But Fr Behan, presiding at the anti-Parnellite demonstration, described the Parnellite one as 'the rag, tag and bobtail of every surrounding parish'.[57] He said that the Parnellites would not be able to say it was clerical dictation which returned Jordan. All he claimed for the priests was the right to vote and to advise the people, as tried friends in every struggle for hundreds of years.

The *Freeman* based much of its optimism about Gibney's prospects on the collapse of William Lawlor's vote in the previous year's Poor Law election in Navan, which was 'proof of 50 per cent of the electorate being transferred from the factionists to the nationalists'.[58] Mahony meanwhile repeated at a meeting in Kingstown that the petitions 'proved that the paid rowdyism was not on our side but on theirs, that thirty men in North Meath, headed by Slasher Geraghty, were paid five shillings a day [by] . . . a priest'.[59] Dalton said at Gormanston that Parnellites were not against the priests but against them telling the people that by voting for a Parnellite 'they would commit a mortal sin'. And did they really imagine that if he and Mahony were elected they would 'vote with the Tories against the Home Rule bill?'

Tim Healy, MP, was welcomed to a major anti-Parnellite demonstration in Gormanlough, about five miles from Navan, with streamers proclaiming 'Meath wants no shame', 'priests and people' and 'long live Dr Nulty'.[60] Fr P. Gallagher, parish priest, College Hill, who presided, said 'it was worth twenty petitions' to witness that meeting. They had not come 'to tap the porter barrels', but they should welcome back those who had been carried away by false issues. Laurence Rowan proposed resolutions supporting 'the choice of the priests and people of Meath'. In a bravura performance, Healy asked them to elect Gibney, who was 'of your own stamp . . . instead of going for broken-down sub-commissioners', or returning a man like Dalton 'simply because he is a brother-in-law of Jack Redmond'. The Meath petitions were not really brought because of priestly dictation: 'It was a bit of spite on the part of John Redmond to injure the priests, because of a story told by Canon Doyle [in Wexford] about his [Redmond's] grandfather. He was a very respectable tailor and . . . the connection he had with the pikemen in the 1798 rebellion was that the government employed him making jackets for the yeomen . . . The honest tailor went down on one knee in the mud of the street while he mended the yeoman's breeches. Trifling as it is . . . that is why Mahony and Redmond . . . are so particular about having nothing said about their grandfathers or mothers.'

Healy said their opponents included men 'not ashamed to be on the same side as the grabbers, the emergencymen, the landlords and the Tories of Meath . . . No matter how much porter he may have drunk, who is such a fool as not to know that the landlords of Meath want Mahony elected . . . the men who have driven out 80,000 from Meath in these last forty years?' Tories would say 'can we give Home Rule to a people that would elect a rowdy like Mahony . . . arrested for blacking a man's eye . . . in a court of justice?' They knew how difficult it was to carry Home Rule in England, 'with the House of Lords with its Tory majority against us, with all the money of the aristocracy'. Parnellites furnished the Tories with ammunition but,

> thanks to the intelligence and patriotism of our priests, the Irish people are re-forming their ranks . . . The Home Rule bill must, before it is presented to parliament, be hammered on the anvil in council between the Irish Party and the English cabinet . . . The duty of the Irish Party will be confined, I hope, to voting . . . with as little talk as possible, but . . . jackasses of the Billy Redmond type . . . will go over there in order to show, not that Ireland is entitled to its rights, but that they are more patriotic . . . than we are . . . While we are fighting for Ireland, don't let Meath stab us from behind . . . How Balfour would clap his hands if he saw the classic face of Mr Pierce Charles de Mongey Mahony in the bar. How the Tory whips would chuckle if they saw Mr Jim Dalton once more at the refreshment counter.

More Navan rioting

In a Parnellite own goal which would have tragic consequences, the *Freeman* reported that when the Navan contingent were returning from Healy's Gormanlough meeting they were attacked by a gang of Parnellites.[61] The *Drogheda Independent* claimed that Mongey was at the head of Cannicetown band, which was joined by about 200 in a howling mob which marched to Flower Hill as 20 cars returned from Gormanlough.[62] The *Argus* reprinted a letter from Fr Patrick Murphy, parish priest, to the *Freeman* about this 'cowardly attack' on Sunday 29 January 1893, in which 'organised rowdyism' prevailed.[63] 'On approaching Market Square, huge stones were thrown from a disused house on the main street and from Timmons's corner . . . we were obliged to descend from the cars and some of our party had to seek protection in the adjoining gateways, where the most odious forms of contumely were heaped upon us . . . This will, I trust, open the eyes of the respectable people of Navan.'

Wooing Parnellite labourers, the *Freeman* claimed 'the working men of Navan' regarded Parnellism as an obstruction to Home Rule, which they hoped would 'advance the industrial interests of the country'.[64] They resented being confused with the 'idlers and loafers' whose 'filthy language, especially to the priests' was recounted at the petitions. The attack on the Navan anti-Parnellites returning from Gormanlough was, the *Freeman* pointed out, organised by a crowd from outside the constituency, brought in by special train to the Parnellite meeting in Navan that day. The police, 'apprehensive of a collision', had drafted in additional forces and had driven them back towards the town. But stones were thrown over the heads of the RIC at the returning cars and the police immediately drew batons. When the procession of cars approached Market Square by Watergate Street, stones were again thrown from the corners and a vacant house. Several of the police were struck and then charged the mob, who scattered in different directions. Fr Patrick Murtagh, parish priest of Stamullen and a former curate in Navan, who was recovering from illness, was set upon and grossly insulted, his assailants 'covering his face and clothes with spittle'.[65]

Meath elections 'proved' unionist case

In Westminster meanwhile, the Speaker having told the reassembled parliament that the elections of Fulham and Davitt had been voided by the Meath petition trials because of spiritual intimidation, the Parnellites tried to move the writ for a new election in South Meath.[66]

But the unionists proposed that this should be suspended until the evidence in the petition had been considered by the house, citing Bishop Nulty's pastoral statement that 'no man can remain a Catholic and continue to cling to Parnellism'. Gladstone said they should adhere to the usage of the House and give two days' notice of moving the writs, the petitions evidence being a separate matter. The *Freeman* feebly alleged collusion between Parnellites and unionists, both in this exchange and in the moving of the North Meath writ some days later.[67]

As debate on the Queen's Speech began, Col. Edward Saunderson, the Unionist leader and member for North Armagh, recalled that at the general election of 1886 they were described as 'Orange bigots' when they said that a Dublin parliament would result in a Catholic ascendancy, but the Meath elections had proven their case.[68] The prime minister had cut down one ascendancy in Ireland because it stood in the way of peace and prosperity, but now at the close of his great career he proposed to found another ascendancy more loathsome. The work of Catholic peasant priests in Ireland had returned 71 members to that house. If they had not interfered, Redmond would have had three times as strong a party as he now had. When Parnell's fall came, the Catholic church made a grab at Ireland, but the clergy never raised a hand against Parnell until the prime minister was quickened into action by the nonconformists. Then, seeing that Parnell had lost his power, the clergy grasped at the reins as they fell from his crime-stained hands. So a Dublin parliament and its executive would be the slaves of the Catholic priests. While unionists might be a minority in Ireland, standing up for the law and the crown, on their side stood the majority of the British people. Now that their worst fears were being realised, the verified prophesies they had made had rallied to their side those who would oppose the Home Rule bill to be introduced. The loyalists of Ireland would never submit to the domination of men who, but for the interference of the police, would at that moment be flying at each other's throats.

When the writ for North Meath was moved, Col. Sanderson again raised the issue of 'priestly intimidation'.[69] As it transpired that both Meath elections could not take place on the same day, there was much bickering among the Irish members about which should occur first, each side believing that whichever won the closer contest in South Meath would enhance their chances in the subsequent North Meath election. The *Irish Independent* accused the anti-Parnellites of trying to delay the elections so that 'irresponsible and unwise young clerics' could again intimidate illiterate voters. 'MPs by grace of the bishops and clergy of Ireland' were humiliating their country in the Commons. They had also failed to gain the support of their government allies, confirming that only an Irish Party which maintained its independence could earn respect. But the *Freeman* said that the Parnellites wished to have the elections over before the Home Rule bill disproved their charges of treachery against the Irish Party and the Liberals.

Back on the campaign trail in Meath, the *Irish Independent* described Mahony's twelve-mile drive from Navan to Moynalty as 'a triumphal procession'.[70] Every cottage had some decorative token and children running onto the road cheered for 'the man that blacked Matt Kenny's eye'. At Carnaross, which the anti-Parnellites claimed to be theirs, a big arch spanned the bridge, surmounted by a portrait of Parnell. At Moynalty, the street in front of the church was filled, while below the platform 'a patient donkey . . . with a battered silk hat fixed between its ears . . . was intended as a representation of Mr Gibney'. Mahony, however, was still having to rebut clerically inspired personal abuse: he challenged the Meath priest who wrote for information about him to a priest who lived near his home in Kerry to publish the answer. 'I believe that they want to know particularly where I was in '67: I was at school.' Acknowledging that he had been dismissed from the Land Commission, Mahony explained that on the Olphert estate in Donegal, in 45 cases, he dissented from the judgement of his fellow commissioners in open court on the ground that the rents they were fixing were too high. As a result, Fr McFadden of Gweedore had described him as one of the best friends of the tenant farmers.

'Our enemies ask why I am interested in old age pensions? Because I know of no reform which could bring a wider blessing to the class in Ireland for whom least has been done but to whom Ireland owes most . . . That reform, although they may sneer at it, will be the law of the land.' Mahony concluded 'we are as capable, as laymen, of judging of matters as any clergyman . . . Slaves cannot free a nation, neither can they use the gift of freedom when they get it . . . Keep the cause pure, remember it is holy and let no meanness or no cowardice stain it.' But other speakers advocated assaulting anyone who maligned Parnellite women, pointing out that the alleged sin of Parnellism was purely geographical. In Dublin, Catholic churchmen shared public platforms for charitable causes with prominent Parnellites who, if they took an hour's railway journey to Navan, would be taunted with immorality.

Mahony's return to Navan was marked by huge bonfires outside the town and he was cheered through the streets.

William O'Brien, MP, told a meeting in Dunshaughlin that the enemies of Ireland clung to the Parnellites because they were their last hope of wrecking Home Rule by appealing to English bigotry against the priests of Ireland.[71] The Parnellites had also tried to terrorise the people of Meath by rowdyism, in which they were encouraged by the then Tory government, and against which the priests of Meath 'resorted to any strong measures that they did' to protect the people. The Parnellites then 'posed as injured archangels', horrified by the violence of the priests. Beaten by the electors of Meath despite their terrorist tactics, they sought vengeance by appealing to English bigotry against their own countrymen and creed. Those responsible for the Meath petitions 'did as foul an injury to Ireland and rendered a better service to the Tory party than the unfortunate man who forged the Pigott letters for the *Times*'. Vengeful Parnellites were like Sadlier and Keogh in robbing Ireland of the liberties within her grasp. But under the new Liberal government, every man in Meath could vote as he pleased without fear of reprisals. If Dalton dressed in orange ribbons, singing 'The Boyne Water' at his meetings, he could not be more the Orange candidate. The *Freeman* commented, 'it is on the plains of Meath and not on the floor of the Commons that the fate of Home Rule will be decided . . . Every coercionist stump orator is provided with the Redmondite pamphlet on the Meath petitions . . . But though they load the Orange cannon, they will not get Meath to put the match to it.'

The former Parnellite MP, Patrick O'Brien, told a rival Parnellite gathering that William O'Brien at the adjoining meeting was condemning the men of Meath for bringing the outrageous conduct of their priests before a court, but he had not been as sympathetic to the Bishop of Limerick when he opposed the plan of campaign, even though Dr O'Dwyer had better grounds 'than Dr Nulty had for opposing Parnell, whose leadership he had previously advocated at the meeting of bishops in Dublin'. The *Freeman* reported that Patrick O'Brien had to be rescued by priests from the anti-Parnellite crowd on which he had been eavesdropping. The *Irish Independent* reported that on that morning's train from Dublin, William O'Brien, MP, had 'a guard of honour' of about a hundred RIC men, armed with rifles, who 'bundled themselves in' behind him at the Broadstone and were met by more police in Dunshaughlin, to prevent clashes with the rival Parnellite gathering. Fr Gallagher, curate, presided at O'Brien's meeting, at which Fr Brady, parish priest, remarked that it was ungrateful to ask the priests to stand aside when they had long been linked to the people of the county 'by a thread of the finest gold and now it is sought to tie their hands'.

John Dillon, MP, said in Burnley that to argue from the Meath case that clerical influence extended to the whole of Ireland was an attempt to trade on the ignorance of the English people.[72] The priests were only human and were subjected to terrible provocation. They had been driven into politics by the persecution of the government and had to take their stand by a persecuted people who, but for their guidance, would have been swept out of existence. In doing so they were true to the teachings of their master and the principles of the gospel. But if Irish priests were to set themselves against the national aspirations of their countrymen, there was not a man in the anti-Parnellite party who would not resist them. Irish priests in Meath and elsewhere had considerable influence in elections because they took the side of the great majority. Sir Henry James had asserted that one-fifth of the illiterate peasants of Meath were coerced to vote according to the orders of the priests, but if that was so then 80 per cent of them voted against the priests in their presence. He admitted that there was intimidation on both sides, but he maintained that that against the priests was far more effectual.

Fr Behan of Trim said in Athboy that their current divisions represented 'a page in Irish history that in years to come will read badly'.[73] Some of those who had opposed Parnell when he accompanied him to that town nearly 18 years before were now opposed 'to the present parish priest, to the priests of Ireland and the majority of the Irish people'. But 'we fought those factionists who were against us before and now, with pepper and ginger as they come on again in this political race, we will beat them again'. Fr P. Callary, parish priest of St Mary's, Drogheda, presided at a meeting in Bettystown, where Jordan said he had always supported the claims of labour. In the North, Tories and Orangemen said the same things of him as Harrington and Redmond. During the last hundred years, with one remarkable exception — Daniel O'Connell — the leaders of the Irish people had also been Protestants. Gibney told a meeting in Carnaross, where Fr James Nulty, parish priest, presided, that if he had not taken action, Clayton's factory in Navan would be closed and its machinery rotting. Fr Gaughran of Kells claimed that Gibney was 'the real Parnellite. There were two Parnells . . . Parnell of the Land League days, that was the real Parnell . . . The other Parnell could not be got for five or six years to

address a meeting of his countrymen.' They excused him, believing that
the reason was sickness or delicacy, but they had seen the spirit and
energy that he displayed when he began to fight for his own ambition
and personal supremacy. Gibney was not a follower of that Parnell.
They made a present of that man to Mahony. It was the splendid unity
of the people that had gained for the labourers their plots of land and
for the farmers their reductions in rents.

As he fixed the nomination and polling dates, with South Meath
first, Captain Uvedale Corbet Singleton, high sheriff of Meath,
haughtily rejected Healy's accusation that he was therefore a Parnellite:
'I am a Conservative but, above all, an Unionist'.[74] The *Freeman*
predicted 'there is not one of Mr Singleton's political brethren in South
Meath' who would not vote for Dalton.[75] Meldon, the Navan RM, wrote
to the Castle on 5 February of his concerns that Navan Parnellites had
transferred their meeting arranged for Slane the following Sunday to
Navan, in order to counter an anti-Parnellite meeting to be held on the
Square.[76] He reckoned that this would risk a breach of the peace, even
if the anti-Parnellites held their meeting on the Fair Green, as their
main contingents would have to pass through the Square 'and we had
serious trouble there last time . . . Party feeling never ran higher,
especially after the riot last Sunday when the Parnellites assaulted first
the anti-Parnellites and then the police, who had to clear the streets by
baton charges. The Parnellites seem anxious to provoke it. A serious
riot in Navan would very much lessen the number of anti-Parnellites
going to the poll.'

At a public meeting in Navan, chaired by James Lawlor, Mahony,
having endured multiple accusations that Parnellites were allied to the
Tories, openly appealed for Protestant votes, as a Protestant himself.[77]
He believed that Home Rule would benefit the Protestants of Ireland.
If Parnellite independence of the priests had calmed fears of Meath
Protestants and encouraged them to vote for him, 'it is a matter not for
opprobrium . . . but for congratulation . . . It augurs well for the future
of Ireland.' For their opponents to suggest that the Parnellites ought
not to have revealed their activities in the petitions, because it struck
a blow at Home Rule, was 'childish nonense. It required no petition
to make public the bishop's pastoral and that pastoral was the most
deadly blow struck at Home Rule for the past ten years.' The priests
of Meath would continue to oppose him, but they had been 'glad
enough to have a Protestant Irishman going on English platforms to
defend the Catholic clergy'.

The Irish Times broke its silence on the Meath elections to note that voters would have sight of the Home Rule bill before the polls, which 'will quite alter the character of the contest'.[78] At present, 'there is nothing beyond the worn-out strife which began in Committee Room 15'. But 'if the measure be a thumping nationalist one, down will go the fortunes of the independents'. If, on the contrary, 'the scheme is Whig . . . full of contrivance and empty of concession . . . the two federation candidates may pack up and quit . . . The elections will be comparable in their consequences to that of Clare in 1829.' The *Freeman* made much of the nine Parnellites abstaining in a Commons division, leaving it to the majority Irish Party to save the liberal 'home rule ministry'.[79] The Parnellites' action 'has considerably weakened their position in Meath'.

Mahony was struck by a stone on the back by Cavan men in Kingscourt, having spent the day there talking to Meath voters at the fair.[80] 'While Mr Mahony was chatting with his supporters on the street, three priests appeared and with an ostentatious display of their breviaries paraded up and down . . . Extra police, with drawn batons, kept the Parnellites and the Cavan seceders apart.' Mahony's charge of assaulting Kenny was abandoned on the instructions of the attorney general, the *Irish Independent* remarking 'neither the crown nor Kenny thought anything could be made out of his black eye[81] . . . Both sides in Navan are glad . . . the Parnellites jubilantly so, the anti-Parnellites quietly, as they would like the whole incident forgotten.' The paper also reported that Gibney 'could not be found around the town, although the oft repeated query . . . "Who is Gibney, where is Gibney, what is Gibney", was in the mouth of everybody', before he emerged from the parochial house. 'Give us a shake of that fist', a man asked Mahony at Kells fair day, when 'children ran around him to put up their tiny fists to be shaken'.[82]

Commons discusses Meath elections

In the Commons, the Belfast Liberal Unionist, Hugh Arnold-Forster, moved an amendment to the queen's address, seeking measures to prevent a repetition of clerical intimidation in Meath.[83] He said they were dealing with a conspiracy against a legal right. The elections in Meath were marked by a brutality of speech and action which happily was rare in contested elections, even in Ireland. A large number of the members opposite owed their seats to this intimidation practised by the priests in Ireland, which was described in the election petitions. Bishop Nulty's sermons and pastoral expressly claimed the right to direct the votes of Catholics. Arnold-Forster noted that he had even declared that no good Catholic could be a Parnellite. Any man who ventured to vote against them was ruined on earth and damned in the world to come. This case of Bishop Nulty was not isolated, but was merely part of a deliberate system which had been inculcated in Ireland and which he and his friends would do their utmost to prevent being extended or continued. They had on the one hand the priests and on the other the law of the House of Commons and although the clergy claimed to decide what were morals, there could not be the slightest hesitation as to which authority should be obeyed. It was useless to expect the present government to prosecute the priests who resorted to intimidation, but it was high time to put an end to voting under the eyes of priests and to what he claimed was the over-representation of the clerically represented Irish constituencies. In nine polling booths in Meath there were 22 priests acting as personating agents and, of eight counting agents, seven were priests.

Horace Plunkett, the Co-operative campaigner, son of Lord Dunsany and south Dublin unionist, seconding the amendment in his maiden speech, said he had lived most of his life in Meath and regarded the Meath elections with 'unfeigned sorrow'. Ireland was a mainly Catholic country and the priests must continue to exercise a mighty influence for good or evil. The Bishop of Meath had laid it down that mere sympathy with a political creed rendered local women guilty of the most atrocious crimes. While the repetition of such a tactical blunder as the pastoral might defeat its own ends, unfortunately the Catholic church in Meath was now constituting itself into a political agency. In the Dunshaughlin area where he lived, the local clergy took no part in the elections, but clergy were sent from other parts of Ireland to make a house-to-house visitation. The clergy were again exercising an influence in the pending election, which he feared would prevent a free vote. Many of those who opposed the clergy at the last election might be led — by a longing to make their peace with heaven, or to secure the offices of the priest in their dying hours — to vote for their nominees at the coming election. He warned the government that the action of the clergy in Meath had made Home Rule morally impossible. If they refused to abolish that influence, they would find themselves confronted with a loyal minority, supported by England, which would make Home Rule physically impossible.

But Herbert Paul, the Edinburgh radical journalist, also in a maiden speech, said that Arnold-Forster had extrapolated the situation in

Meath to the rest of Ireland without evidence. Also, 'he has not shown that a single voter had been induced or compelled to give a vote which he would not otherwise have given'. If spiritual influence had played the part asserted in Meath, it was strange that both the successful and the defeated parties should be equally anxious for new elections and should appeal with equal confidence to the common sense of their countrymen. It was not easy to devise practical means of dealing with undue clerical influence. There was less reason to do so when that influence was exercised to give effect to, rather than to oppose, popular demands. J.G. Butcher, the conservative member for York and son of a former Protestant Bishop of Meath, quoted from Dr Nulty's pastoral and utterances of priests in Meath to challenge the previous speaker: it was 'impossible to believe that such threats addressed to an ignorant and a religious peasantry could fail to produce a great effect'. As to the defence that the issue was not one of politics but of morals, the Liberals had not admitted the claim of the church to decide this when the plan of campaign was in question. The Liberals had done much for liberty and he asked those who were about to propose one man–one vote not to give their sanction to one bishop–10,000 votes.

The attorney general, Sir Charles Russell, who had defended Parnell against the *Times'* allegations, defended John Morley's speech at Newcastle exonerating Irish priests. He said that there was no surer guarantee of civil freedom than to endow a people with their own government. He pointed to the Tories dallying with clerical influence for political purposes, as in the case of the papal rescript which condemned the plan of campaign, 'pulling the sleeve of Monsignor Persico with one hand while with the other beating the Orange drum'. The bishop and clergy in Meath took one side in the contest and were entitled, within certain lines, to use their influence with the people. But they exceeded those lines and in that respect the law had been vindicated. The influence of the priests in Ireland arose from the fact that they stood up in defence of popular rights and they had always stood up against secret societies. Because the people had been influenced by the priests in the direction in which they wished to go, he could not see the case for disenfranchising illiterate voters or reducing parliamentary representation in southern Ireland. The amendment to the address was really aimed at discounting and discrediting the Home Rule measure beforehand.

Justin McCarthy agreed that if there had been intimidation at the Meath elections it had been met by the law. But there was nothing in the nature of extreme intimidation and he and his friends were opposed to any kind of influence, priestly or other, being brought to bear on any voter. Tim Harrington, announcing that the Parnellites would decline to vote, said that the clergy should be left to the judgement of their Catholic fellow-countrymen: clerical influence was not confined to Meath. The ensuing division resulted in 205 for and 248 against, a majority of 43 against the amendment. Earlier, Morley said that as the elections would take place in Meath within five or six days, there was no time to initiate legislation to prevent a recurrence of intimidation by the priests.

The *Irish Independent* accused the anti-Parnellite MPs of failing to defend the bishops and priests of Ireland, 'or even the Bishop and priests of Meath', while Justin McCarthy 'practically admitted the charge against them'.[84] The government had condemned the action of the bishop and clergy of Meath and expressed satisfaction that it had been dealt with by the judges, while Davitt, Healy and O'Brien were silent. The lesson was that the creatures of the clergy at election time were too cowardly to defend their patrons when they got across to Westminster. However, the *Freeman* maintained that Parnellite MPs must have been humiliated 'to hear their calumnies made the text of a venomous attack' on their country and to find their clergy 'so brilliantly championed against their calumnies by an Englishman and a Protestant' (Herbert Paul).[85]

At the beginning of election week in Meath, the *Irish Independent* noted that as a result of the petitions, although the priests were the chief anti-Parnellite canvassers in almost every district, there had been no political sermons and Bishop Nulty had not availed of the opportunity of his Lenten pastoral to allude to the contest.[86] There was no anti-Parnellite meeting in Navan that Sunday to clash with Mahony's, although one was to have been addressed by Healy and Davitt, and special trains to it had been arranged.[87] But the presence in the town of 80 extra police, making the strength of the local force over 100, 'excited suspicions as to the intent of the seceders'.

Gladstone's second Home Rule bill

On 13 February 1893, Gladstone introduced his second Home Rule bill, which unsuccessfully attempted to placate the opposition by providing for continued Irish representation at Westminster, unlike his first measure which had been defeated in the Commons in 1886. The activity of the Bishop of Meath and his priests was again used to good effect in this debate by the enemies of Home Rule.[88] R.M. Dane, Conservative, Fermanagh, and descendant of Speaker Foster of the Irish Commons, warned the government that by handing over to the rule of an Irish parliament the million and a half Protestants who had made Ireland what it was, they were incurring the danger of civil war. They were asked to set up in Ireland a 'Papish' parliament and to establish the ascendancy of the church of Rome, of priests who would follow the directions of that church. If this bill became law, the Protestant people of Ireland would never obey the laws of such a parliament. G.W. Wolff, Conservative member, of the Belfast ship-building firm, said that those he represented rejected the bill because, in furthering the interests of their church, devoted Catholic priests would be bound to put down the Protestant minority, as history had shown.

Col. Saunderson asserted that Healy had admitted that he and his colleagues were the nominees of the Catholic priesthood. Those 71 (anti-Parnellites) might stand up in that House and speak as patriots, but they were really only puppets. Was parliament going to change the constitution, not to meet the overwhelming demands of the Irish people but those of the Catholic church? Mr Paul had told them it was in vain to attempt to deprive the priests of political power. Were the radicals prepared to hand over Ireland to the priestly government, which to radicals of former days was abhorrent? This bill would receive uncompromising resistance from Irish Unionists, because they believed it would be destructive to the liberty and prosperity of Ireland. The minority was strong enough if the military were taken out of the country to make the country their own, the Unionist leader threatened.

The *Irish Independent* said the bill vindicated Parnell's reservations in his manifesto concerning control of the police and the judiciary and the land issue.[89] In further debate in the Commons, the anti-Home Rule Liberal representing Tyrone South, T.W. Russell, maintained that illiterate Irish peasants would be bewildered by simultaneous Irish elections under Home Rule for the Irish parliament, 80 Westminster seats and the Irish legislative council, or upper house.[90] The result would be that priests would be directors of everybody's conscience and the new parliament would be under the control of the Catholic priesthood, despite John Redmond's talk about acting independently. Later, Edward McHugh, Armagh anti-Parnellite, denied that there was any reason to apprehend danger from the intolerance of Catholic priests, after Lord Randolph Churchill raised the Ulster question and predicted the Lords' defeat of the bill, so odious to Unionists.[91] Col.

Thomas Waring, the North Down 'constitutionalist and imperialist', said Englishmen and Scotchmen would not submit to be governed by a parliament which was subject to ecclesiastical domination. The first reading of the bill passed without a division, with the second reading scheduled for 13 March.

Back home, describing Gibney's clerically endorsed candidature as 'an attempt to force into parliament a moneyed fool', the *Irish Independent* reported 'a large force of extra police' in Kells for the formal nominations at the courthouse on 14 February.[92] Mahony, accompanied by his wife and Luke Smyth, John Spicer, James Lawlor and M.A. Manning, arrived by the morning train from Navan, while Gibney, 'followed by a few clergymen and a small crowd, left the parochial house . . . About 50 policemen were extended in a single line in front of the seceders' crowd'. Mahony's main proposers were Smyth and William Lawlor, while James Gibney, Martinstown, Crossakiel, farmer, was nominated by Rev. Peter McNamee, Navan, and Nicholas Kelly. A few days later, as Cavan men were prevented by almost 50 police from attacking a meeting of Mahony's in Oldcastle, he remarked 'boos hurt nobody, but it was sad to see young girls shouting indecencies while three clergymen in the crowd appeared to approve'.[93] About 50 anti-Parnellites drove a horse and car through the police lines after the meeting and then tried unsuccessfully to storm the Parnellite committee rooms, where they were baton-charged. On Mahony's departure from Oldcastle, a meeting in the new parochial hall was addressed by Frs Flood, Brady and Clarke. Earlier, Mahony expressed surprise in Rathkenny that he had been reprimanded for voting for the Tory Land Purchase bill of 1891, even though it had earmarked £33 million for Irish tenant farmers. He said that Parnellites were right not to support Gladstone in divisions after John Morley refused to reduce judicial rents in Ireland following the fall in prices.

It was at this point that the *Irish Independent* reported sadly on the only fatality of the Parnell split in Meath.[94] 'Today in Navan a Parnellite named Edward Burke, who had been batoned by a policeman on the occasion of [the post-Gormanlough rioting on 29 January] . . . succumbed to his injuries. The news created great sensation in the town . . . Aged 50, he was a cattle drover . . . of quiet temper and a rigid teetotaller. His young wife and their child, aged only a few months, are now left dependent.' At the subsequent inquest before coroner, John Reilly, his widow's brother said the deceased told him he got a blow of a baton.[95] Unsuccessfully arguing against an adjournment for Mrs

Burke to have a solicitor present, the coroner asked 'if he does not come, who will pay me for my time?' The *Freeman* said that six police and twenty civilians were treated in hospital after the rioting of 29 January.[96] The *Drogheda Independent* described Edward Burke as being 'of respectable antecedents and quiet disposition and it was well known that beyond being accidentally present on the night of the riot he had not the remotest connection with the wild scenes of disorder'.[97]

Marking a new low for the Catholic church in Meath, the *Irish Independent* reported that Edward Burke's funeral was attended by many, including Mahony and 'some of the most prominent merchants in the town[98] . . . A little after 4 o'clock the remains were removed from a house in Cornmarket and the coffin placed on trestles in the roadway. There was no priest in attendance and the crowd, silently uncovering their heads, prayed for some little time around the corpse before the men shouldered the coffin and set out for the neighbouring graveyard . . . Very pretty wreaths sent by some of the townspeople were laid on the grave, around which the persons present prayed for some time.'

At the resumed inquest in Navan courthouse, several witnesses testified to seeing the police baton-charging the crowd up Trimgate Street and to seeing the deceased being struck by the police or bleeding afterwards.[99] Meldon said he told the people who were stoning them that he would put a stop to it. Some of them were willing to move away, but one shouted out that it was their ground and they meant to hold it. The stoning became heavier and he was compelled to order a charge. He saw the helmet of a police officer crushed in by a blow. Kells band, which belonged to the Parnellites, did everything he asked them. About 50 or 60 policemen had drawn batons. The jury's verdict was that 'Edward Burke came to his death from blood poisoning caused by wounds received on 29th January 1893 on the occasion of a police baton-charge'.

The *Irish Independent* reported on the day before polling that 20 men from the mounted police force at the depot had gone by train from the Broadstone to Trim and would remain in Meath until after the results of the North Meath election.[100] While the petitions had 'done something to prevent the clergy from acting as personation agents in the booths', it had been hoped that they would have abstained altogether. Forty mounted police had been drafted into Trim, 'as well as a regular army of constables'. Priests were still canvassing for Jordan in several districts. Next day the *Irish Times* estimated that 5,000 voted in South Meath, with Trim, Ballivor and Athboy Parnellite, Dunshaughlin and

Dunboyne neutral and the rest anti-Parnellite: Duleek, Julianstown, Clonard, Summerhill and Longwood.[101] 'The principles of Parnell are approved in the largest towns . . . Votes of the rural parts would appear to have been given for Jordan.' Priests were not as active as previously, 'still they have not stood aside', about ten acting as personation agents for Jordan.

As Parnellites alleged clerical intimidation and their opponents accused them of violence, the *Irish Independent* said about 5,350 out of an electorate of 7,000 voted in South Meath, 1,000 more than at the election in July.[102] Priests 'were to be found in the booths in some places and were posted in front of them in almost every polling district'. An 'occult spiritual influence' had pervaded the whole election campaign, but up to the last minute Parnellites believed 'that the priests would not put themselves so strongly forward' on polling day itself. However, the *Freeman* alleged that Parnellite intimidation at the polling booths in Trim was prevented only by a large force of police.[103] 'The Tories turned up in full force . . . Their cars were at the disposal of the Redmondites.' In Dunshaughlin, 'it was rather a curious spectacle to see noted bigoted shoneens abandoning the hunting field and riding up, booted and spurred and bespattered with mud, to record their votes for Mr Dalton'.

Dalton loses by 69 votes

The following day, the *Irish Independent* described Dalton's loss in South Meath by 69 votes in a total poll of over a thousand more than in the previous election as 'a disappointment, but not a defeat'.[104] He had gained 500 voters in eight months, although 'the clerical politicians' had secured the same number, working 'more insidiously', but no less effectively. 'It is absurd to suppose that the altar denunciations of eight months ago have been forgotten.' And the clergy had worked on the revision of the electoral register 'as if some sacred cause depended' on it. The close result — Jordan 2,707, Dalton 2,638 — was 'unsurprising' as priests had 'flocked into and outside the booths' on polling day and if their own votes had not been given for Jordan he would have lost. At the counting of votes in Trim courthouse, 'nobody seemed more surprised' than Jordan, but 'the clergy, who clustered in large numbers on the stairs leading to the counting room and in the hall of the court awaiting the result, seemed to be perfectly confident of the success of their candidate.'

A troop of horse police kept the large crowds back from the courthouse steps, while 'a double line of mounted police rode up and down the principal street . . . When the sheriff appeared, his official declaration was received with respectful silence'. But Jordan was jeered by the crowd as priests shook his hand and waved their hats in the air. Although surrounded by priests, he asked for a police escort to see him safely to the house of the parish priest, Fr Behan. 'About a dozen constables made a ring around the portly figure of the new member for Meath and thus he went off, looking more like a prisoner than one who had been elected.' The priests who accompanied him, incriminated in the petition, 'in the heat and temper of the moment and in a surging crowd, indulged in cross-election and political cries with men who probably were members of their own flock'. Fulham lost Jordan in the crush on the stairs and complained that his friend had gone away without him. But 'another escort was forthcoming for him' to Fr Behan's.

Coming out of the courthouse, the vanquished Dalton, on the other hand, was seized by the crowd 'and chaired on their shoulders across to the house of Mrs Leonard in Market Square, from the windows of which he addressed 2,000 people', after getting Captain Stokes to withdraw the mounted police as 'there was no hostile crowd'. Dalton said they had had to face 'the allied forces of the priests and the government'. The election had been won in the revision courts (a Registration Reform bill aimed to extend the franchise from owners and occupiers of property to all men over 21 years, thereby ending the tedious farce of the revision court, but it would be 1918 before the vote was extended to all adult males and to women over 30). The Parnellite organisation was not as good as it ought to have been, whereas the organisation on the other side, for reasons which they all knew, was the very best. His opponent's canvassers (priests) told the people that the Parnellite members walked out of the Commons and refused to vote for the Home Rule bill. It would have been better if they had quietly remained at home and allowed the people to settle the matter for themselves. There would then have been no doubt of the result, but he would be successful if he was a candidate a third time.

Parnellite organiser and ex-MP, Patrick O'Brien, said they saw Dr Nulty's MP, the representative of the ignorance and cowardice of that division of the county, leave the courthouse and sneak by a back lane with a bodyguard of police up to pay due homage to Fr Behan, although he was not able to muster three votes in Trim. They were unfortunately forced to fight against the priests of their church, as liberty-loving men. Where the priests were abusing their power by interfering with the rights of citizens, they should stop the supplies. The priests would then retire from the field and the Parnellites would win. The greatest argument against Home Rule was the helpless condition of the people who allowed a bishop to compel a whole diocese to vote as he liked. When he saw half a dozen priests walking in the mud outside a polling station he wondered, while they were doing the work of the Whig Party, who were looking after the religious wants of the people?

Luke Smyth appealed for calm when he presided at a meeting on the Square in Navan as the anti-Parnellites held a meeting on the Fair Green, where 'they were guarded by the police, while at all approaches to the town large bodies of constabulary were stationed'.[105] Jordan, Fulham and a contingent from Cavan and Louth arrived by train from Drogheda and were received by a large contingent of police, who escorted them to the parochial house. 'A troop of horse police from the depot were drawn up on the outskirts of the Parnellite crowd . . . to prevent any collision between the Whig crowd which arrived from the Slane direction [who] . . . were accorded a hot reception.' Tim Harrington, MP, said he was proud that 2,600 men voted Parnellite in South Meath 'in spite of unworthy, unChristian and unclerical threats'. In Navan, under the sanction of the bishop, the priests of the diocese had passed a resolution calling on Parnell to stand his ground, but after Gladstone spoke they pretended it was the moral issue which stirred their consciences. They all knew how anxious they were a few years ago to get the political services and able advocacy of a man of Mahony's religion and position. He joined the party at Parnell's urgent request, but in the current struggle 'they were base enough to assert that Mr Mahony was a souper and his family had been soupers'.

The *Irish Independent* reported that Gibney was so unpopular among his neighbours in Oldcastle that Fr Grehan 'addressed a pitiful appeal from the altar for support and, extending the limits of the political influence he has been hitherto claiming, called on the Protestants of the district not to vote for Mahony'. Mahony himself told a meeting in Crossakiel that he remembered when he was the white-haired boy of the priests of Meath. In those days he was 'an honest Protestant', now he was 'a Kerry souper'. That was not the way to make Ireland a free country or 'bring our Protestant fellow-countrymen into line with the nationalists'. They could not make self-government work unless, within a short time, the Irish parliament was supported by the Protestants. The only result of the 'souper' charge had been to make his Catholic fellow-countrymen rally round him and his fellow Protestants in Meath take part in the contest. Many of them would vote for him. Parnellites gave confidence to Irish Protestants and that alone was sufficient reason for asking people to vote for him. Mahony appealed again in Kells for the votes of Protestants and rejected Fr Grehan's appeal to them not to vote for him.

Hailing the South Meath result as 'unity restored', the *Freeman* claimed it was 'an open secret' where the Parnellite increase had come from:[106] the Tories had supported Dalton more than they ever had 'a candidate of their own'. This 'coercionist' support was openly relied upon by the Parnellites, but 'the unholy alliance has been crushed by the honest nationalists of South Meath' and the verdict would be repeated with added emphasis in the northern division. The *Freeman's* report on the count in Trim criticised the 'disgraceful remarks to the priests' of local corner-boys. It described the Parnellite meeting in Navan as a 'police-protected fizzle', but 'a large gathering of priests' attended Jordan's meeting in front of the presbytery on the Fair Green. Up to 260 police were in the town, including 30 on horseback. With Fr McNamee presiding, Jordan claimed that more than half the additional Parnellite votes in South Meath were obtained 'through Tory Protestants and bigoted influences . . . Men came in there from the hunt and got off their horses.' But his own victory had been secured by honest, constitutional means and he was convinced that it was the priests who were intimidated.

The *Irish Independent* was not confident of victory in North Meath, citing the clergy canvassing votes for Gibney 'to show the English that we did not intimidate you at the last election'.[107] In 'the arrogance of their power', they had selected Gibney 'to prove that they hold the keys of the country and that their power is absolute'. If North Meath elected Gibney, 'it would give a majority to a properly accredited broomstick'. Hinting at the possibility of another petition in that eventuality, the *Irish Independent* also noticed that at Mahony's eve-of-poll meeting in Navan, the crowd received each mention of Gibney's name 'with a peculiar cry caused by frequently slapping the hand on the mouth'. But the *Freeman* claimed that when Mahony spoke of his Protestant co-religionists, he 'means Protestant coercionists' — because 'Protestant nationalists of the county' would vote for Gibney, as they had for Davitt — and the basis of Mahony's appeal to them 'is the pillorying of the priests'.[108] On polling day in North Meath, 'priests were in evidence everywhere, but especially in and around the booths, bringing up the voters', said the

Irish Independent.[109] 'Today Bishop Nulty passed through the streets of Navan to vote against Pierce Mahony. His coachman, all the way from Mullingar, turned up in the town on the same business. His clergy all over the constituency worked with might and main', but the petitions had made them 'more cautious, more insidious'. The *Irish Independent* also noted 'the conservatives abstained . . . under the belief that Gibney as an MP of the Irish clergy would be an unanswerable argument against the granting of Home Rule'.

Mahony, his wife and brother, George toured the centre of the constituency on polling day, starting from Navan and covering about 50 miles by road to Wilkinstown, Nobber, Moynalty, Crossakiel, Kells and back to Navan after dark. There they were greeted by 'groups which gathered on the footways as the horses cantered through the town'. In Navan from early morning the pathways had been patrolled by squads of policemen and the principal streets by parties of mounted police. 'Two persons could hardly halt for a moment without being ordered to move on . . . The Ardbraccan men, who marched into town in a body to vote, were dispersed by the mounted police when they halted for a moment in Market Square to divide the voters for the different booths. Persons who booed were immediately pounced upon . . . Bishop Nulty got a fairly vigorous groaning when he went to vote.' Of the 1,292 voters, 1,046 entered the four booths, where 'Frs McNamee, Cole, Murray and Flynn acted as inside agents for the seceders and there were a large number of clergymen active in the streets, buttonholing voters'. Although over 5,000 out of 6,059 voted in the constituency, the *Freeman* complained that there was minor Parnellite intimidation at polling stations in Moynalty, Oldcastle and Kells, while it implausibly alleged Parnellites 'went to Slane armed with revolvers'.[110] It also claimed that over 500 Tory voters 'were received in all cases by the agents of Mr Mahony and directed where to go'. Police confronted 'a musical band accompanying voters led by Fr Mullen of Moynalty' and baton-charged a crowd throwing stones in Drumconrath.

Mahony defeated again

The *Irish Independent* reported next day that Mahony was defeated by 258 votes, reducing Davitt's majority by up to 150 and adding 231 to his July poll.[111] In a poll of 5,047, over 300 more than in the previous election, Gibney got 2,635 votes and Mahony 2,377 (there were 35 spoiled votes). Gibney was booed as he walked off with eight or ten priests to address a small crowd from the steps of Kells parochial house. A large Parnellite meeting in Market Square was addressed from a window of the town hall by Mahony, who congratulated 'the priests of Meath on their paltry little victory', but said he would rather have at his back 'the 2,377 men than six or seven thousand sheep . . . In the face of all their secret work . . . the independent Catholics of Meath . . . have the remedy in their own hands and I must leave it to them to apply [it] . . . Until you get rid of the politically partisan priest you can never bring . . . [with you] that portion of the population of Ireland which I represent in my religion . . . And you can never set up a government in Ireland . . . [answerable to] a free and independent parliament.'

Dalton declared that the priests had won Meath but lost Home Rule. The Parnellites' blood was up and they would return the clergy to 'their own sphere' by stopping 'the supplies'. They had succeeded by the petitions in ending scandalous 'political harangues' from the pulpit and would now advise people everywhere not to contribute to the support of men who had been 'for the last two years simply ministers of dissension and disunion'. Referring to anti-Parnellites in Oldcastle and Slane especially, Dalton warned 'if they attempt to lay a finger upon any of the scattered men of our party who live in their midst, we will exact satisfaction for it where we are strong'. Manning said 'the priests' horses that ate Parnellite oats were used to bring seceders to the poll'. Mahony read a telegram from John and William Redmond congratulating them on 'a magnificent fight'.

The *Irish Independent* said the clergy had demonstrated 'they *can* dictate to a constituency who will be its member. After carrying Gibney, they could carry anybody.' In Navan, Mahony asked a large meeting in the Square were they going to pay priests money so that a political organisation could work against their temporal interests? He had been guaranteed £500 by one man if it were necessary to upset the election by a petition, but another one might not be worthwhile as the priests had been proven to be incapable of shame and as the next election would take place in a year. He considered that the chances of Home Rule becoming law this year had been obliterated by the Meath elections. Mahony also received a big reception in Dublin, where he went in procession from the Broadstone to the *Independent* offices in College Green, from the windows of which he told a large crowd that the Parnellites had shown that in Meath, as well as in every county of Ireland, there were thousands of independent men ready to face intimidation. 'The present parliament may discuss this Home Rule bill, but they will not be able to pass it . . . The lesson of North and South Meath to the English Liberals [is] that there is in Ireland a party with which they will have to account when the final signing of the treaty of peace takes place . . . The lesson to our fellow-countrymen and my co-religionists [is] that there is deep down in the hearts of their Catholic fellow countrymen a determination that, when the doors of that old house [the former parliament building] are open once more . . . Ireland knows no distinction of class or creed.'

However, the *Drogheda Independent* proclaimed that the petition courts' judgement had been reversed, on appeal, by the people.[112] In both divisions, 'the Tory, Unionist vote was wooed and won' for Mahony and Dalton. The paper, along with the *Freeman,* feebly attempted to show that 'where rowdyism was rampant', illiterate voters plumped for the Parnellites. Meldon, the Navan RM, reported a real case of such irresponsibility to the Castle on 23 February:[113] 'The election at Navan and the meetings held by both parties in the town on Sunday passed off peaceably . . . due entirely to the very large body of police present' (210 infantry and 30 cavalry). But on the previous evening when a meeting of about 1,000 of Mahony's supporters was held in the town,

> Mr Manning . . . I regret to say, made a rash, inflammatory harangue. He . . . defied Mr Morley to prosecute him. He denounced the priests, called on the people to boycott cattle and farm produce sent by the anti-Parnellites from Slane to Navan market, should the people of Slane molest or insult their supporters and, referring to band instruments which were in the possession of the parish priest of Navan, said if he had subscribed sixpence towards the purchase of these instruments he would that night wreck the parochial house to get them. His language was so criminal that did I think it would have met the approval of government I would, after warning the speaker, have declared the meeting illegal and dispersed it. As it was, owing to the excitement created, I deemed it necessary to send twenty police to the priests' house to protect it from injury to the windows.

A Navan police report of 26 February added that Manning referred to Fr Woods seizing Navan Brass Band's instruments 'because its members are Parnellites and were going to play at a Parnellite meeting'. Several of the 'more respectable Parnellites have stated their disapproval' of the speech. The *Freeman* reported that the indignation in Slane and Drumconrath at this speech was largely shared by Navan traders, who were apprehensive that any boycott tactics could divert their trade to Drogheda.[114] It condemned the call for an attack on the parochial house, revealing that Bishop Nulty was there at the time.

The *Freeman's* view of the North Meath result was also that 'the Tory rally for faction failed to accomplish its object' and that three-quarters of illiterate voters throughout the division supported Mahony.[115] It quoted Joe Devlin's estimate of 600 Tory votes against them. All the Parnellites had accomplished by the petitions was the substitution of Gibney and Jordan for Davitt and Fulham 'and the provision of Sir Henry James with material for a vicious anti-Home Rule pamphlet . . . If this is the result in Meath, what may Mr Redmond expect throughout the rest of Ireland?' Reporting bonfires in Oldcastle, Slane and Drumconrath, the *Freeman* added that in Mullingar 'popular enthusiasm was unbounded. The men of Westmeath looked on the battle in the sister county as their own.' A torchlight procession was formed as a bonfire of tar barrels blazed in the grounds of St Mary's College. 'Thousands cheered for Dr Nulty, Home Rule and an Irish parliament. Sheaves of telegrams reached the palace, congratulating Dr Nulty.'

The *Freeman's* parliamentary correspondent reported great rejoicing at the news in Westminster, where the majority Irish Party hoped 'that now at last the curse of dissension will disappear'. Agreeing, John Dillon told the federation in Dublin that if the Tory vote for Mahony was discounted, Gibney's majority would have been at least 700. The *Freeman* also quoted the *Daily Chronicle's* claim that the two Meath elections showed 'that the relative strength of the two Irish parties remains substantially what it was at the general election and that it has not been affected by the noise made over the election petitions.[116] The priests have not increased their electioneering influence and if it be contended that Mr Gibney would not have won without their aid, it is equally clear that large numbers of the Irish Catholic electorate are not amenable to their political guidance. The votes polled', the left-wing paper concluded without any basis, 'show conclusively that the cry of priestly intimidation has been exaggerated'.

But Patrick O'Brien told Culmullen Parnellites that the priests had pitted man against man and perpetuated lasting enmity.[117] Dunboyne Parnellites protested at their priests using the parochial house as a committee and refreshment room for Jordan and displaying flags from the parochial house on the declaration of the poll. They called on the bishop 'for the sake of the Catholic religion' to put a stop to it. The Ulster Unionist Association 'looked on all paper safeguards against misgovernment and clerical domination in the Home Rule bill as wholly illusory and unworkable . . . We protest against this project, which would inevitably result in the establishment of an intolerable religious ascendancy.' Edward Carson, MP for Dublin University (Trinity College), who would become Ulster Unionist leader in 1910, also opposed Home Rule at the United Club in London, saying Ulster 'would prefer separation'.

An anonymous Meath writer to the *Irish Independent* asked 'what claim have Dr Nulty, Fr Hugh Behan, Fr Clarke and the scores of other offensively political priests to be kept in opulent luxury by the honest Parnellites whom they scorn?[118] . . . It is generosity and not duty that has enabled Meath priests to ride hunters worth £150 and to have stock by the half dozen or dozen grazing freely on the land of farmers in their parishes.' One Meath priest's alleged threat to close the parish chapel if such privileges were withdrawn was 'idle', because the Parnellites would appeal to Rome. An anonymous Parnellite also wrote that the tyranny of Meath priests left no option but to diminish their supplies: 'Shut the chapels! Let them do so if they wish. Who will suffer most, Dr Nulty and his priests or the people?'[119]

Agreeing, James Lawlor wrote from Navan on 24 February that such opinions 'are those of thousands in Meath and of every independent Irishman[120] . . . Ever since Dr Nulty two years ago claimed a divine right to prevent the election of some of the largest ratepayers and most representative men in Navan to the position of Poor Law guardianship — and with this object denounced them from the altar and returned their offerings — I have kept my money in my pocket and lately others have followed suit.' It was absurd to continue funding political priests, thus 'pulling a rod to beat ourselves' and enabling 'the election of a bosthoon like Gibney . . . If Mr Dillon had been living in Navan during the last couple of years and if he happened to be politically opposed to the clergy, I wonder how he would describe the election of James Gibney . . . The methods exposed at the petition and which are still used in their well-known quiet and insidious manner by the clergy leave life not worth living in small country towns and villages.'

In Trim, where the building of a new parish church was halted for lack of subscriptions, James Collins, presiding at a meeting to reorganise the League in the town, said dues not paid to the clergy could be put into a fund to defray the costs of the petition.[121] Patrick

Supplement given away with
WEEKLY FREEMAN AND NATIONAL PRESS.   March 4th, 1898 Price Three Halfpence

THE MESSAGE OF ROYAL MEATH.   *See page 4.*

ROYAL MEATH (to the Irish Priest)—"You are no Tyrant."   (To the Nationalist Elector)—"You are no Slave."

Courtesy of the National Library of Ireland

O'Brien said this would be necessary as the priests would leave Fulham in the lurch with the costs of the petition, thereby bankrupting him. He queried paying money to priests who had browbeaten them at parliamentary elections. 'Priests went into the streets with blackthorn sticks and beat the heads of men who were as well bred and as good as themselves, because they were safeguarded by their Roman collars.' It was only when 'the battle was between the Irish people and the foreign garrison that their pastors were within their right in aiding in the struggle by their advice'.

That garrison, represented by members of the Grand Jury in Trim, protested in a resolution against Home Rule, as 'such a revolutionary change must lead to the dismemberment of the empire, injure the credit, trade and commerce and endanger the civil and religious liberty and the rights and property of minorities in Ireland'.[122] At Meath assizes, Mr Justice Johnson said that in the two assault cases arising from 'the excitement of the elections' where clergymen were the accused, 'the law made no distinction'.

Amid repeated references to the clergy denouncing secret societies in Cavan and Longford, the RIC merely noted that some of the canvassers 'imported' by the Parnellites 'seemed to be on very intimate terms with all the leading IRB men' of Meath.[123] The police reported that most Unionists, 'especially of the upper classes', abstained from voting. But many 'Unionist farmers, as at the previous election', voted for the Parnellite candidates. 'The bitterness of party feeling in Meath is almost without parallel, as evidenced by the determination of the Parnellites to punish the priests . . . to such an extent that Mrs Leonard, one of the largest shop-keepers in Trim, turned her brother, who is a priest, out of her house and has since refused to speak to him.' But although Trim town commissioners had decided in February by a majority of three that only half the usual dues should be paid to Fr Behan, 'the PP received within three shillings and sixpence of the full amount'. Kildalkey Parnellites resolved to cease clerical subscriptions, amidst increasing enmity in the Trim district.

RIC Captain Stokes referred to the posting of a boycott notice in Navan in February against Bishop Nulty and his priests and to the shooting of Christopher McNamara, 'an ardent anti-Parnellite', by one of four men, three of them from Belfast, canvassing for Dalton and Mahony.[124] 'The injured man recovered but was unable to identify his assailants', which the report, however, does. 'The hostile feeling against the priests in Meath is much more marked in the towns and villages than through the rural districts.' In March, Stokes reported that the loss by the Parnellites of the fresh Meath elections 'has considerably discouraged their followers in the county', an observation which, as we shall see, would be made by others also in the aftermath of their final defeat.

Chapter 7

Parnellite defeat and political apathy

Pierce Mahony, chairing the League in Dublin at the end of February 1893, said he never expected to win.[1] Not only had the bishop's pastoral not been withdrawn, but Healy in his closing speech at the petition in Trim 'distinctly stated that that was the doctrine of the Catholic church and that those who did not like it might seek refuge with the Protestant rector'. As proof that priests interfered in the second election, he quoted a friend who heard Fr Grehan say from the altar in Oldcastle 'how can a person who votes Parnellite approve of the action on his deathbed? No Catholic . . . can vote for Mahony. I can understand Protestants doing so.' However, Mahony regretted that 'I did not receive the full measure of support from the Protestants of Meath to which I think I was entitled, having regard to the magnificent stand which the independent Catholics of Meath were taking in defence of civil liberty in Ireland'. If Protestants had voted for James Dalton and himself 'in their full strength', they would both have been elected. But a federation meeting in Drogheda, chaired by Fr John Woods, St Mary's, applauded Fulham, who condemned Parnellite intimidation 'and masters bringing voters to the poll to vote for the factionists'.[2]

That intimidation appeared to be condoned when William Mongey was acquitted by a jury at Meath assizes of assaulting Michael Davitt in Navan on 1 June and was discharged.[3] Fr P. Clarke, Kingscourt, was found guilty of assaulting Owen Reilly in Nobber on 14 July, but was given bail. John Coyle, labourer, who pleaded guilty to assault by blackening the face of a voter with paint in Navan on 14 July, was bound to the peace. Twelve Navan people were also bound to the peace for rioting in the town on 14 July, but two of them were imprisoned for a fortnight for assaulting two policemen. Fr Christopher Casey, curate, Dunderry, was acquitted by the jury of seriously assaulting Patrick Byrne, Knockumber, in Navan on 14 July.[4] Meldon and District Inspector Duff acknowledged that the 50 police in the town were insufficient to control the mob on polling day. The *Freeman* said Fr Casey had been pilloried by the *Irish Independent* and *Herald* as the perpetrator of the first act of violence in Navan that day and the provoker of the subsequent disorder.[5] But he had been shown to have 'simply intervened, at imminent danger to himself, to prevent an old man and his son from being beaten away from the poll by the Mahonyite mob'. The solitary policeman present 'threatened Fr Casey with arrest for doing what the judge virtually declared he was bound in law to do'. Inadequate policing was due to the benevolence of the then Tory executive towards Parnellism.

Bishop Nulty immediately began his carefully prepared apologia in a series of public utterances discrediting the petitions. Having himself presented with an address in Kells, where he was driven over from Navan for the profession of two Mercy nuns, he said it consoled him after his character had been assailed 'when I could not possibly defend myself[6] . . . That opportunity was not allowed me in South Meath. On a technicality, I was excluded.' The petitions had cast a cloud on his name, but his countrymen had vindicated him by returning candidates pledged to the same policy as those they had elected before 'and they cannot say that I interfered in this election in any way'. He especially thanked 'the electorate of Kells', who had the considerable difficulty of 'living amongst a large Protestant population on terms of harmony . . . But nevertheless you came like men to the poll.' When Parnell was jailed,

> I assailed Mr Gladstone in . . . a letter which pleased Mr Parnell very much. It also put me for a time in danger. They did not arrest me, but if they did I would willingly have gone to jail . . . old as I am . . . It fills my heart with grief to find that dissension prevails in Co. Meath. I don't find it anywhere else . . . I, as a Bishop, look on division in my people as a great evil . . . Who can tell the bitter hatreds and animosities that it has produced? A people who loved each other are now estranged and, instead of charity and love, there have sprung up feelings of estrangement and hatred. The vice of drunkenness has increased and the links of love that bound priests and people together are to a certain extent broken . . . But this [Home Rule] bill of Gladstone's, I have great hope, will re-unite our people . . . please God . . . Parnellite and anti-Parnellite . . . I know that their feelings are strong. Let you therefore treat them with

toleration, moderation and forbearance. We are not here to crow over them or to glory in our triumph. We are quite satisfied that we have won. If it were otherwise, they perhaps would not treat us with the same amount of forebearance . . . [but] we owe it to our dignity and self-respect.

Describing this speech as 'remarkable', the *Irish Independent* said it betrayed uneasiness.[7]

> The Bishop has won at the elections, but the cost . . . fills him with grief . . . What a pity that Dr Nulty did not think of all this sooner . . . in July last, when he wrote his famous pastoral . . . when he urged his clergy to take sides . . . [He] does not realise his own responsibility . . . for the very evils which he now laments, but . . . others do . . . As the independent nationalists of Meath have fought for freedom of opinion and action in politics by the Catholic laity, they cannot make peace or reunite with those who would deny that freedom . . . If Dr Nulty in Kells withdrew his pastoral of July, if he expressed regret for the action of his priests . . . and if he told the people that they were . . . bound to act in political matters in accordance only with their conscience, he would have more correctly apprehended the nature of the situation he chiefly has created.

Patrick O'Brien, speaking on behalf of the League in Dublin at different meetings in Meath, wondered why Dr Nulty 'waited so long to express his regret . . . until they secured the return of his political puppets, Messrs Jordan and Gibney'.[8] On a letter from Fr J. Drum, Bishop Nulty's administrator in Mullingar, to a local guardian saying 'they' would get a candidate to oppose him if he did not stop voting for 'faction', the *Irish Independent* wondered whether Dr Nulty 'considers this letter . . . consistent with the profession of a desire for peace and harmony within his diocese'.[9] In Trim, where he had driven over from Navan for the profession of three Mercy nuns, Bishop Nulty was presented with another address 'in the parochial house by a number of the inhabitants' of the town.[10] He demurred 'I really do not covet these honours, but I cannot of course prevent my people from expressing their confidence and affection for me even still'. It was 45 years since he arrived in Trim as a curate, at a dreadful time of famine and fever: 'The very stones of Trim ought to know my footsteps.' He therefore deplored his estrangement from the people of Trim, but that was not his fault.

Rather, it arose from 'this dreadful fever of Parnellism' which had 'created a schism among my flock here' and 'disunion between the pastor and the people, that fills my heart with sorrow'. Parnellism, which hardly existed outside Co. Meath, had 'led to crime, drunkenness, impurity and disloyalty to the clergy. We had to defend ourselves against this movement and if it were a question of politics alone I would never oppose my people . . . but . . . it is a question of religion as well', although the Parnellites would not agree that it was. However, as 'the accredited pastor sent by God Almighty to the people in this diocese', who had addressed the Vatican Council and studied theology for 54 years, he

> would be a traitor to my religion if I entered into any compromise. They opposed us and we beat them and we will beat them again and again. They gained a temporary triumph over us at the petition inquiries, but their triumph was soon converted into defeat and as we beat them then we will go on beating them forever, as long as they challenge the people's verdict. I am confident that at every new election we will show ourselves growing stronger, for the people will see the justice of our cause and how grievously they have been misled and they will rally round their country and the Church . . . I do not want to say any unkind word of any of these men, many of whom I recognise as my friends of long ago, but I am afraid there is no use in trying to conciliate them . . . Still, there is generosity in the heart of the most mistaken and obdurate Irishman and we cannot tell what time may produce.

Referring to the halt in building a new parish church in Trim, Bishop Nulty said people outside the parish would not contribute to it while they saw the people of the town refusing to do so, but donating their money instead to uphold Parnellism. Those in Trim who considered themselves 'enlightened' were at odds with the majority in the country, but 'they are not all gone wrong in Trim . . . I thank the electors for my vindication. My reputation, not only in the Diocese of Meath but all over the British Empire, was at stake.'

Patrick O'Brien told Boardsmill Parnellites that they would accept Bishop Nulty's challenge to beat them again and again.[11] Regretting that the bishop and his priests were 'again declaring war against the best men in the county', he repeated his call 'to stop supplies'. Their conduct 'has done more to defeat Home Rule than all the bluster and drumming

of the Ulster Orangemen'. Yet the bishop was the only man who could
not or would not see the 'harm done by himself and on his orders in
glorying by anticipation in conquests to come'. O'Brien also told
Castlejordan branch 'to stop supplies'.[12] They were not bound to pay, as
Healy had said in the Cork election of 1880, 'the celebrants of the altar
for acting as touts in the Whig polling booths', or for hurling abuse at
one half of their congregation. When over 400 priests attended the
Home Rule convention in Dublin, who was attending to the spiritual
wants of their respective flocks?

Nicholas Dowd, chairing the Dangan and Summerhill League, said
they needed to be organised to protect themselves from the annoyance
to which they were daily subjected by their Whig neighbours. They
could hardly attend mass without having insults directed at them from
their altar.[13] Patrick O'Brien said Fr Fay should 'retire from public gaze'
and advised Parnellites 'to attack Fr Fay's disease through his breeches
pocket'. But the *Drogheda Independent* said these Parnellite appeals 'will
be abhorrent to every Catholic instinct[14] . . . The party that has stooped
to this anti-Catholic and anti-Irish cry must lose the support of the
Catholics of Meath who may have hitherto stood by it . . . for now the
mask is off.'

Navan Parnellites defeated again

The paper reported that there were ten candidates for five seats in
Navan Poor Law elections, five each nominated by Bishop Nulty and
the Parnellites.[15] The bishop nominated Francis Sheridan,
Cannicetown; M. Kelly, Market Square, and P. Casey, Alexanderaide,
who were sitting guardians, along with James Curran, Donaghmore,
and W. Curry, senior, Bridge Street, as P. Keogan had resigned and M.
Lightholder did not seek re-election. The Parnellites nominated
William Lawlor, Trimgate Street; James Everard, Market Square; Patrick
Blake, Athlumney; Michael Denning, Flower Hill, and John Spicer,
Blackwater House, 'whether with the object of harassing the venerable
Bishop in the declining years of his life or of keeping the ball of
disunion rolling still longer[16] . . . The Poor Law contest in Navan . . .
has more than a political significance and the issues . . . are more
important than those decided at the recent parliamentary conflict.'

The *Drogheda Independent* then rehearsed previous years' arguments
about Bishop Nulty's 'duty' to nominate 'men of thoroughly Catholic
instinct' to 'guide the religious and temporal interests of the poor'. Why
would the electors of Navan defy 'common sense and the wishes of the

poor people themselves', as well as their priests' 'disinterested efforts' in order to elect Parnellites? The bishop could not be accused of political motivation, as two years previously he had 'nominated all the outgoing guardians, regardless of their political opinions, but in spite of his kindly efforts in the interests of peace, a contest was forced . . . and one of his nominees was excluded from the board'. The controversy could have ended there had not some of the Catholic guardians betrayed the best interests of the poor. 'There was witnessed the spectacle — strange in Catholic Ireland — of a few Catholic guardians vieing with the ex-officios [landlords] . . . to exclude the sisters from the workhouse.' These 'betrayers' would again receive landlord support and 'the election of a sister of Mercy may take place at any moment again', so Navan voters should 'never again return . . . men who could be even suspected of joining in a repetition of the unholy alliance'.

In the election, the Parnellite five lost to Bishop Nulty's five nominees, although there was a difference of only 450 votes in the totals of each side: Kelly 461, Sheridan 460, Casey 421, Curry 415 and Curran 409 (elected); Spicer 361, Lawlor 350, Denning 341, Everard and Blake 332 each.[17] Spicer told the League in Dublin that Bishop Nulty was in the habit of claiming divine right and that it was binding on the consciences of his people to elect the men he nominated. But the Parnellites had improved their position and next year he thought they would be elected. Spicer's hope was inspired by the election in Ardbraccan, just outside Navan, of three Parnellites — P. Wall (189), J. Collins (199) and J. Nally (198), who defeated sitting guardians, M. and W. Buchanan (143 and 137) and another anti-Parnellite, W. Martin (136).[18] This may indicate what the result could have been in Navan in the absence of the issue of the nun. But the *Drogheda Independent* put the Ardbraccan victory down to unspecified 'terrorism of mob force and open intimidation' and said the Navan Parnellites 'got such a beating that they are not likely to try a contest again'.

Discounting Spicer's prophecy of the Parnellites winning the following year, as 'in the full blaze of the petition revelations', they 'received an even greater smash' than in the previous year, the paper condemned his 'attempt to sneer . . . at the "claims to divine right" of his Bishop'. Spicer denied sneering at Dr Nulty.[19] At the Dublin meeting, 'I wished to explain a fact not generally known outside Navan, that the clergy do not contest the Poor Law elections here on political grounds but are carrying out the instructions of the bishop, who claims the sole right of appointing guardians. Accordingly the priests canvass the ratepayers, but no sooner are their men elected than the result is hailed as a political victory.' Thus, ratepayers who had to support 'the monstrous system of Poor Law relief' had hardly any control over the expenditure. 'Speaking for myself . . . politics should be excluded from all public boards.' Bishop Nulty demonstrated his use of power on being re-elected chairman of Navan dispensary committee.[20] Warning of cholera from impure water, he criticised the town commissioners for making themselves the sanitary authority, instead of the guardians. The committee agreed to his suggestion that Fr Dooley, president of St Finian's, be their secretary, but found they had no power to pay him, as Bishop Nulty wanted.

Bishop Nulty's defence of his pastoral

'I must ever regard the North and South Meath election petitions as two of the most unpleasant and . . . painful incidents in my whole life', wrote the bishop at the end of March 1893, when he published the brief for his petition counsel as a defence of his pastoral and a reply to Mr Justice O'Brien's judgement.[21] He rejected Parnellite counsel's 'coarse and stupid accusation' that he had said from the altar at Trim that 'all women with Parnellite sympathies are bad women'. This was 'not only a palpable falsehood but a malignant and offensive imputation on the character of hundreds of innocent women who, whatever may have been their other infirmities, were undeniably chaste and virtuous'. He bore testimony to their virtue in his pastoral, which stated: 'It is sad and humiliating to see upright, patriotic, chaste, virtuous Irishwomen striving for the ascendancy of Parnellism and thus doing their very utmost to demolish the "great break-water" which God and nature had raised up to protect Christian society from being submerged by the deluge of adultery and crime with which the unbridled, licentious passions of wicked men and of shameless, abandoned women threaten to overwhelm it.'

Having been subpoenaed by the Parnellites as a witness,

> I did not go into the box because they refused to invite me there. That single manoeuvre . . . robbed me of the right of defending my pastoral and . . . vindicating my character . . . Silently submitting to the foul calumnies and venomous slanders that were circulated against my clergy and myself for fully three months and more is an awfully cruel punishment . . . A Bishop . . . comes as an envoy and a master from Heaven,

commissioned by God to instruct men in the knowledge of the incontestable evangelical truths which their eternal salvation requires . . . To discredit the magisterial authority of the Bishops . . . to bring their sacred character and dignity into popular contempt and destroy the reverence and obedience due to their teaching was the unenviable task to which Parnellism had to address itself . . . Its orators, agents and adherents operated through a splendidly equipped and disciplined organisation, backed up by terrorism of the most tyrannical system of intimidation ever tolerated in any civilised country.

Notably omitting the 'secret societies' excuse used at the petitions, Bishop Nulty colourfully characterised the Parnellites' odious intimidation as being revealed at its fiercest

in the sanguinary ferocity of the Parnellite mobs of Navan and Trim during the elections. These mobs would have certainly murdered Messrs Davitt and Fulham if they could only lay their hands on them. It is mainly through the aid of this execrable force that Parnellism has partially succeeded in extracting from a cowed and terrified section of the public the contributions that are required to meet the expenses of these vexatious election petitions . . . I saw multitudes of 'Red Republicans' in Paris and large Freemason mobs in Rome and I saw and heard of the hatreds and anti-clerical antipathies of the Orange rowdies of Belfast. But I never saw anything that could equal the fierce anti-clerical hatred of the mobs of Meath and especially of the Parnellite mob of Navan. That mob, on polling day, was estimated at fully 1,200 men. It paraded and marched through the streets to the fierce cry of 'to hell with the priests and the peelers'. And yet, these poor misguided men were not ferocious, anti-clerical savages by nature. As a matter of fact, they were the very reverse, till Parnellism had corrupted and depraved them.

Since the publication of the decree of the hierarchy, condemning Parnell for his 'public misconduct' and his 'agents' for their 'open hostility to ecclesiastical authority', he had repeatedly warned his flock against Parnellism 'as being the most aggressive, insidious and dangerous popular movement that appeared in this country within the present century'. The bishop said his pastoral was written without the assistance or knowledge of anyone, least of all of the anti-Parnellite candidates, in whose selection he said he took no part — even though he publicly nominated Davitt, who later made clear, as we shall see, that the bishop and priests asked him to stand; and it is hard to imagine Bishop Nulty being uninvolved in selecting Gibney. He continued:

> I dreaded the Parnellism of a great part of Westmeath and of many parts of King's County . . . I saw vast numbers of my flock swept into what seemed a whirlpool of general apostasy, where many actually lost their faith . . . The judgement of Mr Justice O'Brien . . . pained and grievously disappointed me . . . He exhibits my priests and myself to the whole British Empire as a band of ignorant, blustering and intolerant spiritual bullies who ride rough-shod over the rights, liberties and feelings of our people and who inspire them with a superstitious terror which intimidates them and restricts their liberty in the exercise of the franchise . . . Has a man, because he happens to be a judge, a right of saying of everybody whatever comes into his head? . . . I knew many of [the Parnellite witnesses] personally, I knew them all by repute. Some of them were admittedly regarded as the 'black sheep' of their flocks. A priest who did his duty conscientiously could not live on peaceable and friendly terms with them. They took no pains whatever to conceal the passionate and spiteful feelings which they cherished for the priests against whom they swore . . . One cannot fail to be struck with the manifest discrepancy between the evidence itself and the exaggerated and inaccurate account given of it in the judge's charge . . . The Parnellite witnesses, to a man, scoffed at the idea of being influenced by spiritual intimidation to cast their votes for anyone but the candidate of their own free choice. The anti-Parnellites did exactly the same.

In a footnote, Bishop Nulty wrote that the outcome of the two new elections, where there was no clerical intervention and where two 'weaker' candidates polled about 600 votes more than the stronger ones at the former election 'proves that there was no real spiritual intimidation . . . and therefore that the findings of these two election petitions are all wholly erroneous'. Regarding evidence of alleged canvassing of votes in the confessional, the bishop asked 'what priest can be safe and what priest will be bound to hear the confessions of men who claim the right of revealing in open court the inmost secrets of the sacred tribunal? . . . Every intelligent priest will banish such men from his confessional as spies and hypocrites . . . If Mr Justice O'Brien teaches us law, we will listen with respect, but the reckless audacity with which he presumes to teach us false and immoral theology are simply sickening.' Quoting the Fitzgerald judgement in the Longford petition of 1870, the bishop said that his pastoral 'did not point out expressly the moral duties that bound Catholic electors to vote against Parnellite candidates, it merely insinuated them and left them to be inferred by the unanswerable arguments with which I discredited Parnellism itself'. He had never said that the culpability of not voting for the anti-Parnellite 'would rise to the degree of moral turpitude and guilt that are implied in real, formal sin'. The pastoral 'merely insinuates "the moral duties" by which I proved that Catholic and Christian electors are undoubtedly bound to cast their votes for the suppression of Parnellism'. It was the judge's duty to point out the passage, paragraph, argument, context or feature of the letter in which the illegality lay. 'Until he does so, I cannot persuade myself to believe him.'

Bishop denies slur on Parnellite women

Referring again to criticism of his failure to give evidence at the petitions, Bishop Nulty reverted to a former reason: 'Because a man of my years, of my rank and standing before my countrymen, did not . . . go "into the box" to contradict on my oath a motley parade of witnesses, including our street scavengers, all just then in a high fever of political excitement and of partisan passion, ergo I am guilty of all the crimes that these poor misguided men accused me of.' Again denying attacking Parnellite women, the bishop said that Mr Justice O'Brien credited him with writing with 'great power of expression, moral dignity and severity', but he would prefer to be credited by the judge with 'writing with just as much common sense as would save me from the stupid and thick-witted folly of holding up Parnellite women to the whole world as patterns of virtue and chastity and of stigmatising them, in the same breath, as deplorable samples of vice, sensuality and sin'.

Withdrawing and apologising for any unconscious or inadvertent expression of personal disrespect to Mr Justice O'Brien, Bishop Nulty added that he understood that the other judge, Mr Justice Andrews, was a Unitarian and 'a man who denies the divinity of Our Lord is as incompetent to form clear, correct and reliable conceptions of the feelings, instincts, opinions and religious convictions of an intensely Catholic population as if they were the inhabitants of another planet', so he decided that my 'pastoral alone was sufficient to render the election void'. If Parnell's followers only acknowledged that a Catholic nation could not be led by a man who was guilty of his crimes, 'there would be no difference at all between us, as our political principles are identically the same'.

The Parnellite response came in the *Irish Independent*:[22] Bishop Nulty's apology to those he had vilified 'is tardily made . . . He might as well have left it unexpressed.' Parnellism did not create the petitions; his pastoral and the acts and words of his clergy forced Meath Parnellites to protest in the only available way against an intolerable tyranny. To talk of Davitt and Fulham as having been elected by free votes 'is trifling with the intelligence of the public'. Mr Justice O'Brien, a fervent Catholic, was pained and horrified by the evidence of intimidation and by the pastoral. The bishop's explanation for his attack on Parnellite women 'aggravates the original offence. It is worse, surely . . . to let loose a deluge of crime upon society than to be guilty of a personal act in violation of the moral law.' This

> portion of the pastoral . . . conveyed only one meaning . . . The Bishop admits that he knew what interpretation was put upon the pastoral; he complains bitterly that he was misunderstood and misrepresented. He pathetically invites commiseration for having borne the injustice in patience and silence so long.
>
> The proper time for a withdrawal, defence or explanation of the pastoral was *before* the last elections in North and South Meath. Now that Messrs Jordan and Gibney are members for the county, Dr Nulty claims credit for the patience and fortitude, under suffering, which enabled him to abstain from apologising . . . It was open to his lordship to go into the box on behalf of Mr Fulham or Mr Davitt . . . He could then be cross-examined and if counsel for the petitioners shirked cross-examining him the moral effect would be tremendous. And now we put one straight question to his lordship: Did the counsel for the defence strenuously and emphatically declare against his presenting himself as a witness? . . . If he had any explanation to make, the place to make it from was the witness box, where he could be cross-examined, and the time was the first opportunity which presented itself after he had ascertained that his allusions to Parnellite women and to 'the dying Parnellite' had been

misunderstood. A belated defence in the form of two pamphlets serves no purpose. It will deceive nobody. It will not even placate the independent men of the Diocese of Meath who have recently taken action which cannot be misinterpreted . . . to convince his lordship and the political clergymen of the county that they have gone too far . . . Dr Nulty entertains some singular ideas as to the rights, privileges and duties of a Bishop in relation to the political affairs of the country. His pastoral was, to say the least, a terrible mistake; his defence of it is a blunder.

Patrick O'Brien would later maintain that the bishop's pamphlets 'were intended for foreign — possibly Roman — consumption'.[23] But the *Freeman* claimed that Bishop Nulty had merely waited until the excitement of the Meath elections had passed before vindicating himself and his priests.[24] His pamphlets would have sympathetic readers: 'If some of the Catholics of Meath have forgotten the services of a self-sacrificing life, Ireland is not so ungrateful.' The *Drogheda Independent* noted contradictorily that Dr Nulty, 'for months past the target of every factionist, from the drummed out member for North Meath . . . Mahony, down to town clerk Lawlor and street scavenger Clarke of Navan, has at length broken his long and self-imposed silence'.[25] If it was no offence for the Protestant Bishops of Cork and Derry publicly to protest against Home Rule, it could hardly be one for the Catholic Bishop of Meath to support it. The paper later reported that Fr W.P. Kearney, Mullingar, presided at the annual meeting of *Drogheda Independent* shareholders.[26] Meanwhile, at Navan court, John Whyte, who had pleaded guilty to rioting at the elections, was summonsed for being drunk outside the parochial house, calling out 'to hell with Dr Nulty'.[27] Sentenced to a month in jail, the defendant, who was on a crutch, pleaded 'no fine?' Meldon: 'No, the rowdies of this town will not be let off with fines.'

It is remarkable that the only allegation that Bishop Nulty chose to deny was his slur on Parnellite women in Trim. Supporting his denial was John J. Gilsenan, River Bank, Trim, who wrote to the *Irish Independent* with an affidavit denying a statement by Joseph Moore and a declaration 'purporting to be signed by 13 residents of Trim' which confirmed that they had heard the bishop's sermon in Trim, deposed to by James Collins at the petition, which had characterised Parnellite women as worse than abandoned women.[28] Gilsenan pointed out that Vincent Sheridan, a correspondent for the *Leinster Leader*, who told the petition he took notes of everything said about Parnellism at both masses that day, could not corroborate Collins's evidence. But Sheridan did recall Bishop Nulty saying that a crowd of drunken rowdies and abandoned women in Navan had assailed Davitt: this was what must have confused Collins. 'I was . . . at both masses and I am quite positive that his lordship never used the observation charged against him.' It would appear from this that the bishop may have placed the abandoned women, not in Trim, but in Navan.

In mid-May 1893, the *Irish Independent* reported that Fr Lynch, PP, Donaghmore, near Ashbourne, tore down a Parnellite poster at his chapel and denounced Parnellism yet again, some of his bullocks having been returned by parishioners.[29] Fr Everard, the new parish priest of Ratoath and Ashbourne, replacing the late, non-political Fr Fulham, asked his parishioners as a personal favour not to attend a League meeting organised by Patrick O'Brien, but they ignored his request. On a visit to Fr Fay's parish of Summerhill in late May, Bishop Nulty repeated that Parnellism was an uprising against the authority of the priests and bishops, of whom he was one of the first who had the courage to denounce 'landlord tyranny and oppression'.[30] (Fr Fay next came to prominence in April 1897, when he was ordered by a jury to pay £75 compensation to Patrick Tully, aged 23, from Enfield, whom he had beaten on the head with a shepherd's crook the previous December.)[31] But after Confirmation in Fr Casey's parish of Dunderry in June, the bishop prayed for his people to be re-united, saying anyone who hated a neighbour that differed from him was in a state of perdition and if they died in that state they would be 'lost for all eternity'.[32] However, after Confirmation in Fulham's parish of Donore in July, Dr Nulty said their worst enemies were those who 'created a schism in our ranks', blaming only the Parnellites, who 'invoked the assistance of the law against the registered opinions of the people', which, he blandly asserted, were 'given at an election as fairly and as justly conducted as ever an election was'.[33]

Patrick O'Brien's response to Bishop Nulty's various statements was that the bishop was not prevented from speaking at the petitions by the Parnellites, who would have liked to see him cross-examined on the theology of the pastoral and whether he told Healy after the divorce verdict that the Irish people should stand by Parnell, Healy conveniently being in court as his counsel.[34] He would also have been asked about sanctioning the presence of about a hundred of his priests at conventions in Navan, Tullamore and other places in support of

Parnell in the weeks after the divorce and whether he fought hard to defend Parnell at the meeting of bishops in Dublin, as he told a priest when he returned to Mullingar, regretting that 'a majority of the bishops decided against him'. He could thus explain at what point the Parnellism he espoused became sinful. The bishop was as free as any of his priests to go into the witness box but, after the exhibition some of them made of themselves, he took 'the urgent advice of the Bantry bar [Healy] . . . by bolting out of court'. Bishop Nulty had fiercely attacked the Parnellites but said his priests would do their duty by attending a dying Parnellite, just as they would a Protestant if asked — thereby implying that both were synonymous, despite the financial support of the former. 'If butchers, bakers and drapers are to be boycotted because they are Parnellites in Trim and elsewhere, it cannot be right [for priests] to take their money.'

At the end of June, Trim guardians voted 12 to 4 not to increase the Catholic chaplain's salary from £60 to £70 a year, as his work was reduced when the children were moved to the industrial school.[35] And Trim Parnellites, announcing a contribution of £40 to the Parnellite fund, rejected the parting allegation of Fr Behan that they had not paid their dues. They resented him calling them 'corner boys and porter swillers'. If he had not adopted such an attitude, his mission there would have been a success. Patrick O'Brien said the priests of Meath did not want the unity for which Cardinal Logue had recently appealed. Fr Behan had left Trim because 'Whiggery' could not exist there. A month later, Trim guardians protested at the LGB's reversal of their decision not to increase the chaplain's salary, following which Fr Callery had refused to say mass in the workhouse.[36]

Davitt's and Fulham's bankruptcy

Michael Davitt, faced with bankruptcy proceedings by Pierce Mahony in March for not paying the £1,900 costs of the North Meath petition, refused offers of help and said he would sell his possessions to pay them himself.[37] But he was quickly adjudged a bankrupt, which would result in his losing the Cork North East seat which Justin McCarthy had persuaded him to take because 'your counsel would be so valuable on a hundred questions connected with the Home Rule bill'.[38] The party chairman had also advised him 'your being left to meet the costs of the North Meath election would be . . . a disgrace to Ireland'. Davitt's diary for 1893 reveals how his clerical and party friends deserted him, not altogether surprisingly in view of his repudiation of the bishop and priests of Meath in his *Nineteenth Century* article:[39]

30 Mar — 'Bill of costs re the petition! *Only* £1,870!! Mahony's solicitor asks for this trifle by return of post . . . Pity it could not be sent by telegraph . . . Those whose battle I was asked to fight in Meath will now leave me to pay the Parnellite piper. Well, so be it. The bankruptcy court will be my next experience of reward in Irish politics.' Meath even impinged on Davitt's biggest occasion in the Commons:

11 April — 'Just before rising got wire from Mrs D intimating that Pierce Mahony's bailiffs had not yet put in an appearance! Not very inspiriting frame of mind in which to make a maiden speech.'

29 April — 'Mahony and co. say, I am told, that they don't wish to drive me to resignation — they only want certain sum of money to settle my own and Fulham's costs. They think Irish Party will pay in order to save me from bankruptcy court. We shall see.'

6 May — 'Mahony's solicitor applied for final order to adjudicate me a bankrupt . . . Resolved these lads shall have no more spoil for factions than they can screw out of *me*.'

8 May — 'Wire from wife that receiver for bankruptcy court had come to cottage. Ah! Well . . . malignity itself, if substituted for Mahony, would have stopped short of this . . . Let them do their worst. Multitude . . . begging me not to resign. My course is clear . . . Pay or resign. There is no medium course. I cannot pay in full, therefore I must resign. Offers of friends to pay for me out of question. Mahony shall get all I can give him. That and nothing more. If it was personal ends or needs, case would be totally different. The money is wanted by himself and friends in order to keep up the faction fight in Ireland. They shall not get it, through me at any rate.'

18 May — 'Dillon . . . accused me of having resigned without considering interests [of] party or cause.'

27 June — 'Wonder will party or priests offer to refund me what I have lost in this business? 'Spose not. £1,000 worth of property gone.'

29 June — 'Official assignee hauled off my books today. I feel as if my best friends were taken from me . . . Having failed to steal my wife's furniture and my children's home, they have

succeeded in making off with my little library. Ah well, it is only like the rest of my bitter experience of Irish politics. These books cost me about £70. The other property that has had to be surrendered in this miserable business is value for about £350. The Bishop of Meath and his priests cost me over £1,000, as well as all the mental worry of the petition, bankruptcy, etc. Have not one line from any of them expressing regret or sympathy.'

In fairness to Bishop Nulty, he probably felt that his clergy had done enough by raising funds during Davitt's election campaign — and he could hardly devote diocesan money to paying Mahony's expenses. Naturally, the Parnellites viewed it differently. John Redmond and Tim Harrington accused Davitt of 'a desire for cheap martyrdom, which will deceive nobody'. His party 'have ample means to pay, if they wish to do so'.[40] Denying claims that Redmond and Harrington in fact disapproved of making Davitt pay the costs of the petition, the *Irish Independent* contended that if Davitt had won it, he would have confiscated Mahony's £1,000 security deposit to pay his costs and pursued Mahony for the balance. His language and conduct during the election campaign forfeited any sympathy for him. If Davitt was so valuable to his party, as they frequently stated, why did they not pay up? Partly to punish Mahony, it answered.[41]

Christopher Friery, Mahony's solicitor in the petition, wrote to the paper refuting the 'calumnies' of Davitt's friends that costs were aggravated deliberately.[42] Davitt's counsel had given no indication of abandoning their defence until the court was in session, leaving Friery with no option but to prepare his case fully. Mahony's counsel were ready to accept the decision in the South Meath case, but the judges would not allow this. Davitt's counsel then insisted on cross-examining witnesses. Instead of him paying an honest debt to a Parnellite, his friends claimed sympathy for him becoming a bankrupt.

When Fulham's effects were sold by a bailiff for a nominal sum towards paying the £1,850 claimed by Dalton, the unseated MP said the Parnellites thought he would be weak enough to allow an appeal to the country to pay the costs. But he would go to the workhouse with his wife and nine children before he would allow a penny to be subscribed to sustain faction.[43] Patrick O'Brien maintained, however, that Davitt and Fulham had been left bankrupt by their lords and masters, Dr Nulty and his Whig priests. Even shame had not induced the bishop to appeal to his priests to part with 'a few fat bullocks from their large herds' to save the ex-MPs from bankruptcy. Having served his lordship, they were blunted and used up tools. What did the bishops and priests think of Davitt not allowing his friends to pay his lawful debts? O'Brien asked. How did this fit in with the Ten Commandments?

A 'Meath Parnellite' wrote to the *Irish Independent* that Bishop Nulty and his clergy were morally if not legally responsible for the costs of the petitions 'and out of their pocket the money should come, indirectly if not directly . . . If the men of Meath allow themselves to be swindled out of these law costs . . . they should be left to the tender mercies of Dr Nulty and his browbeating political clergy'.[44] Telling a meeting in Trim that if it was a sin to be a Parnellite it was a sin for priests to share Parnellite money, Patrick O'Brien said he did not wish to see Fulham's children paying the price of their father's folly, but it was a disgrace to Bishop Nulty that Davitt and Fulham were subjected to bankruptcy because of their non-payment of the costs of the petitions. The Parnellites were now forced to pay the bishop's debts and should stop the money out of their church contributions.[45]

In the bankruptcy court in October, Judge Boyd refused to certify that Davitt was not responsible for his bankruptcy and for the non-payment of 10 shillings in the £.[46] He was 'the selected candidate of the clergy' and had benefited from Bishop Nulty's pastoral, which 'had been condemned by four judges', who 'could not have come to any other conclusion', as it was a 'shocking piece of intimidation'. Davitt had told Fr McNamee that he did not want it published, but when it was, 'Davitt did not withdraw but went on . . . with his eyes open . . . into the contest . . . subsequently relying on it; and those associated with him . . . made use of it to the utmost'. Davitt's personal expenses had all been paid, but those of 'the gentleman who had the misfortune to unseat him' had not. Consequently, Mahony had proceedings against him in bankruptcy. He (judge) did not think that any gentleman who aspired to represent a constituency and was not able to pay 10 shillings in the £ had a right to put his opponent to expense which he could not meet if he were defeated. Davitt need not have aspired to be member for North Meath. He had indulged in a speculation and the result was that he had to pay over £1,800 and his answer was 'I have not a farthing to pay, parliament does not require me to be a wealthy man.'

On 31 December 1893, Davitt confided in his diary:[47] 'I end this year in indifferent health and under a load of debt. To the Irish cause it has been a memorable year in the passage through the British House of Commons of the Home Rule bill. To me it has been a year of singular misfortune. I began it with the judgement of the Meath petition . . . end it with the position of a bankruptcy . . . Neither the priests or people of Meath who got me into this mess have offered to pay me one cent of this money which I have lost in this business. Being as always in money matters a damned fool I have been left in the lurch with my foolishness this time also.' Davitt estimated the cost to him of the bankruptcy at £1,018–10–0. However, the appeal court in February 1894 reversed the bankruptcy court's decision and discharged Davitt from bankruptcy.[48] Navan guardians congratulated him, recalling 'how he had been deprived of his seat, which he had won fairly, honestly, having been struck down by the hand of a dastard in Navan'.[49]

Redmond cautiously defends Irish democracy

The unionist polemicist, Philip H. Bagenal, maintained in his 1893 book, *The Priest in Politics*, that the fresh elections in Meath showed that John Redmond's independent party could not be relied on by Protestants to withstand the 'tremendous forces' of 'priestly intolerance'.[50] John Redmond's response to such contentions was noticeably guarded as the parliamentary debate continued on the Home Rule bill. Again addressing British public opinion, this time in the *Pall Mall Gazette,* he conceded that the church was 'under certain conditions, omnipotent in Irish politics', but the spirit of independence was spreading, so that there need be no fear of a future Irish parliament 'being for any long period dominated by clerical influence'.[51] Parnell's movement, the Land League and the plan of campaign had all been initially opposed by the clergy but, being supported by the people, they were ultimately successful. There were three reasons for the clergy's success in the split: they were not opposing Home Rule, they were not opposing a majority of the Irish Party and they could maintain that a religious and not a political issue was involved, as Bishop Nulty repeatedly stated. Yet in the boroughs, politically advanced voters polled three to two for Parnellites in the general election and over 70,000 Catholic votes were given for Parnellites in the whole country, despite the active opposition of the bishops and priests, while Dublin was solidly Parnellite.

Such favourable conditions for the clergy would not arise again, wrote Redmond. The days of 'wholesale clerical intimidation' in Irish politics were numbered and in an Irish parliament political freedom would be 'speedily established and jealously guarded'. Highlighting the absence of sectarian bigotry in the conflict by pointing to each side in the recent Meath elections running both a Protestant and a Catholic candidate, Redmond stressed that the influence of priests in Irish politics was 'rapidly waning', the contest of the previous two years having injured their political prestige 'almost beyond recovery'. Within five years the new Irish parliament would be free of improper clerical influence. In a subsequent interview with the *Freeman*, Redmond not unreasonably argued that if the general election had been by proportional representation there would be far more Parnellite MPs. But he conceded 'I believe that the first Irish parliament will be elected by the priests.'[52]

So fierce was the opposition in the Commons to the Home Rule bill, particularly from the Ulster Unionists, that the government had to pre-empt further debate in order to force it through by September. Clerical influence on Irish politics continued to be a theme of the bill's opponents. During its second reading, for instance, David Robert Plunket, Conservative member for Dublin University and a former solicitor-general for Ireland, said members of an Irish parliament 'would generally be small tenant farmers who are almost entirely under the influence of the Catholic church'.[53] But Joseph Albert Pease, Liberal Home Rule member for Tyneside and private secretary to John Morley as Irish secretary, maintained that Home Rule would be the greatest security against the domination of the priesthood. Michael Davitt, in his maiden speech, asserted that the Protestants of Ireland had nothing to fear from their Catholic fellow-subjects.[54] But T.W. Russell said he had no respect for any church that sought to put political pressure upon the consciences of men. Edmund Francis Vesey Knox, the Oxford-educated barrister and anti-Parnellite member for Cavan West, expressed confidence in the just and generous liberality of Irish Catholics towards their Protestant fellow-countrymen. John Redmond again referred to recent events in Ireland as proof that Protestants would not be oppressed by a largely Catholic Home Rule parliament: 'I and my comrades sit in this house as the result of defeating the unanimous opposition of the priests and bishops of Ireland' — 70,000 had voted against such influence.[55] But Col. Saunderson, envisaging manipulation by the priests under Irish Home Rule, described the anti-Parnellites as 'mere [Archbishop of Dublin] Walsh's removables'.[56]

During the committee stage of the bill, Col. Saunderson again described anti-Parnellites as a party elected by the Catholic priests.[57]

Sir Henry James withdrew an amendment that the second chamber of an Irish parliament be equal in power to the first (aimed at balancing such priestly influence), only on receiving assurances from Gladstone.[58] The bill was finally passed by 34 votes in the Commons and sent to the Lords.[59] There the Duke of Devonshire, Spencer Compton Cavendish, a Liberal who had been Irish secretary and had held many government offices, feared that an Irish parliament elected on the orders of the hierarchy would threaten the interests of the minority.[60] The Marquis of Londonderry, Charles Stewart Vane-Tempest-Stewart, former Conservative MP for Co. Down and lord lieutenant of Ireland, said that the 80 nationalists were mostly returned by the votes of the most ignorant, who were largely influenced by clerical intimidation, so the majority should not be heeded.[61] The Marquis of Salisbury, the previous (Conservative) prime minister, said that the 80 members 'sent us mainly by Archbishop Walsh' would insist on denominational education in Ireland.[62] After just a week, the Lords overwhelmingly rejected the Home Rule bill (on 8 September 1893, on its second reading).

Gladstone reluctantly opted to let the bill drop, rather than resign or go to the country on the issue of removing the Lords' veto on legislation. The Meath evidence of clerical involvement in politics would not have helped him to galvanise the support of the nonconformist and radical elements in his party which would have been essential in attempting such constitutional change — quite apart from its effect in antagonising Irish Protestants, Ulster Unionists and their Conservative allies in Britain. When Gladstone resigned the premiership in March the following year, his foreign secretary, Lord Rosebery, became prime minister but showed little interest in Home Rule. His public shelving of the issue was seen by the Parnellites to justify their independent stance and discomforted their hapless colleagues in the majority Irish Party. Rosebery understandably therefore had only reluctant support from the Irish Home Rulers on whom he depended and his government resigned in June 1895, to be succeeded by a coalition of Conservatives and Unionists. At a general election in July this new government secured a large majority over the Liberals and Home Rulers.

As the Unionists held the balance of power for the next decade, there was no further prospect of Irish Home Rule. It would take the Parliament Act of 1911 to deprive the Lords of their veto, allowing their rejection of a measure only to delay its implementation for two years.

The third Home Rule bill, passed by the Commons against fierce Unionist opposition in 1913 and again defeated in the Lords, was thus delayed and then put off by the First World War — before the end of which everything had changed.

Navan versus Mullingar

As we have seen, rivalry simmered between the two towns between which Bishop Nulty divided his residency and of each of which he was parish priest. He again seemed to favour Mullingar over Navan when, in February 1894, he presented the Westmeath town with 'a turret clock and chime of bells', the town commissioners thanking him 'for this latest mark of your attachment to your cathedral parish'.[63] He replied that he hoped to see the cathedral improved further, while two months later indicating that Navan would continue to be the location of a new St Finian's seminary. Contesting an application at Navan court by James Powderly, road contractor, to open a gravel pit on his land at Athlumney, Navan, the bishop said he had bought it from Lord Athlumney to build a new seminary to replace that which had been in existence for nearly a hundred years.[64] He had spent the previous 29 years collecting £15,000 and just as he was about to carry out his plan, this business was sprung upon him. If the application succeeded, the school would have to be sited 'somewhere else' and 'it will be an irreparable loss to us and to the town of Navan'. Cross-examined, the bishop said 'I have the money ready and the plans are in the hands of the architect.' The contractor's application was refused. In November, Navan guardians resolved that a new cemetery, to be provided by the bishop near the old one at Athlumney, which was 'fully occupied . . . is much needed'.[65] This was to help Bishop Nulty get a long lease from Lord Athlumney.

In July 1893, William Lawlor had presided at a meeting of the Navan league which appealed to Parnellites to ensure they were on the voters' register 'to wipe out the eternal disgrace of having a non-entity like Gibney in parliament, who represents nothing but despotism and ignorance', and suggested that a selection convention be held soon. But the sterility of political wrangling following the disappointment of the defeat of Home Rule — contrasted with the excitement and promise of the Parnell days — induced a nation-wide despair and apathy which was more marked perhaps in Meath than anywhere. There, a long decline in political activity of any kind was beginning as, the following year, Navan Parnell anniversary committee, 'consisting of labourers and artisans', urged 'every Irishman worthy of the name to again wend his sorrowful way to Glasnevin next October and there renew his vow to give no quarter to the Chief's and his country's betrayers'.[66] They summarised the Parnellite viewpoint: 'Three years ago, Parnell was removed at the dictation of an Englishman, backed by the nonconformist conscience and tyranny masquerading in the garb of religion. Parnell was driven to his grave, sold without a price, Home Rule is shelved, the political prisoners are rotting in English dungeons, the duped evicted tenants are still on the hillsides. Is there any further proof wanted of the weakness of the Union Jack federation and the incompetency of the 71 West Britons [anti-Parnellites]? If so, give the Whigs a further chance and you will have it.'

Two years later, *The Parnellite* magazine echoed Joseph Cooke and James Lawlor in deploring the lack of organisation in North Meath and called again for the holding of a selection convention:[67] 'The brave people who rallied round us in the teeth of cruel insults and petty persecution are practically forgotten. But the insults and persecution too often continue unabated. Small wonder that stout hearts sometimes grow sore.' In July 1895, an anti-Parnellite convention in the exam hall of St Finian's seminary, Navan, with a large number of clergy present, re-selected James Gibney and Jeremiah Jordan for North and South Meath (against John Howard Parnell, brother of the dead leader).[68] Shortly afterwards, Luke Smyth presided at a meeting on the Square in Navan to ratify the Parnellite candidate, John Sweetman.[69] In the ensuing campaign, the chairman of Meath GAA, R.T. Blake, resigned after being accused of publishing 'rule 3' against GAA participation in politics while simultaneously issuing a pamphlet on behalf of Gibney, who was re-elected by only 32 votes.[70] But John Howard Parnell defeated Jordan in the South Meath contest, though by a mere 43 votes.

At the end of 1895, when Bishop Nulty was welcomed home from Rome at a banquet in Mullingar, he deplored the disunity of the Irish Party, with Parnellite, Dillonite and Healyite factions making 'our parliamentary representation . . . worthless'.[71] After the split, 'people lost hope and in the last election I saw honest, honourable men, when asked to vote, refuse, saying "what's the use to put them in, they will do nothing but fight amongst themselves". Hence the political activity to which I attach so much importance is lost and my fear is that the country . . . will return to the old ways of arson, outrage and murder to redress their wrongs.' But the bishop himself 'dissented' from the expulsion by the majority of Healy, 'one of the most honourable men' who, along with Sullivan, had come to his rescue 'without fee or reward' at the petitions three years earlier, when 'I dared not open my mouth to defend myself'.

Also eschewing unity, James Lawlor told a Parnellite meeting of over 1,000 in Carlanstown, Kells, in February 1896 'those mercenary traitors who have backed up Whiggery for the past few years . . . this wretched band of Irish vultures . . . will have to repent and [even] then . . . I will not trust them.'[72] In May 1896, Patrick Fulham was evicted from his home in Donore as a result of his bankruptcy following the petition, but he was reinstated after a major public demonstration.[73] In June 1896, when Francis Sheridan, still chairman of Navan guardians, read a draft address to Bishop Nulty on the 50th anniversary of his ordination, the former MP, Robert Metge objected that, although he was the oldest friend of Dr Nulty present and held him, as a clergyman, second to none, he was entirely averse to the address mentioning the bishop's political ideas.[74] 'Having regard to the bishop's pastoral on one occasion, no liberal men could for one moment endorse the address.' Major Everard, agreeing, said there were parts of the address which no landlord could agree to, although he greatly respected Dr Nulty. T. Boylan said it was only bad landlords the bishop was down on.

But Metge again referred to the 'famous pastoral, trying to coerce the vote of his people by using his spiritual influence. I was astonished at it and horrified and it did more to influence my political view than anything that ever happened in this county.' Sheridan said that history would prove that the pastoral and pamphlets of the bishop had enlightened the present and past governments into giving concessions such as land bills and education measures. Major Everard said the board was a composite body, with representatives of the three great parties in Ireland, against two of which the pastoral was addressed. Therefore, it was not reasonable that they should approve of the address. Speaking in Mullingar on his golden jubilee, Bishop Nulty confined his remarks to aspects of the Land Acts, while carefully avoiding current politics, as his priests presented him with an oil painting and a bust of himself.[75] The *Argus* quoted the *Westmeath Nationalist*: he had 'endured the extremes of popular love and esteem and of mob fury and violence' as 'he held aloft the banner of Ireland's faith and chastity'. It also quoted the *Skibbereen Eagle*: 'In his jubilee address, Bishop Nulty goes straight for land nationalisation . . . stronger than ever on the policy of the land for the people, that is the nation . . .

the great gospel truth that the profit of the earth is for all and not for a few private individuals.'

The opening of Meath home industries exhibition by Lady Cadogan, the viceroy's wife, in Navan in May 1898 represented the last hurrah for the landed gentry.[76] A crimson carpet was laid at the Great Northern Railway (GNR) station, where she was met by Major Everard, who introduced her to the chairman of the town commissioners, John Spicer, whose daughter Magdalen, 'a handsome young lady, elegantly attired', presented a bouquet. Spicer read the address, 'which was the expression of the opinion of all parties in the town, conservative, Parnellite and anti-Parnellite'. The RIC band played 'God Save the Queen' as the vice-regal carriage, 'preceded by mounted police and followed by the carriages and wagonettes of the country gentry then drove over by Railway Street and through the principal streets of the town to the old barracks [Abbey Road], in which the exhibition was held . . . The ladies' committee had the honour of entertaining Her Excellency at luncheon in the Clubhouse' (Russell Arms hotel) before she returned by train. But at a 1798 centenary demonstration on the Hill of Tara the following week, Christopher Quinn said the people of the town had expressed their feelings about the 'renegades' who had hung out Union Jacks for Countess Cadogan's visit:[77] 'The Emmet Band . . . turned out and played as a protest. The men who were responsible for these decorations . . . some of them pledged their support to Parnell and then ran away. The men of Navan, with the exception of half a dozen or so, had nothing to do with the unfurling of the Union Jack.'

As late as March 1897, Fr P. Farrell, curate, Navan, had told a local government board inquiry into a proposed new water supply scheme for the town that the bishop intended building a new diocesan seminary in Navan, the lowest possible cost of which would be £15,000.[78] A further application at Navan court to open a quarry on Bishop Nulty's land at Athlumney was refused in December 1898,[79] just before the bishop died in Mullingar on Christmas Eve.[80] Navan town commissioners met specially 'to publicly place on record our deep sorrow and regret at the sad event which has deprived us of our beloved Bishop'.[81] Bishop Nulty in his will, made at Navan on 27 April 1897, had bequeathed his books to the seminary in Navan 'or wherever else in Ireland it may be situated'.[82] An affidavit by his executors gave his personal wealth as £2,647, but the will contained no reference to the money he had collected for the new seminary in Navan.

Te Deum and fireworks

In January 1899 William Lawlor presided at the unanimous election of John Spicer as first chairman of Navan urban council, established under the 1898 Local Government Act and following elections earlier in the month.[83] Around the same time, a meeting of parish priests in the cathedral, Mullingar, chaired by Cardinal Logue, selected three names to be sent to Rome to succeed Bishop Nulty:[84] Monsignor Matthew Gaffney, parish priest of Clara (29 votes), Dr Higgins, auxiliary bishop of Sydney and formerly president of the diocesan seminary in Navan and parish priest of Navan (15) and Monsignor Laurence Gaughran, parish priest of Kells (7). In May the pope named Mons. Gaffney Bishop of Meath.[85] Bishop Gaffney, in reply to addresses from local councils at his consecration in June, said he hoped 'the differences which affected the past would be forgotten by all in the future in the universal desire to equip the diocese of Meath in every requisite of intellectual and spiritual life'.[86] A 'hastily summoned' meeting in the CYMS hall, chaired by Spicer, appointed a committee to suitably receive Dr Gaffney on his first visit to Navan as bishop in July.[87]

Such mottoes as 'faith and fatherland', 'welcome', 'priests and people' and 'peace and unity' adorned Navan for Bishop Gaffney's visit.[88] The CYMS band led a procession around the town, during which 'the people cheered His Lordship'. Then a *Te Deum* (hymn of praise) was sung in the parish church, the bishop presiding at the altar. Afterwards, in the CYMS hall, Spicer read an address which was also signed by William Curry, chairman of Navan guardians and William C. Smith, secretary of the organising committee. It offered Bishop Gaffney 'fealty and obedience' and assured him that 'in the wide province where it is yours to command and counsel, it will be ever ours to obey and reverence'. Hoping that this was 'but the beginning of many happy days to be spent in our midst . . . to give us the benefits of your comprehensive views on the many social questions that are of such vital importance to us', the address concluded 'that all past differences may be forgotten and that we may all be more united, pastor and people, by the bonds of loyalty and love'.

Dr Gaffney replied that since beginning his ministry in the diocese, he had never had any connection with Navan or with the Meath portion of it. He noticed that although the town had good natural resources and commercial transport links, it had declined economically since he was a boy in the seminary there, due to the de-population of the surrounding countryside. This was a result of British policy, under which several poorhouses had also been provided for Meath's 'banished peasantry'. Characterising the 11-months competitive setting system as 'a second landlordism', he advocated farmer ownership of the land as an overall economic solution.

Referring to the expressed desire for peace and unity, Bishop Gaffney said as 'a high priest of the God of peace . . . The war has been too long prolonged and no one wishes it to continue except he have private ends to serve. In God's name, let it stop. Let an impenetrable veil be drawn over the past and let us devote our energies to higher and better work . . . I hope and trust that the spirit of old Ireland will be revived this day and that the spirit and union cemented between people and priests . . . will survive even the wreck of Navan.' Fr Woods said the bishop's reception in Navan told him unmistakably that the Catholic heart of Navan and Meath was in the right place and that, 'no matter what little aberrations might have occurred in the past', they were in truth a thing of the past. Any little differences they had were amongst themselves and were 'only ruffles on the surface' and did not at all disturb the depth of feeling of the Catholic people. He thanked the people of Navan from his heart for the demonstration they had made that when their bishop came to their town, 'all old quarrels were forgotten and past' and hearts and hands and voices were joined together, of priests and people. The bishop would look after not only the spiritual interests of his people but also their temporal interests and lead them in the path of propriety in their national and independent aspirations. They should recognise the power they had in the new county councils to start a new era, Fr Woods concluded.

A display of fireworks in the seminary grounds in the evening before an immense crowd on the Fair Green, evoked 'a good deal of enthusiastic cheering . . . [it] being quite a novelty in Navan'. There is no record of any objection to the reassertion of the bishop's and clergy's right to political leadership. In further comments in Meath, the new bishop condemned the evil consequences of athletic sports on Sundays, along with intemperance at markets and fairs, wakes and threshings.[89] He immediately announced that he would reside in Mullingar (an indication in itself that the location of the See of Meath was not finally fixed at this time). He told a deputation on the education of workhouse children there in August that he knew nothing about the United Irish League (founded by William O'Brien, MP, in 1898 to reinvigorate the Home Rule movement and ultimately to help reunite the party) and 'as regards matters of civil import, my sphere is outside these things'.[90]

However, three years later, he attacked the government as representing only 'an intolerant minority, hardly one-tenth of the population' and denying 'justice and equity' to the majority:[91] 'The whole system of government is a pantomime.' Bishop Gaffney also felt free to intervene with local bodies, on one occasion writing to Oldcastle guardians to complain about a member using the Holy Name.[92] He called for 'the suppression of such iniquity' and that otherwise 'the constituency would not again send such a representative'. In a departure from the less careful practice of his predecessor, Bishop Gaffney also wrote to Navan rural council refusing permission for a church gate collection for the evicted tenants, because it would 'impede the way that leads to the church of God.[93] It is every man's right to enter there without any challenge of his opinions.'

The bishop was of course a staunch upholder of Catholic sexual mores. Sir Horace Plunkett, now vice-president of the new department of agriculture which he was instrumental in establishing, in his 1904 book, *Ireland in the New Century*, blamed Irish priests for the depopulation of the countryside because the dullness of life resulting from their discouragement of young people's amusements in order to preserve their chastity forced them to emigrate. Dr Gaffney attacked Sir Horace[94], who,

> in his wanton insult to our Catholic beliefs and practices, thinks his economics will do more for the liberation of Ireland from the dark bondage of Catholicism than the gibbet had done for 300 years. How silly. Nor do I think that, hailing from Dunsany and seeing the devastation before the windows of his paternal mansion within living memory, he ought to feel any philosophic doubt about the causes of depopulation of the country and ascribe the widespread ruin to the chastity of our girls or the absence of the cross-roads dance. The chastity of our girls does not belong in his department and we repudiate his right to lecture us or to damage his public office by his unhappy allusions. I doubt if any cross-roads dance could be gathered on the Dunsany estate — the 11-months system holds the field. Men who have sounded the philosophy of history to its depths have drawn a widely different conclusion, viz. that a chaste people are a marrying people. The reason is not difficult to see.

After officiating at Bishop Nulty's anniversary mass in Mullingar cathedral at the end of 1899, Dr Gaffney had discussions with priests and people about a memorial to his predecessor, a Virgin's chapel, but in a new cathedral of Mullingar.[95] On the proposal of Laurence Rowan, Navan rural council in February 1900 unanimously congratulated Irish MPs on re-uniting in one party under John Redmond.[96] Clusker: 'Amen' (laughter). But the local row between Navan and the bishop threatened to re-ignite when Dr Gaffney wrote to Navan guardians that month threatening to withdraw nuns from the workhouse 'if this guerrilla warfare continue'.[97] He was referring to two members, J.P. Cooke and J. Maguire, complaining of extravagance in the nuns' running of the workhouse.[98] Cooke told the next meeting that he doubted the wisdom of the bishop 'in addressing the board in a controversial [manner], rather than a spirit of admonishment[99] . . . It has been regarded in Navan by large numbers of His Lordship's parishioners . . . as if he had taken in his hands a petroleum can and poured its contents onto the smouldering embers of that fire which has raged so fiercely in Navan during the past several years . . . He could not be more pained by the introduction of those ladies' names into the debates of this board than I was myself. But unfortunately His Lordship has fallen into the error' The chairman interjected to ask Cooke to withdraw the word 'error'. — During further wrangling, Cooke left, saying 'a man only stultifies himself to take part with such a lot of slaves'.

St Finian's move to Mullingar

Shortly afterwards, Bishop Gaffney, in his 1900 Lenten pastoral announced two new projects: a diocesan college and a cathedral, both in Mullingar.[100] The Westmeath town had been chosen for the new school instead of Navan by a large majority of priests (73 to 31),[101] who would fund its cost. 'It is the law and spirit of the Church that the Diocesan College should be under the Bishop's eye, attached to the Cathedral, and the priests have rightly given effect to her mind.' Reviewing the existing schools provision in Navan, Dr Gaffney promised 'there will also be an intermediate school under clerical management and no intellectual advantage at present enjoyed will be wanting.'

A new cathedral was necessary, as the existing church in Mullingar was old and badly constructed, too small for a growing parish and not even as suitable 'for a bishop's cathedral [as] some of the diocesan churches' (including, presumably, Navan). As the mother church of the diocese, every other parish should contribute to funding the new cathedral, while in Mullingar itself there were several promises of

£1,000. In a later pastoral, Dr Gaffney further explained his cathedral decision: 'Since the days when the small dioceses of which Meath is composed were confederated into one, it is not clear that the Catholic Bishop's See was ever fixed or determined.[102] He lived in Clonard, Kells, Navan, Mullingar or in his hiding place — there was no proper . . . Canonical Cathedral. After some years of his episcopacy, Dr Cantwell fixed his home here and built a parochial church for Mullingar . . . We are thus left without a cathedral . . . [in] Meath, which is not only a diocese but an historic kingdom.'

On 1 January 1901, Bishop Gaffney told a cathedral inauguration meeting in Mullingar 'the priests of the Diocese voted that the College would be in Mullingar, because at that time it was intended and he was sure it would be effected that the Cathedral would be in Mullingar'.[103] The only Navan representative listed as present was Fr M. Dooley, president of the doomed St Finian's seminary there. Among subscriptions received were £1,000 from Loreto Convents, Mullingar and Navan, and £500 from Convent of Mercy, Navan. But it was May 1902 before Fr D. Flynn, Dr Gaffney's administrator, told his Navan parishioners that they were as much bound to contribute towards the new cathedral as the people of any other parish.[104] The *Argus* reported 'the collection has been prosecuted in the town with much success' by Fr McNamee, parish priest, Lobinstown.

In a pastoral in August 1903, Bishop Gaffney mentioned 'the commencement of the new college and the strengthening of the teaching staff in the present college', while 'the nuns of Navan have built a new convent' above the confluence of the Boyne and Blackwater.[105] In December 1904, the bishop attended a farewell concert in Loreto Convent, Navan, 'the community of which are removing to their spacious buildings along the banks of the Boyne'.[106] In August 1905, Dr Gaffney petitioned the pope to retire due to failing health, particularly his eyesight, with 'the building of the magnificent new Diocesan College now in course'.[107] (The real reason for Bishop Gaffney's resignation appears to have centred on mistaken allegations of an improper relationship with a nun who was his nurse. It was presumably fear of this episode becoming widely known which in 1909 led Bishop Gaughran to destroy Meath's diocesan archive.) While Navan guardians expressed regret, C. Owens complained that for the previous six years the bishop had never encouraged the people to become united and never supported the national movement, unlike every other bishop in Ireland.[108] Chairman (P. Mangan): 'Dr Gaffney has not been

Portrait of Matthew Gaffney, Bishop of Meath, who decided to move St Finian's diocesan seminary from Navan to Mullingar and to build a cathedral there (courtesy of the President, St Finian's College, Mullingar).

James Gibney, anti-Parnellite MP for Meath, who was 'as unaware as that he could catch the man in the moon by the leg' that he would be selected (photograph courtesy of Hugh Gibney, Athboy).

Laurence Gaughran, Bishop of Meath, formerly parish priest of Kells – 'There were two Parnells' (photograph courtesy of Fr Pat McManus, St Columban's, Dalgan, Navan).

John Spicer, Navan Parnellite town commissioner – Bishop Nulty 'claims the sole right of appointing guardians' (photograph courtesy of Philip Smyth, Ardmulchan, Navan).

very liberal to Navan people or the parishioners.' This appears to have been the only public complaint about the moving of St Finian's college from Navan and the confirmation of Mullingar as the centre of the diocese. In December Rome accepted Bishop Gaffney's resignation, with parish priests meeting in the chapel of St Finian's seminary, Navan, to appoint a vicar capitular, pending the election of a bishop.[109]

Monsignor Gaughran of Kells summoned parish priests to a meeting in the 'parochial church of Navan' in January 1906 to select the names of three clergymen to submit to Rome.[110] Such ceremonies, to commence with votive mass at which Cardinal Logue would preside, 'have not been seen in Navan since 1864, when Dr Nulty was selected as co-adjutor to Dr Cantwell', the *Meath Chronicle* noted. Monsignor Gaughran, with 43 votes, easily beat five other contenders to head the list. A former secretary to Bishop Nulty, he was confirmed as bishop in May.[111] In October he told massgoers in Mullingar that Bishop Gaffney had given him £47,082 for the erection of the new cathedral, which would commence when the diocesan college was built.[112] At the beginning of 1908, the *Chronicle* reported 'about 15th January a large number of students, many of them from Navan, are coming to pursue their studies at the new diocesan college in Mullingar', which it described as 'a glorious adornment to the Diocese of Meath and particularly to Mullingar town and parish'.[113] It did not mention the closure of St Finian's in Navan, where the buildings were sold, leaving the national school the only educational establishment for Catholic boys until the arrival of the De La Salle brothers in 1917.[114]

When Kells councillor, P. Maguire, had chaired the Meath executive of the United Irish League in Navan in April 1902, he looked forward to the people of the town changing, to become once again the leaders of political thought in the county.[115] He remembered when Kells also led public opinion and he was 'sorry for the position occupied by these towns' currently. He acknowledged that it would be premature to start a branch in Navan, but a meeting on the Square in September did form one, urban councillor Simon Murray noting that 'the nationalism of Navan, where they had hitherto been so dilatory, was not yet dead'.[116] Patrick White, MP (who had beaten Gibney in the election of October 1900)[117] hoped that past differences, however bitter, would now be forgotten. Maguire said the nationalists of Navan would be as loyal to Redmond as in the past to Parnell. But '*Sacerdos Midensis*' (a priest of Meath) complained to the *Chronicle* in March 1906 about 'the universal torpor and lack of intelligent interest in politics' in Navan and Meath:[118]

'A deadly creeping paralysis has succeeded the spasmodic and unnatural excitement which accompanied the growth and development of the awful "split" of the early 1890s and as an inevitable result the people have sunk into a state of hapless apathy and despair.'

A different reason was advanced by Navan councillor, P. Collins, who told the inaugural meeting of Meath Labour Union in Navan that as there was 'too much grass in Meath' they were 'more asleep than awake'.[119] But when P. Byrne at Navan guardians in January 1907 quoted the new bishop as stating that the average attendance in Navan schools had decreased by 30 per cent, Collins explained that 'owing to political causes, the priests had not the same influence over the parents as they formerly had' and it was resolved to ask the urban council to re-introduce compulsion.[120] Fr P. Flanagan, the bishop's administrator in Navan, retorted that school absenteeism was the same as when attendance was compulsory:[121] 'I should like to know what the result would be if the influence of the priests was not exercised in this respect.' Fr Flanagan, after being made an honorary member of Navan Foresters in March 1907, said he regretted that the town, formerly known for its patriotism, had not contributed to the Parliamentary Fund.[122] He urged them to form a branch of the League and to raise subscriptions for the fund, to which he gave £1, after which 30 more subscribed. Presiding at a meeting shortly afterwards in the Foresters' Hall to re-form a League branch in the town, Fr Flanagan said that Navan was nationalist to the core.[123] Collins said that whenever priests and people united they would have a gratifying result in Meath. The cause of Ireland could not succeed unless it was sanctified by the presence of the priests. Elected president of Meath executive of the League, Fr Flanagan said 'notwithstanding the little apathy that prevented Navan and other places taking a prominent part in the movement', he was sure it was not for want of nationality:[124] 'What Navan is today, Meath will be tomorrow.'

Despite failing to be re-elected in Meath, Mahony had remained extremely active in the party, as well as being a director of the *Irish Independent*. In the following six months, for instance, he addressed Protestant Home Rulers in Dublin,[125] lamented the lack of Parnellite organisation in Meath, which allowed Navan to be represented on its board of guardians by 'seceders',[126] spoke on the union at a Dublin meeting,[127] chaired a Dublin meeting to plan the Parnell anniversary demonstration[128] and, as president of the Amnesty Association, chaired a large meeting in Dublin supporting political prisoners.[129] He was rewarded by being selected for the St Stephen's Green constituency in Dublin in 1895, but failed to be elected.[130] For an account of his extraordinary later life, see Maria Spassova's and Seamus Shortall's *Pierce O'Mahony — an Irishman in Bulgaria* (Dublin, 1999). He became 'The O'Mahony' and took to wearing a kilt. He funded an orphanage in Sofia in Bulgaria, where a chapel in his honour features his likeness as St Patrick, complete with the mitre and crosier of a bishop — his nemesis. He died on 31 October 1930, having become a Catholic the previous year. To this day, he is commemorated in the name of Navan's GAA club, the O'Mahonys.

Mahony's former colleague, James Dalton, had returned to Australia in June 1893.[131] The Gaelic League was first mentioned in print in Meath in September 1902, when the organisation in Navan sought the appointment of extern Irish teachers in schools and resolved to hold a *feis*.[132] The following year, Navan guardians accepted the League's proposal to have St Patrick's Day observed as a general holiday in the town for the first time, with a procession of all national and religious organisations, the merchants and traders closing their establishments.[133] In July 1902, Bishop Gaffney had consecrated a new cemetery on land bequeathed by Luke Smyth, about a mile from the centre of Navan, along the Beauparc Road.[134] There the remains of Luke Smyth, who had died in December 1899, were exhumed from Ardmulchan cemetery at the request of his wife and re-interred.[135] Francis Sheridan died in March 1904,[136] followed in December by William Lawlor,[137] whose son, James, retired as town clerk the year before he died in 1922.[138] Laurence Rowan died in 1930. When Navan workhouse became Our Lady's hospital, a Mercy nun continued as matron for many years. Navan was without a boys' secondary school until 1930, when Bishop Thomas Mulvany (1929–43) resolved what he termed Navan people's 'grievance' by opening St Patrick's classical school in the study hall of the old St Finian's.[139] Dr Mulvany dedicated the new cathedral in Mullingar to Christ the King in 1936. It has been described as 'one of the most stylishly triumphant Irish cathedrals' by one expert,[140] and as 'grandiose' and 'triumphalist' by others, who also ascribe 'the sheer scale' of St Finian's college in Mullingar to 'the confidence of the Catholic Church at the turn of the [nineteenth century]'.[141] The Bishop of Meath has not resided in Navan since Bishop Nulty's time, although he is still the town's parish priest.

Epilogue

This study of the actual events of the split in Meath affirms the urban–rural (rather than, say, social or economic) determinant of political affiliation, as noted by C.J. Woods and others. The three larger towns of Navan, Kells and Trim remained Parnellite in the face of vehement clerical opposition, while smaller towns like Slane and Oldcastle followed their anti-Parnellite priests, just as the village of Moynalty followed its Parnellite Fr Mullen. While these facts could be argued either to uphold or discount the accepted view of J.H. Whyte and others, this study suggests that, overall, priests could, in Meath at least, lead their people in a different direction to that in which they would otherwise go. This does not imply that without their intervention there would have been no opposition to the Parnellites in Meath. However, it would be difficult to imagine the sitting MP, Pierce Mahony, being ousted by a candidate, even of Michael Davitt's stature, without the strategic planning, organisation and activity of the bishop and priests, as described here.

A.C. Murray reached a similar conclusion in his study of Bishop Nulty's influence on politics in Co. Westmeath. But in that county, opposition to the bishop and priests was much less than in Meath, people there being politically 'apathetic'. A documented reason for this difference is the immense pride of Meathmen in Parnell as their former MP, but the same independent reaction in Meath — and again not in Westmeath — has been noted in relation to Dr Nulty's banning of gaelic games throughout his diocese in the year before the split.[142] Perhaps, as Murray noted, many inhabitants of the western half of the diocese had been beaten into submission even before the defeat of the Parnellites in 1892.

Was Bishop Nulty's power therefore unique — the constituencies of his Meath diocese being the only ones in which the clergy could determine the outcome of electoral contests? Probably not, if one accepts the considerable evidence of clerical involvement in the Kilkenny and other by-election campaigns after the split, which Conor Cruise O'Brien described as 'decisive'. There is also John Redmond's belief that the Parnellites would have won many more seats in the 1892 general election if the priests had 'stood aside' — not to mention his conviction that the first Irish parliament would be elected by the priests. But this question can only be satisfactorily answered by similar studies to this one of other constituencies, in many of which priests were deeply involved in selecting anti-Parnellite candidates, whom they were very likely to have then striven to get elected. Perhaps such studies would show that bishops and priests in other constituencies were merely less overt and therefore more subtly influential — arousing less opposition to their political activity — than Bishop Nulty and his clergy. Of course the devastating effect on Parnellite support of the hierarchy's condemnation of Parnell's moral lapse, although difficult to measure, affected even constituencies devoid of clerical activity in politics.

As well as helping to spoil the political atmosphere necessary for Gladstone's second Home Rule bill to succeed or for the House of Lords' veto to be confronted, the events of the Parnell split in Meath accentuated the bitterness which political divisions engendered among former allies. Pierce Mahony and Michael Davitt, once good friends, epitomise the enmity which stymied efforts towards peace by moderates on both sides. In particular, the failure to agree on not contesting seats which either side was likely to win led to unnecessary animosity in the 1892 general election. This replicated the bitterness of the preceding by-elections throughout the whole country, nowhere more than in Meath. Thus the split settled into open conflict between the majority Irish Party and the much smaller but persistently critical band of followers of the 'lost leader' who would himself, however, capture the imagination of succeeding generations.

Appendices

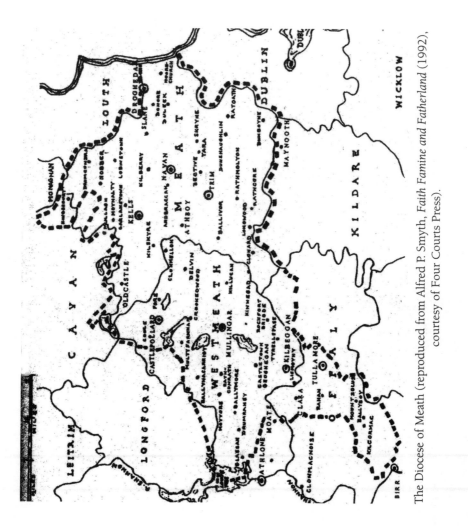

The Diocese of Meath (reproduced from Alfred P. Smyth, *Faith Famine and Fatherland* (1992), courtesy of Four Courts Press).

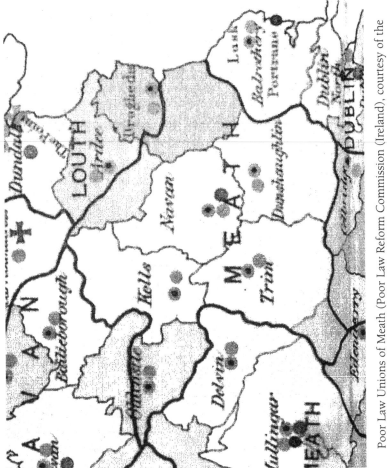

Poor Law Unions of Meath (Poor Law Reform Commission (Ireland), courtesy of the National Library of Ireland).

North and South Meath parliamentary constituencies (reproduced from parliamentary papers, courtesy of the National Library of Ireland).

References and notes

Chapter 1 — The Parnell split and priests in politics, pp. 1–8

1. F.S.L. Lyons, *Charles Stewart Parnell* (London, 1977), p. 611.
2. R. Barry O'Brien, *The Life of Parnell* (two volumes, London, 1898; reprinted, one volume, 1910).
3. For an analysis of the revolution in Irish history writing pioneered from the 1930s by Professors T.W. Moody and R. Dudley Edwards, see Ciaran Brady (ed.), *Interpreting Irish History* (Dublin 1994), pp. 3–31.
4. Lyons, *The Irish Parliamentary Party,1890–1910* (London, 1951) and Conor Cruise O'Brien, *Parnell and His Party, 1880–90* (Oxford, 1957).
5. Cruise O'Brien, *Parnell and His Party*, p. 352.
6. Lyons, *The Fall of Parnell* (London, 1960), pp. 266–70.
7. J.H. Whyte, 'The Role of the Catholic Clergy in Nineteenth Century Elections', in *English Historical Review*, April 1960, p. 249.
8. Emmet Larkin's foreword in William L. Feingold, *The Revolt of the Tenantry: The Transformation of Local Government in Ireland, 1872–1886* (Boston, 1984), pp. xiii–xvii, and Virginia Crossman, *Local Government in Nineteenth Century Ireland* (Belfast, 1994), p. 53.
9. Tom Garvin, 'The strange death of clerical politics in UCD', *Irish University Review*, spring/summer 1998, pp. 308–14. See also Garvin, *Preventing the Future: Why was Ireland so poor for so long?* (Dublin 2004), p. 57.
10. Larkin, *The Roman Catholic Church and the Creation of the Modern Irish State* (Philadelphia, 1975), prologue, pp. xxi–xxiv.
11. Lyons, *Charles Stewart Parnell*, pp. 619–21.
12. Larkin, *The Roman Catholic Church in Ireland and the Fall of Parnell, 1888–91* (Liverpool, 1979), p. 259.
13. D. George Boyce, *Nineteenth Century Ireland, The Search for Stability* (Dublin, 1990), p. 181.
14. Larkin's foreword in Feingold, *Revolt of the Tenantry*, pp. xvi–xvii.
15. E.R. Norman, *The Catholic Church and Ireland in the Age of Rebellion* (London, 1965), pp. 160–82.
16. Patrick J. Corish, 'Guide to material of public and political interest in the Kirby papers, Irish College, Rome, 1862–94', in *Archivium Hibernicum*, nos 30 (1972), 31 (1973) and 32 (1974).
17. Paul Connell, *The Diocese of Meath under Bishop John Cantwell, 1830–66* (Dublin, 2004), p. 149.
18. Whyte, 'The Role of the Catholic Clergy', p. 249.
19. Cruise O'Brien, *Parnell and his Party*, pp. 42–3.

20. C.J. Woods, 'The General Election of 1892: The Catholic Clergy and the Defeat of the Parnellites', in F.S.L. Lyons and R.A.J. Hawkins (eds), *Ireland Under the Union, Varieties of Tension: Essays in Honour of T.W. Moody* (Oxford, 1980), pp. 289–319.

21. Joe Lee, *The Modernisation of Irish Society, 1848–1918* (Dublin, 1973, reprinted 1989), pp. 120–1.

22. Lee, 'On the birth of the modern Irish state: the Larkin thesis', in Stewart J. Brown and David W. Miller (eds), *Piety and Power in Ireland, 1760–1960, Essays in Honour of Emmet Larkin* (Indiana, 2000), pp. 130–157.

23. Sean Connolly, *Religion and Society in Nineteenth Century Ireland* (Dundalk, 1985), pp. 37–9.

24. James Loughlin, *Gladstone, Home Rule and the Ulster Question* (Dublin, 1986), p. 250.

25. K.T. Hoppen, *Elections, Politics and Society in Ireland, 1832–85* (Oxford, 1984), pp. vii–ix.

26. Ibid., p. 255.

27. A.C. Murray, 'Nationality and local politics in late 19th century Ireland: the case of Co. Westmeath', in *Irish Historical Studies*, xxv, no. 98 (Nov. 1986), pp. 144–58.

28. Archbishop Walsh papers, Dublin Diocesan Archive: Croke to Walsh, 8 Nov. 1891.

29. Frank Callanan, '"Clerical Dictation:" Reflections on the Catholic Church and the Parnell split', in *Archivium Hibernicum,* vol. xlv, 1990, pp. 64–75.

30. Callanan, *The Parnell Split* (Cork, 1992), pp. 266–7.

31. Callanan, 'Parnell: The Great Pretender?' in *History Ireland*, autumn 1993, pp. 54–55.

32. Lyons, *Culture and Anarchy in Ireland, 1890–1939* (Oxford, 1979).

33. Cruise O'Brien, *States of Ireland* (Dublin, 1972) and *Ancestral Voices, Religion and Nationalism in Ireland* (Dublin, 1994).

Chapter 2 — Bishop Nulty's 'divine right', pp. 9–47

1. *Freeman's Journal (F.J.),*18 Nov. 1890, p. 5; *Drogheda Argus (D.A.),* 22 Nov. 1890, p. 6; *Drogheda Independent (D.I.),* 22 Nov. 1890, p. 3.

2. Bishop Thomas Nulty, pastoral, 20 Feb. 1871; also *D.A.*, 19 Oct. & 9 Nov. 1889.

3. Bishop Nulty, *Back to the Land* (Manchester, 1881), National Library of Ireland (N.L.I.).

4. L. Fogarty, *James Fintan Lalor* (Dublin, 1919), p. 102.

5. Michael Davitt, *The Fall of Feudalism in Ireland* (London, 1904), pp. 656–7.

6. See Bishop Nulty's obituary in the *Irish Catholic Directory,* 1900, p. 366; also P.J. Markham's memoir on Nulty and his times in the Henry George foundation edition of the bishop's *Back to the Land* (Melbourne, 1939), pp. 6–11.

7. See *United Ireland,* 16 October 1888, for Bishop Nulty's account of Parnell's visit to seek the Meath nomination in 1875 and Corish, 'Guide to Kirby Papers', in *Archivium Hibernicum,* 32 (1974), p. 12, no. 215,

Nulty to Kirby, Navan, 22 April 1887: '. . . he was in trouble with Rome two years ago. Does not regret this trouble, arising out of a warning to Rome of the danger of going against the strong popular feeling in Ireland.'

8. Anthony Cogan, *Diocese of Meath* (re-issued Dublin, 1992), vol. 1, pp. 234–40 & vol. 2, pp. 181–2.

9. Bishop Nulty, *The Land Agitation in Ireland* (letter to the clergy and laity of Meath), Mullingar, 1881, N.L.I.

10. Minutes of Navan town commissioners, 19 Nov. 1890, Meath Co. Library, Navan. Voting with Smyth, Lawlor and Spicer were Peter Finegan, Patrick McNamara, John McKieren, Matthew Tormey, Peter Murray and Thomas Nugent (9), against Laurence O'Reilly, Thomas Reilly, Patrick Sheridan and Edward Crinion (4).

11. Ibid., 7 Jan. 1890.

12. *F.J.*, 21 Nov. 1890, p. 6; *D.A.*, 22 Nov. 1890, p. 4; *D.I.*, 22 Nov. 1890, p. 3.

13. Maria Spassova and Seamus Shortall, *Pierce Mahony–an Irishman in Bulgaria* (Dublin, 1999), p. 194.

14. *The Irish Times (I.T.)*, 21 Nov. 1890, p. 6.

15. *F.J.*, 2 Dec. 1890, p. 6.

16. *F.J.*, 4 Dec. 1890, p. 5.

17. *F.J.*, 5 Dec. 1890, p. 4.

18. *IDI*, 7 June 1893, p. 5.

19. Margaret Leamy, *Parnell's Faithful Few* (New York, 1936), p. 30.

20. *United Ireland,* 16 Oct. 1888.

21. *D.A.*, 3, 10, 17 & 24 April 1875.

22. *F.J.*, 8 Dec. 1890, p. 7.

23. *D.A.*, 6 Dec. 1890, p. 4.

24. *D.I.*, 13 Dec. 1890, p. 5.

25. *D.A.*, 13 Dec. 1890, p. 4.

26. *D.A.*, 20 Dec. 1890, p. 7.

27. *D.A.*, 20 Dec. 1890, p. 7.

28. *F.J.*, 17 Dec. 1890, p. 7.

29. *D.I.*, 20 Dec. 1890, p. 5.

30. *D.A.*, 20 Dec. 1890, p. 4.

31. *I.T.*, 23 Dec. 1890, p. 5.

32. Crime branch special, division commander's confidential information (CBSDCC1), box 9, National Archives (N.A.).

33. *D.A.*, 27 Dec. 1890, p. 4.

34. *D.I.*, 3 Jan. 1891, p. 5.

35. *D.I.*, 31 Jan. 1891, p. 5.

36. *The Nation,* 24 Jan. 1891 & T.M. Healy, *Letters and Leaders of My Day* (London, 1928), vol. 1, p. 352: 22 Jan. 1891 to his brother, Maurice.

37. *F.J.*, 12 Jan. 1891, p. 6.

38. *F.J.*, 16 Jan. 1891, p. 5.

39. *D.I.*, 7 Feb. 1891, p. 6.

40. *D.A.*, 7 Feb. 1891, p. 7.

41. *D.A.*, 21 Feb. 1891, p. 3.
42. *D.A.*, 21 Feb. 1891, p. 4.
43. *D.A.*, 7 March 1891, p. 5.
44. *F.J.*, 5 March 1891, p. 6.
45. *F.J.*, 2 March 1891, p. 5.
46. Navan TC minutes, 23 May 1887.
47. Navan TC minutes, 27 Feb. 1891.
48. Chief secretary's office registered papers (CSORP), 1891, no. 6163, N.A.
49. *F.J.*, 2 March 1891, p. 5.
50. *F.J.*, 2 March 1891, p. 4.
51. *I.T.*, 2 March 1891, pp. 4 & 7.
52. *D.I.*, 7 March 1891, p. 3.
53. *D.A.*, 14 March 1891, p. 3.
54. *D.I.*, 7 March 1891, p. 4.
55. *D.I.*, 7 March 1891, p. 4.
56. Crime branch special, district inspector's confidential summary (CBS DICS), box 4, N.A.
57. CBSDCCI, box 9, N.A.
58. *F.J.*, 14 March 1891, pp. 5–6.
59. *D.A.*, 14 March 1891, p. 4.
60. *I.T.*, 12 March 1891, p. 3.
61. *D.A.*, 21 March 1891, p. 3.
62. CSORP 1891, no. 15846, N.A.
63. *I.T.*, 25, 26, 27 March 1891, p. 6 & *D.A.*, 28 March, 4 April 1891, p. 7.
64. Letter from Bishop Nulty to Fr Woods, 13 March 1891, Meath diocesan archive, Mullingar. It includes John Spicer in the deputation, which the RIC report does not. The writing, incidentally, does not provide evidence of a sight problem, despite Navan rowdies' appellation the following year of 'blind Tom'.
65. *D.I.*, 28 March 1891, p. 4.
66. *National Press (N.P.)*, 25 March 1891, p. 7.
67. *D.A.*, 14 March 1891, p. 6.
68. *F.J.*, 14 March 1891, p. 5.
69. *D.A.*, 21 March 1891, p. 7.
70. *D.I.*, 4 April 1891, p. 5.
71. *D.A.*, 4 April 1891, p. 4.
72. *N.P.*, 30 July 1891, p. 5.
73. Corish, 'Guide to the Kirby papers', in *Archivium Hibernicum*, no. 32 (1974), p. 31 (no. 212).
74. *D.A.*, 4 April 1891, p. 7.
75. *D.I.*, 4 April 1891, p. 3.
76. *D.I.*, 4 April 1891, p. 4.
77. *N.P.*, 2 April 1891, p. 7.
78. *D.A.*, 16 May 1891, p. 3.
79. *D.A*, 11 April 1891, p. 7.
80. *F.J.*, 15 April 1891, p. 6. The 28 were William Lawlor, Michael Denning,

Patrick Smyth, John Spicer, Francis Loughran, John Quinn, Patrick Clusker, James Finucane, Patrick Coldrick, Joseph Cregan, Joseph Cooke, James Duffy, James Lawlor, James Everard, George Jones, Peter Finegan, John McKiever, John Coogan, Peter Murray, John Beggan, James Finnegan, Joseph Harlin, Bernard Reilly, Matthew Rice, Henry Loughran, Matthew Tormey, Patrick Foley and Patrick McNamara.

81. D.A., 8, 15 & 22 May, 1880 and 12 March and 3 & 9 April 1881. See also Frank Callanan, *T.M. Healy* (Cork, 1996), pp. 39–40, for reference to his subject's failure to secure the nomination for the Meath by-election in 1880 at 'a conference of the clergy' convened and re-convened in Navan, chaired by Bishop Nulty (*F.J.*, 5 & 18 May 1880; *The Nation*, 8 & 22 May 1880). Callanan's notes refer to T.D. Sullivan, *A.M. Sullivan, A Memoir* (Dublin, 1885), pp. 135–7, and Gavan Duffy to T.D. Sullivan, 28 November & 8 December, 1884, N.L.I. MS 82317 (2) about Duffy also being ditched by a conference of clergy in Navan in 1875, when Parnell got the nomination.

82. D.I., 18 April 1891, p. 4.

83. D.I., 25 April 1891, p. 3. They were Frs Woods, Claffy and McNamee (curates), John Cassidy, president of St Finian's, who chaired the meeting, M. Dooley, vice-president and C. Murray, do., with Nicholas Kelly, Laurence Reilly, Patrick Sheridan, Thomas Reilly, Francis Sheridan, Patrick Allen, Joseph Keappock, James Maguire, James Sheridan, John Lightholder, Peter Gaughran and Laurence Carpenter.

84. D.A., 11 April 1891, p. 3.

85. D.A., 18 April 1891, p. 3.

86. Only odd issues of the *Meath Reporter* (M.R.), from 14 January 1888 to 29 June 1901, are bound in one volume in N.L.I.

87. D.A., 2 May 1891, pp. 3 & 4.

88. D.I., 2 May 1891, p. 6.

89. D.I., 23 May 1891, p. 2.

90. D.A., 16 May 1891, p. 3.

91. D.A., 30 May 1891, p. 4.

92. N.P., 2 May 1891, p. 6.

93. N.P., 19 May 1891, p. 6.

94. N.P., 9 May 1891, p. 3.

95. N.P., 11 May 1891, p. 2.

96. N.P., 12 May 1891, p. 5.

97. N.P., 19 May 1891, p. 3.

98. N.P., 23 May 1891, p. 6.

99. N.P., 25 May 1891, p. 5.

100. N.P., 27 May 1891, p. 5.

101. D.A., 30 May 1891, p. 7.

102. F.J., 25 May 1891, p. 5.

103. F.J., 30 May 1891.

104. F.J., 1 June 1891, p. 3.

105. F.J., 3 June 1891, p. 7.

106. I.D.I., 23 Nov. 1892, p. 7.

107. *D.A.*, 20 June 1891, p. 6.
108. *F.J.*, 15 June 1891, pp. 4 & 7.
109. *D.I.*, 27 June 1891, p. 2.
110. *N.P.*, 2 July 1891.
111. *D.A.*, 18 July 1891, p. 3.
112. *D.A.*, 11 July 1891, p. 3.
113. *D.A.*, 18 July 1891, p. 3.
114. *D.A.*, 8 Aug. 1891, p. 3.
115. *D.A.*, 3 Oct. 1891, p. 3.
116. *N.P.*, 22 June 1891, p. 2.
117. *D.A.*, 1 Aug. 1891, p. 7; *N.P.*, 27 July 1891, p. 5; *F.J.*, 27 July 1891, p. 5.
118. CBSDICS, box 4, N.A.
119. *F.J.*, 31 July 1891, p. 5.
120. CBSDICS, box 4, N.A.
121. *N.P.*, 3 Aug. 1891, p. 5.
122. *N.P.*, 8 Aug. 1891, p. 5.
123. *D.I.*, 8 Aug. 1891, p. 3.
124. *N.P.*, 10 Aug. 1891, p. 7.
125. *F.J.*, 8 Aug. 1891, p. 6. The Parnellite justification was signed by Smyth, Spicer, W. Lawlor, Peter Finegan, John McKeever, Michael Rogers, Thomas Nugent, Peter Murray, Matthew Tormey, Patrick McNamara, Michael Denning, Patrick Clusker, Joseph Cooke, Christopher Quinn, Joseph Cregan, Matthew Rice, C. Monaghan, Peter Biggan, Patrick McEvoy, Patrick Smyth, Edward Guiry, C. McCoogan, Denis Donnolly, F.Loughran, Patrick Fagan, William Ludlow, Peter Byrne, Thomas Lowe, John Farrelly, J. Harkin, James Everard, Patrick Sherlock, James Finucane, James Finnegan, James Foley, John Coogan, Richard Ludlow, James Lawlor, H. Loughran, James Carpenter and John Quinn.
126. *N.P.*, 11 Aug. 1891, p. 5.
127. *F.J.*, 17 Aug. 1891, p. 4.
128. CBSDICS, box 4, N.A.
129. *N.P.*, 17 Aug. 1891, p. 6.
130. *D.I.*, 22 Aug. 1891, p. 5.
131. *D.A.*, 22 Aug. 1891, p. 6 & *I.T.*, 17 Aug. 1891, p. 5.
132. CBSDICS, box 4, N.A.
133. *N.P.*, 26 Sept. 1891, p. 7.
134. Navan TC minutes, 8 Oct. 1891.
135. *F.J.*, 20 Oct. 1891, p. 2.
136. *D.A.*, 10 Oct. 1891, p. 4.
137. *D.A.*, & *D.I.*, 17 Oct. 1891, p. 3.
138. *D.I.*, 17 Oct. 1891, p. 3.
139. *F.J.* & *I.T.*, 13 Oct. 1891, p. 5.
140. *F.J.*, 13 Oct. 1891, p. 6.
141. *F.J.*, 15 Oct. 1891, p. 5.
142. *I.T.*, 14 Oct. 1891, p. 5.
143. *D.I.*, 7 Nov. 1891, p. 7.

144. *F.J.*, 2 Nov. 1891, p. 7.
145. *F.J.*, 9 Nov. 1891, p. 5.
146. *Irish Catholic (I.C.)*, 14 Nov. 1891, p. 5.

Chapter 3 — A nun for Navan workhouse, pp. 48–62

1.   *D.A.*, 2 Nov. 1891, p. 7.
2.   *D.I.*, 14 Nov. 1891, pp. 2 & 4.
3.   *D.I.*, 28 Nov. 1891, pp. 2 & 4.
4.   *D.A.*, 28 Nov. 1891, p. 6.
5.   *D.I.*, 5 Dec. 1891, p. 6.
6.   *D.I.*, 12 Dec. 1891, p. 2 & *D.A.*, 12 Dec. 1891, p. 3.
7.   *I.C.*, 19 Dec. 1891, p. 6.
8.   *D.I.*, 12 Dec. 1891, p. 4.
9.   *D.I.*, 2 Jan. 1891, p. 6.
10. CBSDICS, box 4, N.A.
11. *D.A.*, 19 Dec. 1891, p. 4.
12. *F.J.*, 12 Dec. 1891, p. 5.
13. *D.A.*, 24 Oct. 1891, p. 7.
14. *F.J.*, 16 Dec. 1891, p. 4.
15. *I.T.*, 14 & 15 Dec., 1891.
16. *I.T.*, 26 Dec., 1891.
17. *Irish Daily Independent (I.D.I.)* 28 Dec. 1891, p. 7.
18. Trinity College Dublin (TCD) MS 9403.
19. *F.J.*, 22 Jan. 1892, p. 6.
20. *D.A.*, 30 Jan. 1892.
21. *I.C.*, 30 Jan. 1892, p. 1.
22. *D.I.*, 23 Jan. 1892, p. 4.
23. CBSDICS, box 4, N.A.
24. *I.D.I.*, 23 Jan. 1892, p. 4.
25. *I.D.I.*, 23 Jan. 1892, p. 6.
26. *I.D.I.*, 27 Jan. 1892, p. 4.
27. *I.D.I.*, 1 Feb. 1892, p. 4.
28. *I.D.I.*, 3 Feb. 1892, p. 6.
29. *D.I.*, 5 March 1892, pp. 4–5.
30. *I.D.I.*, 8 March 1892, p. 5.
31. *I.D.I.*, 9 March 1892, p. 4.
32. *D.I.*, 12 March 1892, p. 4.
33. *D.I.*, 12 March 1892, p. 4.
34. *D.I.*, 19 March 1892, p. 5.
35. *D.I.*, 19 March 1892, p. 5.
36. *I.D.I.*, 18 March 1892, p. 4.
37. *D.I.*, 19 March 1892, p. 5.
38. Olive C. Curran, *History of the Diocese of Meath, 1860–1993*, 3 vols. (Bishop of Meath, 1995), vol. 1, p. 2.
39. *I.D.I.*, 24 March 1892.
40. *I.D.I.*, 25 March 1892, p. 4.
41. *D.I.*, 26 March 1892, p. 4.

42. *F.J.*, 29 March 1892, p. 7.
43. CBSDICS, box 4, N.A.
44. *D.I.*, 4 June 1892, p. 3.
45. *I.D.I.*, 30 March 1892, p. 5.
46. *D.I.*, 2 April 1892, p. 4.
47. *D.A.*, 2 April 1892, p. 4.
48. *F.J.*, 29 March 1892, p. 4.
49. *F.J.*, 30 March 1892, p. 4.
50. *D.A.*, 9 April 1892.
51. *D.A.*, 16 April 1892.
52. *I.D.I.*, 13 April 1892, p. 2. Attending were Smyth, Denning, P. Clusker, J. Quinn, T. Loughran, P.McNamara, J. Spicer, C. Quinn and J. Lawlor.
53. CBSDICS, box 4, N.A.
54. *F.J.*, 14 June 1892, p. 4.
55. *D.I.*, 11 June 1892, p. 4.
56. *D.A.*, 23 April 1892.
57. *D.A.*, 2 Feb. 1901, p. 3.
58. *D.A.*, 30 April & 14 May 1892, p. 7.

Chapter 4 — Michael Davitt in the 1892 election, pp. 63–98

1.   *D.I.*, 16 April 1892, p. 4.
2.   See Carla King (ed.) introduction to *Jottings in Solitary, Michael Davitt* (Dublin, 2003) and *F.J.*, 24 May 1882, p. 3.
3.   See Fintan Lane, *The Origins of Modern Irish Socialism* (Cork, 1997), pp. 71–2.
4.   CBSDICS, box 4, N.A. From April 1892 the signature is no longer Bell's and is indecipherable.
5.   *F.J.*, 25 April 1892, p. 5 & *D.A.*, 30 April 1892.
6.   *D.I.*, 30 April 1892, p. 4.
7.   *F.J.*, 27 April 1892, pp. 3 & 4.
8.   Harrington papers, N.L.I. MS 8576 (14), Dillon to Harrington, 27 April 1892.
9.   T.M. Healy, *Why Ireland Is Not Free* (Dublin, 1898), pp. 56–7 & 72–3.
10. *I.D.I.*, 27 April 1892, p. 6.
11. *F.J.*, 10 May 1892, p. 5.
12. *D.I.*, 14 May 1892, p. 4.
13. *I.D.I.*, 10 May 1892, p. 6.
14. *I.D.I.*, 26 May 1892, p. 4.
15. *I.D.I.*, 30 May 1892, p. 5. The *Argus* agreed on the 4,000 attendance (see *D.A.*, 4 June 1892, p. 3), but the *Drogheda Independent* put it at only 1,500 (see *D.I.*, 4 June 1892, p. 3), while the police said 3,000 (see report of RIC midland division commander, Captain Robert B. Stokes, to the Castle for June 1892 — Special list 392 on microfilm (CO 904 classification), reels 27 & 28, boxes 60 & 61, call nos P8218–9, N.L.I., hereafter cited as Special list 392).
16. *D.I.*, 28 May 1892, p. 4.
17. *F.J.*, 2 June 1892, p. 5 & *I.D.I.*, 2 June 1892, p. 6. The Navan delegates

were given as F. Sheridan, N. Kelly, P. Casey, M. Lightholder, P. Sheridan, E. Crinion, J. Keappock, P. Gaughran, W. Walsh, T. Reilly, F. Fitzgerald, P. Potts, Thomas McGuerk, James Higgins, P. Allen and J. McNally.

18. D.A., 15 April 1882, pp. 5 & 7.
19. D.A., 8 April 1882, p. 4.
20. I.D.I., 2 June 1892, p. 4.
21. D.I., 4 June 1892, p. 4.
22. D.A., 4 June 1892, p. 4.
23. Special list 392, N.L.I.
24. D.I., 11 June 1892, pp. 4 & 6.
25. I.D.I., 13 June 1892, p. 5.
26. I.D.I., 17 June 1892, p. 5.
27. D.I., 11 June 1892, p. 5.
28. D.I., 11 June 1892, p. 4.
29. D.I., 18 June 1892, p. 5.
30. I.D.I., 25 June 1892, p. 5.
31. D.I., 2 July 1892, p. 5.
32. I.D.I., 27 June 1892, p. 6.
33. F.J., 27 June 1892, p. 7.
34. I.D.I., 29 June 1892, p. 5.
35. I.D.I., 1 July 1892, p. 6.
36. F.J., 28 June 1892, p. 7.
37. F.J., 29 June 1892, p. 4.
38. F.J., 30 June 1892, p. 6.
39. D.I., 2 July 1892, p. 5.
40. D.I., 2 July 1892, p. 2.
41. D.I., 2 July 1892, p. 4.
42. F.J., 4 July 1892, p. 7.
43. D.I., 9 July 1892, p. 6.
44. I.D.I., 4 July 1892, pp. 4, 5 & 6.
45. I.D.I., 5 July 1892, p. 4.
46. F.J., 8 July 1892, p. 6.
47. D.A., 9 July 1892, p. 4.
48. T.M. Healy, Letters and Leaders of My Day (London, 1928), vol. 2, p. 386.
49. Mark Tierney, Croke of Cashel (Dublin, 1976), p. 248.
50. Spassova and Shortall, Pierce Mahony, p. 193.
51. CSORP 1892, no. 9117, N.A.
52. D.I., 9 July 1892, p. 5.
53. CBSDICS, box 4, N.A.
54. Special list 392, N.L.I.
55. I.C., 9 July 1892, p. 4.
56. I.T., 29 July 1892, p. 3.
57. CSORP 1892, no. 9117, N.A.
58. I.D.I., 11 July 1892, p. 6.
59. F.J., 11 July 1892, p. 6. Assenting electors were John Rice, Athlumney; Thomas Keappock, Watergate Street; Thomas Sheridan, do.; James Sheridan, Trimgate Street; Laurence Reilly, Bridge Street; Peter

Gaughran, Watergate Street; Jospeh Keappock, do.; Thomas Walshe, do.; Francis Sheridan, Thomas Reilly, Edward Crinion, Patrick Sheridan, Patrick Allen, James Curran, James Maguire and Bertie Casey.

60. *D.I.*, 16 July 1892, p. 6.
61. CSORP 1892, no. 9275, N.A.
62. TCD MS 9621, p. 28.
63. TCD MS 9328–181/19.
64. *I.D.I.*, 12 July 1892, p. 4.
65. *I.D.I.*, 13 July 1892, p. 4.
66. *I.D.I.*, 13 July 1892, p. 5.
67. *I.D.I.*, 14 July 1892, pp. 4 & 5.
68. *I.D.I.*, 15 July 1892, p. 2.
69. *I.D.I.*, 15 July 1892, p. 5.
70. CSORP 1892, no. 9607, N.A.
71. *I.D.I.*, 18 July 1892, p. 6.
72. *F.J.*, 15 July 1892, p. 5.
73. *F.J.*, 16 July 1892, pp. 4 & 5.
74. *F.J.*, 18 July 1892, p. 5.
75. *I.D.I.*, 16 July 1892, p. 4.
76. *D.I.*, 16 July 1892, pp. 4 & 6.
77. *I.D.I.*, 19 July 1892, p. 5.
78. *D.I.*, 23 July 1892, p. 5.
79. *D.A.*, 23 July 1892.
80. *F.J.*, 19 July 1892, p. 5.
81. *D.I.*, 30 July 1892, p. 4.
82. *F.J.*, 21 July 1892, p. 5.
83. *F.J.*, 23 July 1892, p. 5.
84. *F.J.*, 27 July 1892, p. 4.
85. Special list 392, N.L.I.
86. *F.J.*, 28 July 1892, p. 5.
87. *F.J.*, 29 July 1892, p. 5.
88. *I.D.I.*, 28 July 1892, p. 5.
89. *F.J.*, 2 Aug. 1892, pp. 4 & 5.
90. *I.D.I.*, 2 Aug. 1892, p. 6.

Chapter 5 — South and North Meath election petitions, pp. 99–148

1. *F.J.*, 28 July 1892, p. 2.
2. *I.D.I.*, 28 July 1892, p. 6.
3. *I.D.I.*, 4 Aug. 1892, p. 5.
4. *I.D.I.*, 4 Aug. 1892, p. 5.
5. *I.D.I.*, 4 Aug. 1892, p. 4.
6. *I.D.I.*, 5 Aug. 1892, p. 4.
7. *I.D.I.*, 5 Aug. 1892, p. 5.
8. Reprinted in *I.D.I.*, 5 Aug. 1892, p. 5.
9. *I.D.I.*, 8 Aug. 1892, p. 4.
10. *D.I.*, 6 Aug. 1892, p. 2.

11. *D.I.*, 6 Aug. 1892, p. 4.
12. *I.D.I.*, 9 Aug. 1892, p. 4.
13. *I.D.I.*, 9 Aug. 1892, p. 4.
14. *D.I.*, 13 Aug. 1892, p. 4.
15. *I.D.I.*, 9 Aug. 1892, p. 6.
16. *I.D.I.*, 10 Aug. 1892, p. 5.
17. *I.D.I.*, 11 Aug. 1892, p. 4.
18. *D.I.*, 13 Aug. 1892, p. 4.
19. *D.I.*, 3 Sept. 1892, p. 5.
20. *I.D.I.*, 31 Aug. 1892, p. 2.
21. *F.J.*, 10 Sept. 1892, p. 5.
22. *F.J.*, 10 Sept. 1892, p. 4.
23. *M.R.*, 27 Aug. 1892.
24. *I.D.I.*, 6 Sept. 1892, p. 2.
25. *F.J.*, 19 & 27 Sept. 1892, p. 7.
26. *D.A.*, 17 & 24 Sept. 1892, p. 3.
27. *D.I.*, 1 Oct. 1892, p. 7.
28. *F.J.*, 26 Oct. 1892, p. 5.
29. *D.A.*, 29 Oct. 1892.
30. *F.J.*, 27 Oct. 1892, p. 4.
31. *I.D.I.*, 7 Sept. 1892, p. 4.
32. *I.D.I.*, 7 Oct. 1892, p. 4.
33. *I.D.I.*, 11 Oct. 1892, p. 4.
34. *D.A.*, 4 Oct. 1892, p. 5.
35. *I.D.I.*, 2 Nov. 1892, p. 2.
36. *I.D.I.*, 7 Nov. 1892, p. 5.
37. *I.D.I.*, 14 Nov. 1892, p. 6.
38. *I.D.I.*, 23 Sept. 1892, p. 4.
39. *I.D.I.*, 24 Sept. 1892, p. 5.
40. *I.D.I.*, 6 Oct. 1892, p. 4.
41. *D.I.*, 8 Oct. 1892, p. 3.
42. *I.D.I.*, 29 Oct. 1892, p. 2.
43. *I.D.I.*, 1 Nov. 1892, p. 6.
44. *I.D.I.*, 16 Nov. 1892, p. 4.
45. *I.D.I.*, 7 Nov. 1892, p. 6.
46. *I.D.I.*, 8 Nov. 1892, p. 2.
47. *I.D.I.*, 9 Nov. 1892, p. 6.
48. *I.D.I.*, 12 Nov. 1892, p. 2.
49. *I.D.I.*, 14 Nov. 1892, p. 4.
50. *F.J.*, 14 Nov. 1892, p. 5.
51. *I.C.*, 19 Nov. 1892, p. 5.
52. *I.D.I.*, 15 Nov. 1892, p. 6.
53. *I.D.I.*, 17 Nov. 1892, p. 5.
54. *D.I.*, 12 Nov. 1892, p. 4.
55. *D.I.*, 19 Nov. 1892, pp. 2–4.
56. *F.J.*, 17 Nov. 1892, pp. 4 & 6.
57. *I.D.I.*, 18 Nov. 1892, p. 5.

58. *I.D.I.*, 19 Nov. 1892, p. 5.
59. *I.D.I.*, 24 Nov. 1892, p. 6.
60. *I.D.I.*, 25 & 26 Nov. 1892, p. 5.
61. *I.D.I.*, 28 Nov. 1892, p. 5.
62. *I.D.I.*, 30 Nov. 1892, pp. 5 & 6.
63. *I.D.I.*, 1 Dec. 1892, p. 5.
64. *I.D.I.*, 1 Dec. 1892, pp. 5 & 6.
65. *I.D.I.*, 2 Dec. 1892, pp. 4, 5 & 6.
66. *I.D.I.*, 5 Dec. 1892, p. 5.
67. *F.J.*, 1 Dec. 1892, pp. 4–5.
68. *I.T.*, 1 Dec. 1892, p. 4.
69. *F.J.*, 2 Dec. 1892, p. 4.
70. *F.J.*, 3 Dec. 1892, p. 5.
71. *I.C.*, 3 Dec. 1892, pp. 4–5.
72. *I.C.*, 10 Dec. 1892, p. 4.
73. *D.I.*, 3 Dec. 1892, p. 4.
74. *F.J.*, 9 Dec. 1892, p. 5.
75. *D.I.*, 10 Dec. 1892, p. 4.
76. *F.J.*, 12 Dec. 1892, pp. 4–5.
77. *I.D.I.*, 14 Dec. 1892, p. 4.
78. *I.D.I.*, 13 Dec. 1892, p. 4.
79. *I.D.I.*, 14 Dec. 1892, p. 6.
80. *I.D.I.*, 19 Dec. 1892, p. 5.
81. *F.J.*, 8 Dec. 1892, p. 5.
82. TCD MS 9403–1570.
83. *I.D.I.*, 15 Dec. 1892, p. 5.
84. The *North Meath Election Petition, Tried at Trim, December 1892, Verbatim Report reprinted from the Irish Daily Independent* (N.L.I.), pp. 3–29 (hereafter cited as Petition report).
85. Petition report, pp. 30–58.
86. Petition report, pp. 59–78.
87. Petition report, pp. 79–107.
88. Petition report, pp. 108–131.
89. Petition report, pp. 132–169.
90. Petition report, pp. 170–90.
91. Petition report, pp. 191–6.
92. *I.D.I.*, 24 Dec. 1892, p. 4.
93. *F.J.*, 24 Dec. 1892, p. 5.
94. *I.T.*, 24 Dec. 1892, p. 4.
95. *I.D.I.*, 24 Dec. 1892, pp. 5 & 6.
96. *I.D.I.*, 26 Dec. 1892, p. 6.
97. *D.I.*, 24 Dec. 1892, p. 4.
98. *I.D.I.*, 30 Dec. 1892, p. 5, reprinted from *Fortnightly Review,* vol. 59 (January 1893), pp. 1–6.
99. *I.D.I.*, 30 Dec. 1892, p. 6.
100. *F.J.*, 30 Dec. 1892, p. 5, reprinted from *Nineteenth Century,* vol. 33 (January 1893), pp. 139–51.

101. *I.C.*, 18 Feb. 1893, p. 5.

Chapter 6 — New elections in Meath as Commons debates Home Rule, pp. 149–191

1. *I.D.I.*, 31 Dec. 1892, p. 4.
2. *FJ.*, 31 Dec. 1892, p. 4.
3. CBSDICS, box 4, N.A.
4. *I.C.*, 31 Dec. 1892, p. 5.
5. *I.C.*, 21 Jan. 1893, p. 5.
6. *D.I.*, 31 Dec. 1892, p. 4.
7. *I.D.I.*, 2 Jan. 1893, p. 7.
8. *I.D.I.*, 2 Jan. 1893, p. 4.
9. *I.D.I.*, 3 Jan. 1893, p. 4.
10. Reported in *I.D.I.*, 4 Jan. 1893, p. 4.
11. Reported in *I.D.I.*, 5 Jan. 1893, p. 5.
12. *I.D.I.*, 4 Jan. 1893, pp. 5–6.
13. *I.D.I.*, 3 & 6 Jan. 1893, p. 4.
14. *I.D.I.*, 7 Jan. 1893, p. 5.
15. *I.D.I.*, 7 Jan. 1893, p. 4.
16. *FJ.*, 7 Jan. 1893, p. 4.
17. TCD MS 9404/1575.
18. *I.D.I.*, 7 Jan. 1893, pp. 4–5 & *FJ.*, 7 Jan. 1893, p. 6.
19. TCD MS 9404/1579.
20. *D.I.*, 7 Jan. 1893, p. 4.
21. *D.I.*, 14 Jan. 1893, p. 6.
22. *I.D.I.*, 10 Jan. 1893, p. 5.
23. *FJ.*, 9 Jan. 1893, p. 5.
24. *I.D.I.*, 12 Jan. 1893, pp. 4–6 & *FJ.*, 12 Jan. 1893, p. 6.
25. *I.D.I.*, 16 Jan. 1893, p. 5.
26. *I.D.I.*, 16 Jan. 1893, pp. 5 & 6.
27. *I.D.I.*, 17 Jan. 1893, p. 2.
28. *FJ.*, 16 Jan. 1893, p. 6.
29. *FJ.*, 14 Jan. 1893, p. 4.
30. *I.D.I.*, 18 Jan. 1893, p. 6.
31. A.M. Sullivan, *Old Ireland, Reminiscences of an Irish KC* (London, 1927), pp. 102–3.
32. TCD MS 9328–181/21.
33. *FJ.*, 16 Jan. 1893, p. 6.
34. *FJ.*, 18 Jan. 1893, p. 5.
35. *D.I.*, 21 Jan. 1893, p. 4.
36. *I.D.I.*, 19 Jan 1893, p. 7.
37. *FJ.*, 21 Jan. 1893, p. 5.
38. *I.D.I.*, 23 Jan. 1893, pp. 4–6 & *FJ.*, 23 Jan. 1893, p. 5.
39. *I.D.I.*, 23 Jan 1893, p. 6.
40. *I.D.I.*, 24 Jan. 1892, p. 6.
41. *FJ.*, 23 Jan. 1893, p. 7.
42. Lt. Col. Richard K. Page, *The O'Mahonys of Grange Con*, an unpublished

family history, of which a copy is in the possession of Seamus Shortall, who kindly supplied this reference.

43. *I.D.I.*, 25 Jan. 1893, pp. 4, 5 & 6.
44. *F.J.*, 25 Jan. 1893, p. 6.
45. TCD MS 6728/18.
46. *F.J.*, 28 Jan. 1893, pp. 4, 5 & 6. See also Sir Henry James, MP, *The evidence of priestly influence in Ireland, as shown by the North and South Meath election petitions* (London, 1893).
47. *F.J.*, 30 Jan. 1893, pp. 4–5.
48. *I.D.I.*, 7 Feb. 1893, pp. 4–5.
49. *F.J.*, 28 Jan. 1893, p. 5.
50. *F.J.*, 8 Feb. 1893, p. 4.
51. *I.D.I. & F.J.*, 6 Feb. 1893, pp. 4 & 5.
52. *Irish Weekly Independent,* 7 Oct. 1893, p. 1.
53. R. Barry O'Brien, *The Life of Parnell,* p. 476.
54. *I.D.I.*, 30 Jan. 1893, p. 4.
55. *F.J.*, 30 Jan. 1893, p. 4.
56. *I.D.I.*, 30 Jan. 1893, p. 5.
57. *F.J.*, 30 Jan. 1893, p. 6.
58. *F.J.*, 2 Feb. 1893, p. 6.
59. *I.D.I.*, 31 Jan. 1893, p. 2.
60. *F.J.*, 30 Jan. 1893, p. 5.
61. *F.J.*, 30 Jan. 1893, p. 6.
62. *D.I.*, 4 Feb. 1893, p. 5.
63. *D.A.*, 4 Feb. 1893, p. 3.
64. *F.J.*, 1 Feb. 1893, p. 7.
65. *F.J.*, 2 Feb. 1893, p. 6.
66. *I.D.I.*, 1 Feb. 1893, p. 5.
67. *F.J.*, 2 Feb. 1893, pp. 4–5.
68. *I.T. & I.D.I.*, 3 Feb. 1893, p. 6.
69. *I.D.I. & F.J.*, 4 Feb. 1893, pp. 4–5.
70. *I.D.I. & F.J.*, 6 Feb. 1893, pp. 4 & 5.
71. *F.J.*, 6 Feb. 1983.
72. *F.J.*, 6 Feb. 1893, p. 5.
73. *F.J.*, 6 Feb. 1893.
74. *I.D.I.*, 7 Feb. 1893, pp. 4–5.
75. *F.J.*, 7 Feb. 1893, p. 4.
76. CSORP 1893, no. 3039, N.A.
77. *I.D.I.*, 7 Feb. 1893, p. 6.
78. *I.T.*, 8 Feb. 1893, p. 4.
79. *F.J.*, 9 Feb. 1893, pp. 4 & 7.
80. *I.D.I.*, 8 Feb. 1893, p. 6.
81. *I.D.I.*, 9 Feb. 1893, pp. 2–4.
82. *I.D.I.*, 11 Feb. 1893, p. 5.
83. *I.D.I.*, 11 Feb. 1893, p. 6.
84. *I.D.I.*, 13 Feb. 1893, pp. 4–6.
85. *F.J.*, 11 Feb. 1893, p. 4.

86. *I.D.I.*, 13 Feb. 1893, pp. 4–6.
87. *I.D.I.*, 13 Feb. 1893, p. 6.
88. *I.T.*, 14 Feb. 1893, p. 6.
89. *I.D.I.*, 14 Feb. 1893, p. 4.
90. *I.T.*, 15 Feb. 1893, p. 5.
91. *I.T.*, 17 Feb. 1893, p. 6.
92. *I.D.I.*, 15 Feb. 1893, pp. 4 & 6. Assenting electors for Mahony were: John McKeever, Market Square; John Spicer, Blackwater; Patrick McNamara, Ludlow Street; James Ludlow, Polbwee; John Farrelly, do; Joseph Cooke, Ludlow Street; Michael Nevin, Polbwee, and Peter Byrne, Abbeylands. A second paper was signed exclusively by Navan labourers, on the proposal of William Gerrard, Brewshill, seconded by Bernard Clarke, Barrack Lane. Assenting nominators for Gibney were: Peter Rogers, do; Christopher Carpenter, do; Cornelius Corcoran, Canon Row; Christopher Gargan, Townparks; John Pierce, Metges Lane; John Brady, Townparks, and Laurence Dowd, Chapel Lane. Nine other nomination papers came from different parts of the constituency. Assenting electors were: Patrick Sheridan, Watergate Street; Peter Gaughran, do; Patrick Allen, do; Joseph Keappock, do; Bartle Casey, Market Square; Thomas Reilly, Trimgate Street; James Maguire, do. and Francis Swan, Bridge Street. In a second paper, he was proposed by James Buchanan, Market Square, and Edward Crinion, do. In each of five other papers he was proposed by clergymen and seconded by laymen.
93. *I.D.I.*, 18 Feb. 1893, p. 6.
94. *I.D.I.*, 14 Feb. 1893, p. 7.
95. *I.D.I.*, 15 Feb. 1893, p. 6.
96. *F.J.*, 16 Feb. 1893, p. 6.
97. *D.I.*, 18 Feb. 1893, p. 5.
98. *I.D.I.*, 16 Feb. 1893, p. 5.
99. *I.D.I.*, 18 Feb. 1893, p. 7.
100. *I.D.I.*, 17 Feb. 1893, pp. 4 & 7.
101. *I.T.*, 18 Feb. 1893, p. 6.
102. *I.D.I.*, 18 Feb. 1893, pp. 4–5.
103. *F.J.*, 18 Feb. 1893, p. 7.
104. *I.D.I.*, 20 Feb. 1893, p. 4.
105. *I.D.I.*, 20 Feb. 1893, pp. 5 & 6.
106. *F.J.*, 20 Feb. 1893, pp. 4–6.
107. *I.D.I.*, 21 Feb. 1893, pp. 4 & 5.
108. *F.J.*, 21 Feb. 1893, p. 4.
109. *I.D.I.*, 22 Feb. 1893, pp. 4–5.
110. *F.J.*, 22 Feb. 1893, p. 5.
111. *I.D.I.*, 23 Feb. 1893, pp. 4–5.
112. *D.I.*, 25 Feb. 1893, pp. 4 & 6.
113. CSORP 1893, no. 3035, N.A.
114. *F.J.*, 24 Feb. 1893, p. 4.
115. *F.J.*, 23 Feb. 1893, pp. 4–5.

116. *F.J.*, 24 Feb. 1893, p. 4.
117. *I.D.I.*, 21 Feb. 1893, p. 2.
118. *I.D.I.*, 24 Feb. 1893, p. 4.
119. *I.D.I.*, 25 Feb. 1893, p. 5.
120. *I.D.I.*, 27 Feb. 1893, p. 2.
121. *I.D.I.*, 27 Feb. 1893, p. 5.
122. *I.D.I.*, 28 Feb. 1893, pp. 2 & 4.
123. CBSDICS, box 4, N.A.
124. Special list 392, N.L.I.

Chapter 7 — Parnellite defeat and political apathy, pp. 192–226

1. *I.D.I.*, 1 March 1893, p. 5.
2. *F.J.*, 1 March 1893, p. 5.
3. *I.D.I.*, 1 March 1893, p. 2.
4. *I.D.I.*, 2 March 1893, p. 2.
5. *F.J.*, 2 March 1893, p. 4.
6. *F.J.*, 3 March 1893, p. 5 & *D.A.*, 4 March 1893, p. 4.
7. *I.D.I.*, 4 March 1893, p. 4.
8. *I.D.I.*, 7 March 1893, pp. 4 & 6.
9. *I.D.I.*, 14 March 1893, p. 4.
10. *F.J.*, 10 March 1893, pp. 5–6.
11. *I.D.I.*, 22 March 1893, p. 2.
12. *I.D.I.*, 23 March 1893, p. 6.
13. *I.D.I.*, 30 March 1893, p. 2.
14. *D.I.*, 4 March 1893, p. 4.
15. *D.I.*, 11 March 1893, p. 2.
16. *D.I.*, 18 March 1893, p. 4.
17. *D.A.*, 1 April 1893, pp. 6–7.
18. *D.I.*, 25 March 1893, p. 5.
19. *D.I.*, 8 April 1893, p. 4.
20. *D.A.*, 15 April 1893, p. 7.
21. Nulty, *Defence of the Pastoral*, Mullingar, 25 March 1893, N.L.I., reported in *D.I.*, 25 March 1893, p. 4 & 8 April 1893, p. 6.
22. *I.D.I.*, 24 March 1893, p. 4.
23. *I.D.I.*, 18 April 1893, p. 6.
24. *F.J.*, 23 March 1893, p. 4.
25. *D.I.*, 25 March 1893, p. 4.
26. *D.I.*, 8 April 1893, p. 4.
27. *D.A.*, 25 March 1893, p. 7.
28. *I.D.I.*, 6 April 1893, p. 6.
29. *I.D.I.*, 17 May 1893, p. 6.
30. *D.A.*, 27 May 1893, p. 5.
31. *D.A.*, 17 April 1897.
32. *D.A.*, 10 June 1893, p. 4.
33. *D.A.*, 8 July 1893, p. 6.
34. *I.D.I.*, 7 June 1893, p. 5.
35. *I.D.I.*, 27 June 1893, p. 5.

36.   *I.D.I.*, 1 Aug. 1893, p. 4.
37.   *D.A.*, 22 April 1893, pp. 5–6 & 13 May 1893, p. 7.
38.   TCD MS 9473/4280.
39.   TCD MS 9554.
40.   *I.D.I.*, 12 May 1893, p. 5.
41.   *I.D.I.*, 12 May 1893, p. 4.
42.   *I.D.I.*, 13 May 1893, p. 4.
43.   *I.D.I.*, 17 May 1893, p. 2.
44.   *I.D.I.*, 30 May 1893, p. 5.
45.   *I.D.I.*, 12 June 1893, p. 5.
46.   *D.A.*, 28 Oct. 1893, p. 2.
47.   TCD MS 9554.
48.   *D.A.*, 3 Feb. 1894.
49.   *D.A.*, 10 Feb. 1894.
50.   Philip H. Bagenal, *The Priest in Politics* (London, 1893).
51.   *I.D.I.*, 5 July 1893, p. 5, reprinted from the *Pall Mall Gazette*.
52.   *I.D.I.*, 1 Aug. 1893, p. 4.
53.   *I.D.I.*, 11 April 1893, p. 6.
54.   *I.D.I.*, 12 April 1893, p. 6.
55.   *I.D.I.*, 14 April 1893, p. 6.
56.   *I.D.I.*, 21 April 1893, p. 6.
57.   *I.D.I.*, 13 May 1893, p. 6.
58.   *I.D.I.*, 17 May 1893, p. 6.
59.   *I.D.I.*, 2 Sept. 1893, p. 4.
60.   *I.D.I.*, 6 Sept. 1893, p. 6.
61.   *I.D.I.*, 7 Sept. 1893, p. 5.
62.   *I.D.I.*, 9 Sept. 1893, p. 5.
63.   *D.A.*, 10 Feb. 1894.
64.   *D.A.*, 7 April 1894, pp. 3,4 & 7.
65.   *D.A.*, 24 Nov. 1894, p. 7.
66.   *D.A.*, 25 Aug. 1894, p. 3.
67.   *The Parnellite*, 6 April 1895, p. 8.
68.   *D.A.*, 13 July 1895.
69.   *D.A.*, 20 July 1895, p. 3.
70.   *D.A.*, 10 Aug. 1895, p. 3.
71.   *D.A.*, 4 Jan. 1896.
72.   *D.A.*, 8 Feb. 1896, p. 3.
73.   *D.A.*, 9 May 1896, p. 3.
74.   *D.A.*, 6 June 1896.
75.   *D.A.*, 13 June 1896, pp. 5 & 7.
76.   *D.A.*, 28 May 1898, p. 3.
77.   *D.A.*, 4 June 1898, p. 4.
78.   *D.A.*, 27 March 1897, p. 5.
79.   *D.A.*, 24 Dec. 1898, p. 7.
80.   *D.A.*, 31 Dec. 1898, p. 3.
81.   *D.A.*, 7 Jan. 1899, p. 3.
82.   Will of Bishop Nulty, N.A.

83. *D.A.,* 28 Jan. 1899, p. 3.
84. *D.A.,* 28 Jan. 1899, p. 4.
85. *D.A.,* 20 May 1899, p. 3.
86. *D.A.,* 1 July 1899, p. 7.
87. *D.A.,* 8 July 1899, p. 4.
88. *D.A.,* 15 July 1899, p. 7.
89. *D.A.,* 22 July 1899, p. 4.
90. *D.A.,* 12 Aug. 1899, p. 7.
91. *D.A.,* 1 Nov. 1902, p. 6.
92. *D.A.,* 22 Aug. 1903, p. 6.
93. *D.A.,* 7 April 1900, p. 4.
94. *D.A.,* 26 March 1904, p. 6.
95. *D.A.,* 6 Jan. 1900, p. 5.
96. *D.A.,* 10 Feb. 1900, p. 3.
97. Minutes of Navan guardians, 14 Feb. 1900, Navan library.
98. *D.A.,* 17 Feb. 1900, p. 3.
99. *D.A.,* 3 March 1900, p. 5.
100. Bishop Gaffney Lenten pastoral, 1900, Meath diocesan archive, Mullingar.
101. *Meath Chronicle (M.C.)* centenary publication, 1997, p. 43 (reference kindly supplied by Bishop Michael Smith).
102. *D.A.,* 5 Jan. 1901, p. 7.
103. *D.A.,* 3 May 1902, p. 4.
104. *D.A.,* 29 Sept. 1900, pp. 3 & 5.
105. *D.A.,* 22 Aug. 1903, p. 7.
106. *D.A.,* 17 Dec. 1904, p. 4.
107. *M.C.,* 2 Sept. 1905, p. 5. *See also* Archbishop Walsh papers, Dublin diocesan archive: Logue to Walsh, 21 Aug. 1905; Gaffney to Walsh, 28 Aug. 1905; Logue to Walsh, 28 Aug. 1905; and *F.J.,* 26 Aug. 1905, p. 7. Bishop Gaffney's writing, incidentally, does not provide evidence of impaired sight.
108. *M.C.,* 9 Sept. 1905, p. 3.
109. *M.C.,* 23 Dec. 1905, p. 5.
110. *M.C.,* 6 Jan. 1906, p. 3.
111. *M.C.,* 26 May 1906, p. 5.
112. *M.C.,* 27 Oct. 1906, p. 5.
113. *M.C.,* 4 Jan. 1908, p. 1.
114. Curran, *History of the Diocese,* vol. 3, p. 979.
115. *D.A.,* 3 May 1902, p. 5.
116. *D.A.,* 27 Sept. 1902, p. 3.
117. *D.A.,* 20 Oct. 1900, p. 4.
118. *M.C.,* 17 March 1906, p. 6.
119. *M.C.,* 27 Jan. 1906, p. 5.
120. *M.C.,* 2 Feb. 1907, p. 8.
121. *M.C.,* 9 Feb. 1907, p. 8.
122. *M.C.,* 23 March 1907, p. 5.
123. *M.C.,* 6 April 1907, p. 1.

124. *M.C.*, 4 May 1907, p. 2.
125. *I.D.I.*, 6 April 1893, p. 5.
126. *I.D.I.*, 17 April 1893, p. 5.
127. *I.D.I.*, 12 May 1893, p. 4.
128. *I.D.I.*, 31 Aug. 1893, p. 5.
129. *I.D.I.*, 11 Sept. 1893, p. 5.
130. See Spassova, Shortall, *Pierce O'Mahony*.
131. *I.D.I.*, 2 June 1893, p. 4.
132. *D.A.*, 13 Sept. 1902, p. 6.
133. *D.A.*, 14 Feb. 1903, p. 8.
134. *D.A.*, 19 July 1902, p. 5.
135. *D.A.*, 20 Sept. 1902, p. 5 & 14 Oct. 1902, p. 3.
136. *D.A.*, 26 March 1904, pp. 6 & 7.
137. *D.A.*, 31 Dec. 1904, p. 5.
138. *M.C.*, 4 Feb. 1922, p. 1.
139. Curran, *History of the Diocese*, vol. 3, p. 979.
140. Peter Galloway, *Cathedrals of Ireland* (Belfast, 1992), p. 184.
141. Christine Casey and Alistair Rowan, *The Buildings of Ireland — North Leinster* (London, 1993), pp. 415 & 419.
142. See Michael O'Brien, *Royal and Loyal, Meath GAA History, 1884–1940*, pp. 24–55 & 32–35.

Bibliography

Primary sources

Freemans Journal
National Press
Irish Daily Independent
Irish Weekly Independent
Irish Times
Irish Catholic
North Meath Election Petition, Irish Daily Independent, December 1892.
South Meath Election Petition, Irish Daily Independent, December 1892.
Drogheda Argus
Drogheda Independent
Meath Reporter
Meath Chronicle
Meath Chronicle centenary publication, 1997
United Ireland
The Nation
Nineteenth Century
Fortnightly Review
Lyceum
The Parnellite
Catholic Directory
Slater's Directory
Dod's Parliamentary Companion
The O'Mahonys of Grange Con, an unpublished family history by Lt. Col.
Richard K. Page (copy in possession of Seamus Shortall)

Meath Diocesan Archive, Bishop's House, Mullingar.
Walsh Papers, Dublin Diocesan Archive, Archbishop's House, Drumcondra,
Dublin.
Minutes of Navan Town Commissioners, Meath County Library, Navan.
Minutes of Navan Poor Law Guardians, do.
Crime Branch Special, District Inspectors Confidential Summaries, National
Archives.
Crime Branch Special, Divisional Commanders Confidential Information, do.
Chief Secretary's Office Registered Papers, do.
Royal Irish Constabulary reports, Special list 392 (CO 904), National Library
of Ireland.
Parliamentary papers, do.
T.C. Harrington papers, do.
Michael Davitt and John Dillon Papers, Trinity College Dublin.

Secondary sources

Bagenal, Philip H., *The Priest in Politics*, London, 1893.

Boyce, D. George, *Nineteenth Century Ireland, The Search for Stability*, Dublin, 1990.

Brady, Ciaran, '"Constructive and Instrumental": The Dilemma of Ireland's First "New Historians",' in Ciaran Brady (ed.), *Interpreting Irish History, The Debate on Historical Revisionism*, Dublin, 1994.

Brown, Stewart J. and Miller, David W. (eds), *Piety and Power in Ireland, 1760–1960, Essays in Honour of Emmet Larkin*, Indiana, 2000.

Callanan, Frank, '"Clerical Dictation": Reflections on the Catholic Church and the Parnell Split', in *Archivium Hibernicum*, vol. xlv, 1990.

Callanan, Frank, *The Parnell Split, 1890–91*, Cork, 1992.

Callanan, Frank, 'Parnell: The Great Pretender?' in *History Ireland*, autumn, 1993.

Casey, Christine and Alistair Rowan, *The Buildings of Ireland – North Leinster*, London 1993.

Cogan, Anthony, *Diocese of Meath*, 3 volumes, re-issued Dublin, 1992.

Connell, Paul, *The Diocese of Meath under Bishop John Cantwell, 1830–66*, Dublin, 2004.

Connell, Peter, *The Land and People of Co. Meath, 1750–1850*, Dublin, 2004.

Connolly, Sean, *Religion and Society in Nineteenth Century Ireland*, Dundalk, 1985.

Corish, Patrick J., 'Guide to material of public and political interest in the Kirby papers, Irish College, Rome, 1862–94', in *Archivium Hibernicum*, nos 30 (1972), 31 (1973) and 32 (1974).

Crossman, Virginia, *Local Government in Nineteenth Century Ireland*, Belfast, 1994.

Curran, Olive C., *History of the Diocese of Meath, 1860–1993*, 3 vols, Bishop of Meath, 1995.

Curtis, L. Perry, jnr., *Images of Erin in the Age of Parnell*, N.L.I., 2000.

Davitt, Michael, 'The Priest in Politics', in *Nineteenth Century*, January 1893.

Davitt, Michael, *The Fall of Feudalism in Ireland*, London, 1904.

Feingold, William L., *The Revolt of the Tenantry: The Transformation of Local Government in Ireland, 1872–86*, Boston, 1984.

Flynn, Gabriel, 'Bishop Thomas Nulty and the Irish Land Question', in *Ríocht na Midhe*, 1984, pp. 14–28 and 1985–86, pp. 93–110.

Fogarty, L., *James Fintan Lalor*, Dublin, 1919.

Foster, R.F., *Charles Stewart Parnell: The Man and His Family*, Sussex, 1976.

Galloway, Peter, *Cathedrals of Ireland*, Belfast, 1992.

Garvin, Tom, 'The Strange Death of Clerical Politics in UCD', in *Irish University Review*, spring/summer 1998.

Garvin, Tom, *Preventing the Future: Why was Ireland so Poor for so Long?* Dublin 2004.

Harrison, Henry, *Parnell Vindicated: The Lifting of the Veil*, London, 1931.

Healy, T.M., *Why Ireland Is Not Free*, Dublin, 1898.

Healy, T.M., *Letters and Leaders of My Day*, 2 vols, London, 1928.

Hoppen, K.T., *Elections, Politics and Society in Ireland, 1832–85*, Oxford, 1984.

James, Sir Henry, MP, *The Evidence of Priestly Influence in Ireland, as Shown by the North and South Meath Election Petitions*, London, 1893.

King, Carla (ed.), *Jottings in Solitary, Michael Davitt*, Dublin, 2003.

Fogarty, L., *James Fintan Lalor*, Dublin, 1919.

Lane, Fintan, *The Origins of Modern Irish Socialism*, Cork, 1997.

Larkin, Emmet, *The Roman Catholic Church and the Creation of the Modern Irish State*, Philadelphia, 1975.

Larkin, Emmet, *The Roman Catholic Church in Ireland and the Fall of Parnell, 1888–91*, Liverpool, 1979.

Leamy, Margaret, *Parnell's Faithful Few*, New York, 1936.

Lee, Joe, *The Modernisation of Irish Society, 1848–1918*, Dublin, 1973 & 1989.

Lee, Joe 'On the birth of the modern Irish state: the Larkin thesis', in Brown and Miller, *Piety and Power*, pp. 130–157.

Loughlin, James, *Gladstone, Home Rule and the Ulster Question*, Dublin, 1986.

Lyons, F.S.L., *The Irish Parliamentary Party, 1890–1910*, London, 1951.

Lyons, F.S.L., *The Fall of Parnell, 1890–91*, London, 1960.

Lyons, F.S.L., *Charles Stewart Parnell*, London, 1977.

Lyons, F.S.L., *Culture and Anarchy in Ireland, 1890–1939*, Oxford, 1979.

Macaulay, Ambrose, *The Holy See, British Policy and the Plan of Campaign in Ireland, 1885–93*, Dublin 2002.

Markham, P.J., 'Memoir on Dr Nulty and his Times', in Bishop Thomas Nulty, *Back to the Land*, 1881, reprinted by Henry George foundation, Melbourne, 1939.

McCaffrey, Lawrence J., 'Emmet Larkin, A Memoir', in Brown and Miller, *Piety and Power*.

Murray, A.C., 'Nationality and local politics in late 19th century Ireland: the case of Co. Westmeath', in *Irish Historical Studies*, xxv, no. 98 (Nov. 1986).

Norman, E.R., *The Catholic Church and Ireland in the Age of Rebellion*, London, 1965.

Nulty, Bishop Thomas, *The Land Agitation in Ireland*, Mullingar, 1881.

Nulty, Bishop Thomas, *Defence of the Pastoral*, Mullingar, 1893.

O'Brien, R. Barry, *The Life of Charles Stewart Parnell, 1846–91*, 2 vols, London, 1898, reprinted in 1 vol., 1910.

O'Brien, Conor Cruise, *Parnell and His Party, 1880–90*, first published Oxford, 1957, corrected impressions 1964, 1968, reprinted 1968.

O'Brien, Conor Cruise, *States of Ireland*, Dublin, 1972.

O'Brien, Conor Cruise, *Ancestral Voices, Religion and Nationalism in Ireland*, Dublin, 1994.

O'Brien, Michael, *Royal and Loyal, Meath GAA History, 1884–1940*.

Plunkett, Sir Horace, *Ireland in the New Century*, London, 1904.

Redmond, John, 'The Lesson of South Meath', in *Fortnightly Review*, January, London, January 1893.

Smyth, Alfred P., *Faith, Famine and Fatherland in the Irish Midlands*, Dublin, 1992.

Spassova, Maria, and Shortall, Seamus, *Pierce Mahony — an Irishman in Bulgaria*, Dublin, 1999.

Sullivan, A.M., *Old Ireland, Reminiscences of an Irish KC,* London, 1927.

Sullivan, T.D., *A.M. Sullivan, A Memoir,* Dublin, 1885.

Tierney, Mark, 'Dr Croke, the Irish Bishops and the Parnell Crisis', in *Collectanea Hibernica,* no. 11 (1968).

Tierney, Mark, Calendar of Archbishop Croke Papers in Cashel, in *Collectanea Hibernica,* nos 13 (1970), 16 (1973) and 17 (1974–5).

Tierney, Mark, *Croke of Cashel,* Dublin, 1976.

Walker, Brian M. (ed.), *Parliamentary Election Results in Ireland, 1801–1922,* Dublin, 1978.

Whyte, J.H., 'The Role of the Catholic Clergy in Nineteenth Century Elections', in *English Historical Review,* April 1960.

Whyte, J.H., *Church and State in Modern Ireland, 1923–70,* Dublin, 1971, revised edition to 1979, New Jersey, 1980.

Woods, C.J., 'The General Election of 1892: The Catholic Clergy and the Defeat of the Parnellites', in F.S.L. Lyons and R.A.J. Harkin (eds), *Ireland Under the Union, Varieties of Tension: Essays in Honour of T.W. Moody,* Oxford, 1980.

Index